A War Too Far

Also by Paul Rogers from Pluto Press:

Losing Control: Global Security in the Twenty-first Century (Second edition) (2002)

A War On Terror: Afghanistan and After (2004)

A War Too Far

Iraq, Iran and the New American Century

Paul Rogers

LONDON • ANN ARBOR, MI

First published 2006 by Pluto Press
345 Archway Road, London N6 5AA
and 839 Greene Street, Ann Arbor, MI 48106

www.plutobooks.com

British Library Cataloguing in Publication Data
A catalogue record for this book is available from the British Library

ISBN 0 7453 2432 0 hardback
ISBN 0 7453 2431 2 paperback

Library of Congress Cataloging-in-Publication Data applied for

10 9 8 7 6 5 4 3 2 1

Designed and produced for Pluto Press by
Chase Publishing Services Ltd, Fortescue, Sidmouth, EX10 9QG, England
Typeset from disk by Stanford DTP Services, Northampton, England
Printed and bound in the European Union by
Antony Rowe Ltd, Chippenham and Eastbourne, England

Contents

Introduction

THE NEW AMERICAN CENTURY

In March 2003, the United States and its coalition partners commenced a large-scale military assault on Iraq in order to terminate the Saddam Hussein regime. This followed the 9/11 attacks in New York and Washington, the subsequent termination of the Taliban regime in Afghanistan and the start of the global war on terror. The Iraq War was said to be concerned with Iraq's development and deployment of weapons of mass destruction, but that was disregarded after such systems could not be found and a second motivation, Iraq's support for al-Qaida and other paramilitary groups, was emphasised, even though there was little evidence of any such relationship.

In the four years since 9/11, the global war on terror resulted in many tens of thousands of people being killed and many more seriously injured. By mid-2005, well over 10,000 people were being detained without trial in Iraq, Afghanistan, Guantanamo and elsewhere, a bitter insurgency in Iraq was continuing, security in much of Afghanistan was deeply problematic and the determined if disparate al-Qaida movement continued its many activities, not least with the London bombings in early July.

Even so, and in spite of the many problems the United States faces in the Middle East and Central Asia, President Bush has made it clear that a military confrontation with Iran should not be ruled out. With the deep US antipathy to the government in Tehran, the presumption of a nuclear weapons programme and the suspicions of a developing Iran/Iraq Shi'a axis, there is now the prospect of a third war in the region, adding Iran to Iraq and Afghanistan.

To a large extent, the current US military posture in President Bush's global war on terror stems from the powerfully expressed vision of a New American Century – an international system built on American economic values and orientations. It is a vision of almost messianic proportions, has been present within American conservatism for several generations, but has come to the fore in the ten years from 1995.

After the election of George W Bush in November 2000, the outlook of a New American Century was very quickly evident in US policies on issues such as arms control, trade and climate change, with a vigorous unilateralism frequently replacing a rather more multilateral norm. The outlook became much more heightened in the immediate wake of the 9/11 attacks but the resultant military actions have failed to bring stability and peace to Iraq and Afghanistan, neither have they prevented many further attacks by paramilitaries linked to the al-Qaida movement. It is therefore open to question whether the idea of a New American Century will survive and thrive, or whether it will be a short-lived phenomenon as the United States is forced to come to terms with its current predicament. This book seeks, in one particular way, to throw light on this.

THE OPEN DEMOCRACY GLOBAL SECURITY SERIES

Shortly before 9/11, an unusual new web journal was started, Open Democracy, describing itself as 'a channel for knowledge, learning, participation and understanding that is not owned by a media corporation, does not serve a special interest and does not adhere to a single ideological position'. As part of its early development, and just after 9/11, a weekly Global Security column was started that sought to analyse the developing war on terror, trying to put in perspective the unfolding conflict. Since October 2001, some 200 articles have been published on a weekly basis.

An earlier book (*A War on Terror: Afghanistan and After*, Pluto Press, 2004) brought together about 40 articles written between October 2001 and December 2002, and tracking the development of the war in Afghanistan and the subsequent evolution of al-Qaida and US counter-terrorism actions. It covered a period in which the prospects of a war with Iraq were increasing but did not deal specifically with it. As the introduction to that book concluded:

> Some mention is made of the developing crisis with Iraq, but that is in many ways a separate and very substantive issue. It is not central to this particular set of articles and perhaps deserves more detailed attention on another occasion.

This book is that 'occasion' and uses a similar format, with around 55 articles brought together in chronological order and grouped into chapters, each with a short introduction. The first four chapters give an almost week-by-week account of the Iraq War from the start in March 2003 through to September of that year. Later chapters extend the period for close to another two years, with the focus on Iraq but covering the developing crisis with Iran.

The articles constitute an attempt at contemporary analysis with the disadvantages and advantages of that approach, and might best be taken with other published analysis produced with the benefit of hindsight. The normal mechanism has been for a particular contribution to be written mid-week, for publication on the Open Democracy website on the Thursday evening of a given week. The articles are therefore very *immediate* in their perspective. Moreover, since they persistently attempt to analyse events and developments in a predictive context, they can certainly prove at fault on occasions. At the same time, the series builds up into an overall narrative that can also serve as a reminder of how ideas developed and changed, pointing to issues that can easily be lost a few months or years later.

The articles are reproduced here almost exactly as written, with just minor grammatical corrections and a small amount of editing to avoid excessive repetition, but with no adjustments in analysis. The information contained in them is gained from a very wide range of sources, some of the most commonly used being US broadsheets such as the *New York Times*, *Washington Post*, *Boston Globe* and *Los Angeles Times*, other newspapers from the UK, France, Israel, Pakistan and elsewhere, military journals such as *Defense News*, *International Defence Review*, *Jane's Defence Weekly*, *Jane's Intelligence Review* and *Aviation Week* and numerous websites but especially the BBC, al-Jazeera, Juan Cole's *Informed Comment*, *Truthout* and *Asia Times*.

Some particularly significant news items are sourced to sites in the articles and a few are given as detailed references. Much more comprehensive sourcing is available by going to the individual articles, all of which are available with free access on the Open Democracy website – <www.opendemocracy.net>, and following the links provided.

ACKNOWLEDGEMENTS

I would like to thank the numerous people who have helped me with this book, most notably Anthony Barnett of Open Democracy who got me involved in the first place, and David Hayes, Isabel Hilton and other members of staff with whom I have worked over the past four years. In the period covered by this book I have been able to talk to many journalists, military officers, public officials and activists with direct experience of Iraq, to many Iraqis and Iranians, and to academic and policy specialists in the United States, the United Kingdom and elsewhere.

Visits to Iran, Pakistan, China, the United Arab Emirates, the United States and Japan have supplemented these discussions and I have particularly valued a long-term and continuing association with the Oxford Research Group and the UN University for Peace in Costa Rica. Working at the Department of Peace Studies at Bradford University has been a particular pleasure. Fellow members of staff have been a continual source of information and ideas, and the 350 students from over 40 countries, some of them with many years of experience in conflict zones, bring a quite extraordinary wealth of knowledge to the Department.

Paul Rogers
August 2005

1
War

INTRODUCTION

When the war started in March 2003, there was a high expectation that the 'shock and awe' bombing tactics and a sense of liberation from most ordinary Iraqis would lead to a very rapid collapse of the regime followed by an early transition to peace and stability. Some of the problems experienced early in the campaign, including adverse weather and attacks on supply routes by irregular forces, resulted in a degree of consternation and critical analysis in some sectors of the media. That was quickly forgotten when the regime collapsed within three weeks, the overall view being that the pulling down of the statue of Saddam Hussein near the centre of Baghdad was the iconic demonstration of the success of the US forces and their coalition partners.

In the Open Democracy analyses reprinted here, a different view was taken right from the start, and within a few days of the outbreak of the war some of the comments were suggesting a protracted conflict that might stretch over a number of years. This view was predicated on the probability that there would be an organised guerrilla resistance centred on the Special Republican Guard, and that US forces would find urban conflict particularly difficult. With the benefit of hindsight, the analysis has proved to be wrong in one sense and right in most others.

It was wrong in suggesting that the regime as a whole would survive for many weeks or even months, but it quickly became apparent that units of the Special Republican Guard largely melted away rather than take on the overwhelming firepower of the US forces. Because of this, the regime itself collapsed, although many elements of the leadership evaded initial capture, and there were indications of some initial resistance to occupation within days of the taking of Baghdad.

In other respects, the analysis has proved sadly accurate in predicting a long-lasting conflict that would be costly to the United States and its coalition partners and even more so to tens of thousands of ordinary Iraqis. Its consistent focus during these first three weeks of the war on casualties has also proved apposite, given what is now known about the thousands of civilians killed in that period alone. It also correctly highlighted incidents of suicide bombings that occurred right at the start of the war and have, since then, become a major feature of the insurgency.

At the time, the fall of the regime was greeted with great enthusiasm within the Bush administration, and there were frequent suggestions that the more pessimistic analysts and commentators had been proved wrong. The achievement of the New American Century was on course, and diversions from this aim were highly unlikely. As the following accounts suggest, though, even at the height of this brief phase of the war, there were all too many signs that this was to be an entirely false prospect.

THE QUICKSAND OF WAR *24 March 2003*

The first indication of the unexpected nature of the war with Iraq came just a few hours into the ground invasion. At about 05.30 (London time) on 21 March, the BBC's 24-hour news channel called up one of its correspondents, Adam Mynott, who was with a group of US soldiers as they crossed the border from Kuwait into Iraq.

Whereas other reports had indicated rapid progress of US and British troops, Mynott came on air breathless from having to take cover as the convoy he was with faced up to small arms and rocket attack from Iraqi forces. It was clearly unexpected, and gave the first indication that the Iraqi resistance to the invasion would be fierce.

Umm Qasr

Four days on, US troops are still trying to defeat a group of Iraqi soldiers in the port of Umm Qasr, and substantial British troop deployments are stuck outside of Basra. While the major US forces are moving rapidly up the Tigris/Euphrates valley towards Baghdad, what is happening in south-east Iraq is highly significant.

According to informed sources just before the war started, one of the first major ground campaigns would be the liberation of Basra, Iraq's second city and a centre for the Shi'a population that had been treated so badly by the Saddam Hussein regime.

As a *New York Times* article put it, 'a successful and "benign" occupation that results in flag-waving crowds hugging British and American soldiers will create an immediate positive image worldwide of American and British war aims while also undermining Iraqi resistance elsewhere in the country'. Five days into the war, and with US forces facing substantial resistance in several towns and cities, the liberation of Basra is still awaited.

This may seem a small sign, but it is important in the context of the expectation that this would be a straightforward war of liberation for the Iraqi people, with the US demonstrating such firepower and determination that the regime would fall within days – or that there would, at minimum, be massive desertions and surrenders, with resistance limited to a hard core of regime supporters.

It is still possible that the regime will collapse in the next few days, but the least that can be said now is that it seems unlikely. Moreover, whereas resistance was expected in Baghdad, one surprise to invading forces has been the frequent problems posed by small numbers of Iraqi forces operating in areas remote from the regime's control, and possibly not even in communication with Baghdad.

A Conflict of Surprises

Any attempt to predict the further development of the war is highly risky, but there are three significant indicators of the unfolding character of the war.

The first is that the bombing of Baghdad, while intensive, has not been on the overwhelming scale expected by many analysts and predicted by US administration officials. Most of the attacks have been directed at narrow military targets, including command and control centres; civilian casualties have been relatively low, at least during the first four nights.

A likely reason for this relative restraint is the necessity of limiting the political impact of civilian casualties. The British prime minister Tony Blair is in an especially vulnerable political position, and even within the Bush administration there will be some idea of the extent of international opposition to the war (although its sheer intensity is largely unreported by the US and UK media).

The second indicator is that the US war plan calls for a very rapid advance towards Baghdad by the equivalent of three divisions numbering perhaps 60,000 troops. This is not actually a very large force and the advance is dependent on secure supply lines and overwhelming use of firepower against any opposition facing the advancing forces.

The use of multiple launch rocket systems, cluster bombs and other area impact weapons is almost certainly causing many deaths and serious injuries among Iraqi conscripts. This is speeding the advance, but does not address the serious security problem presented by small Iraqi units that choose to engage US forces only after the main advance has gone through.

Something similar is happening around Basra, and a picture is now starting to emerge of a risk of guerrilla activity in the coming days, with actions aimed at the more lightly-armed US and British troops that are deployed behind the main advances.

The third indicator is the civilian context of the military campaign. US troops are, unsurprisingly, simply not being welcomed in the way that was confidently expected in Washington, as liberators. There are several possible factors involved here: memories of the failure of the US to support the Shi'a revolt in 1991, the effectiveness of regime propaganda, the underlying force of Iraqi nationalism.

In the light of the military setbacks of the first days of the war, it is possible that the US may yet return to the 'shock and awe' bombing tactics that were originally expected, whatever their wider political consequences.

A New Timetable?

After five days of war, the regime in Baghdad still seems in control, US forces are moving towards the city, Iraqi resistance is stronger than expected and the whole war is becoming steadily more complex.

There are other complicating factors. Turkish involvement in northern Iraq and Israeli action in Lebanon are both possible, and the US is simultaneously involved in a substantial military operation in Afghanistan.

A quick war with few casualties looks increasingly unlikely. There could be dramatic changes but the second Gulf war seems likely to last not days, but weeks or even months.

A LONG OR A SHORT WAR? *27 March 2003*

After eight days of war in Iraq, there is growing evidence that the campaign is not going the way the US and Britain wanted or expected. The situation remains very fluid, with an enormous amount of misinformation coming from both sides.

One way to try and make some sense of it is to examine the range of possible outcomes. On this basis, and on a best estimate, there were at the outset of war five ways in which it could have been expected to go to a conclusion. Each outcome had a different duration, ranging from one-to-two weeks to a year or more. These will be examined in turn.

The First Outcome: 'Shock and Awe'

The 'shock and awe' tactic of massive bombing of the Iraqi leadership and military causes the immediate collapse of the regime, and the assassination of Saddam Hussein, with little or no fighting on the ground. *Duration: 3–5 days.*

While events have already made this estimate redundant, a version of it is still just possible over a longer timescale, especially if the US returns to the intensive city-centre bombing of the third night of the war and succeeds in destroying the Iraqi leadership, including Saddam Hussein himself. It remains unlikely, partly because the US is limited in its bombing campaign by the need to avoid civilian casualties, and because the Iraqi leadership is both dispersed and well protected.

The Second Outcome: Quick Victory

The leadership survives the initial bombing, coalition troops move rapidly towards Baghdad, unimpeded by Iraqi forces. In southern cities they are welcomed and there are anti-regime rebellions. The Republican Guard is engaged and defeated, largely by air power, outside of Baghdad, and the Special

Republican Guard disperses. Baghdad is occupied with little conflict. The regime collapses. *Duration: 1–3 weeks.*

This is still possible but frankly very unlikely. There has been surprisingly little welcome for coalition troops. Basra was expected to be liberated within a couple of days but remains in regime hands. US troops are being harried by militia and fedayeen and neither they nor the British have achieved full control of south-east Iraq. The regime appears firmly in control in Baghdad. There has been little in the way of rebellion.

There is now some evidence that the Republican Guard is willing to fight, contrary to the expectations of many analysts who saw the much smaller Special Republican Guard as being the main problem for the US. The Republican Guard has forces deeply protected south of Baghdad and is subject to intensive bombing, but some units repelled a substantial air attack by US Apache helicopters earlier this week, bringing one and possibly two down and damaging many more, much to the surprise of US commanders. Attacks against extended supply lines from Kuwait towards Baghdad are causing problems. The weather has not helped.

The Third Outcome: Slow Victory

The Republican Guard fights but is defeated. The Special Republican Guard is eventually defeated in Baghdad. There are limited uprisings. The regime collapses with thousands of military casualties and hundreds of civilians killed. *Duration: 4–8 weeks.*

This is certainly still possible, but would require substantial US reinforcements into southern Iraq accompanied by air-lifted troops to open a new front north of Baghdad, splitting Iraqi defences. Both may now be happening, but heavy resistance by the Special Republican Guard and Iraqi Special Forces could lead to substantial US casualties. The regional and international political impact would be considerable, with the anti-American and anti-British mood increasing greatly.

The Fourth Outcome: Long War

The Republican Guard fights outside Baghdad first and then retreats to pre-prepared defensive positions in the suburbs. There is an eventual defeat but the Special Republican Guard, fedayeen and other forces fight on for weeks in the city. Substantial further US reinforcements are called in and there is consistent use of heavy firepower in the city during a siege in which US forces slowly encroach on the centre. They eventually occupy Baghdad and destroy the regime but not without even higher civilian casualties. The US is unable to succeed by the end of May; the war slows down through the heat of the summer until the autumn. *Duration: up to 8 months.*

This is quite possible and would be a humanitarian disaster. It would also have huge political implications for George Bush and would threaten Tony Blair's position. The regional and international impact of sustained warfare in an ancient Arab city, as well as considerable loss of civilian life, would further intensify anti-American and anti-British feelings across the region, with unpredictable consequences.

The Fifth Outcome: Defeat

This is an extension of the previous outcome, except that the elite Iraqi forces and irregular guerrilla groups tie down US forces for an extended period, with the regime surviving through next winter. There is instability in several Arab states as popular sentiments require support for Iraq. This instability is compounded by harsh action by Ariel Sharon's Israeli government in southern Lebanon following missile attacks directed at Haifa. US and UK forces in the region are subject to paramilitary attacks. A messy ceasefire is eventually agreed under UN auspices, and the UN takes a leading role in trying to restore some sense of stability in the face of many tens of thousands of casualties and a wrecked Iraq. *Duration: uncertain.*

The Probable Outcome

At present the US and Britain are obliged to face up to something between a slow victory and a long war. The extent of Iraqi guerrilla actions has come as a surprise, but even more remarkable has been the ability of Iraqi forces to inflict damage on US equipment, most notably the response to the Apache helicopter attack.

Although there could still be a sudden and rapid collapse of the Saddam Hussein regime, this looks decreasingly likely. One consequence is that the US plan for a rapid march on Baghdad using relatively light but highly mobile forces is proving difficult to carry out.

At the same time, we should not underestimate the absolute determination of the Bush administration to succeed in terminating the Iraqi regime. If there were any prospect of the war dragging on into the summer, there would be a major intensification of US operations in late April and May.

'Defeat', the fifth option, is utterly unthinkable. If it were to happen, it would destroy not just the US strategy for the region, threatening its control of Gulf oil, but would fatally damage the whole Project for the New American Century that lies at the heart of the neo-conservative security agenda in Washington.

A CHANGE OF STRATEGY? *31 March 2003*

The US war plan in Iraq depended on massive air bombardments and rapid movements of ground troops towards Baghdad to bring the regime to its knees, possibly in a matter of days and certainly in a very few weeks. The war in Iraq is not going according to this plan. The main reason is simple: the strategy was flawed from the start, and has been further thrown off course by short-term surprises and specific failures.

A Shifting Timetable

The US military planners had originally hoped to begin the war towards the end of March, when all of its intended troop deployments were to have been completed.

Three factors disrupted this. First, the reluctance of the UN Security Council to accede to pressure over a possible second resolution (as a follow-up to Resolution 1441) influenced the decision to launch the war a few days earlier than planned.

Second, the refusal of the Turkish parliament to allow US troops to move through Turkey into northern Iraq refocused attention on the southern front, with US planners believing that there would be sufficient US forces in Kuwait by around 26 March to begin the war from that direction alone.

These two events led war planners to bring the schedule forward by several days, probably to the night of 21–22 March. In turn, however, that was changed again in the light of credible intelligence reports locating Saddam Hussein and other Iraqi leaders at a leadership compound in the vicinity of one of the homes of Saddam Hussein's younger son (and leader of the Republican Guard), Qusay.

At short notice, and at least two full days before the intended start of the war, President Bush authorised a massive attack on the compound. The assault on the night of 19–20 March used about 40 cruise missiles fired from four ships and two submarines, along with two 1,000-kilogram bombs dropped by F-117A stealth strike aircraft.

The attack failed in its targeting of Saddam, yet it also gave the Iraqis clear notice of the onset of war; this meant that the rest of the US forces had to be rushed into action. The US journal *Aviation Week* (one of the most reliable sources of information on the war) reported that the new situation 'left military commanders in the Middle East scrambling to move up their schedules. The attack may have come as a surprise to the Iraqis, but equally shocked were US troops assembled in the region and America's British allies' (*Aviation Week*, 24 March 2003).

As war plans were brought forward, US and British troops crossed the border from Kuwait, and substantial air raids were mounted on many parts of Iraq, notably Baghdad itself. These caused considerable destruction and substantial loss of life, yet even the massive attacks of the third night of the war failed to make the regime capitulate. Thus, within days of the start of the war, the ground offensive became essential to the central US war aim of terminating the regime.

Now, twelve days into the war, and with the ground offensive virtually stalled, military and political leaders frequently deny making any pre-war promise of a short war.

This is, at best, disingenuous. In the run-up to the war there were numerous briefings from within the Bush administration to selected journalists that confidently predicted that the intense use of air power combined with a rapid march on Baghdad would guarantee a quick victory. At their more optimistic, this even extended to a belief that three or four nights of intensive bombing alone would be enough to destroy the regime.

The Iraqi Factor

In practice, and almost from the start, it became clear that US plans were not going to work as planned. Yet the full extent of early failures was concealed by the coalition's effective news management, which consistently overestimated its progress – from the Basra 'uprising' to the premature 'capture' of Umm Qasr.

Four distinct factors combined to ensure the problems that handicapped the US and British from the outset. First, the severe weather, including lengthy sandstorms; second, the constraints on actions that might inflict especially high civilian casualties, which were partly a testimony to the enormous anti-war movements that have developed (especially in Britain).

The other two factors require more elaboration. Third, then, is the amount of resistance mounted by lightly-armed but determined Iraqi units, many of them targeting the long supply lines established as a consequence of the rapid initial movement of US troops from Kuwait towards Baghdad.

The extent of this disruption is extraordinary, considering that the confrontations involve the use of light weapons against the world's best-equipped forces. The equivalent of three US Army brigades are tied down protecting the supply lines, with additional fighting taking place in many of the urban centres on the route to Baghdad.

These three brigades represent about half of the army currently in Iraq and close to 30 per cent of the combined force of army and Marine Corps units. These troops are facing a level of resistance that was completely unexpected and is now affecting the entire operation.

A complicating factor here is the 'embedding' of correspondents with army and Marine Corps units. This kind of media coverage is predicated on a successful war – with the victor gaining not just the spoils of war but its media glamour. If however, a war does not go as expected, media correspondents are on hand to report its failures and setbacks too.

Correspondents with the troops are, of course, operating with 'minders' and may often be limited in what they can report, especially through the all-important medium of television. But what is forgotten is that such reporters also have satellite phones and can communicate direct with their offices, giving private indications of damaging circumstances that they cannot cover fully in their 'live' reports.

The fourth factor is the failure of ordinary Iraqi people even to welcome US and British troops as liberators, let alone rise up against the regime. The reasons may vary. Shi'a memories of US inaction during the bloody 1991 uprising are often cited; but a more general pattern of sullen and suspicious attitudes throughout the southern areas subject to coalition control is becoming evident.

This situation is made worse by the increasingly tough behaviour of US troops, especially jittery after the recent suicide bombing, an incident with profound significance to US forces. In October 1983, the US Marine Corps lost 241 of its members to a massive truck bomb detonated outside a barracks block at Beirut airport, an event that precipitated the end of US intervention in Lebanon. This disaster is ingrained in the mindset of the modern Marine Corps.

Suicide bombings by people connected with the Iraqi army have an even greater symbolic impact than those from a paramilitary group, not least because the Iraqi armed forces have access to far more powerful weapons than, for example, Hamas.

What Now?

The failed US strategy has in turn created a very dangerous set of circumstances.

At present, there are three possible options. First, the one formally announced by official US sources: a pause of several more days before an attack on Baghdad is launched. This would be highly risky and could be achieved only by combining a ground offensive with a very heavy use of air power that would result in large numbers of civilian casualties – measured in the thousands rather than the hundreds as at present.

If this option was followed through, it could start within a week, and build on the intensive bombardment of Republican Guard divisions that is currently underway (which includes extensive carpet-bombing by B-52s from RAF Fairford in England). The success of this policy is dependent on the aerial destruction of the Republican Guard, though there are indications of their capacity to regroup along pre-existing defensive positions in the southern suburbs of Baghdad.

The second option available is to await the arrival of another US Army division of around 18,000 troops, originally intended for the northern front through Turkey. This would certainly reinforce existing capabilities. The equipment for the division is currently in transit from the eastern Mediterranean to Kuwait.

The problem is that the necessary equipment will not all be in place until 11 April, and it will take several more days to get the division ready for action and move it through southern Iraq. This would delay the offensive until the second half of April, closer to the hottest time of year when hostilities are likely to be much harder to wage.

The third option is for the US to bring in substantial reinforcements, comprising the 120,000 or so troops that are now being prepared for deployment in the region, before resuming its major advance. This would delay the war even further, certainly through the summer months.

The US Dilemma: Intensify, or Delay?

The overall predicament for the US is whether to try and terminate the Iraqi regime with the forces now available. It has the ability to do so, but only through the use of its massive advantage in firepower. This would entail thousands of civilian deaths. The alternative is to wait until there are far greater forces in the area. This, however, might delay a conclusion to the war by some months, giving greater opportunity for an even more vigorous anti-war mood throughout the Middle East and beyond.

Both these possibilities could be pre-empted by the assassination of Saddam Hussein (and other members of the Iraqi leadership) in a US bombing raid, but that seems unlikely given the deception and concealment tactics now being practised.

In conclusion, what was expected to be a quick and easy victory is turning into something far more complex and difficult. The gravest result for the US would be severe damage to the neo-conservative security agenda in Washington, one built around the extraordinary yet deeply entrenched idea of a New American Century. This vision will not be readily abandoned. As a result, and in the face of the problems that have arisen, an intensification of the US war effort is highly likely.

A 30-YEAR WAR *4 April 2003*

The Iraq war is only two weeks old yet the Iraqi civilian death toll is already in the high hundreds, and Iraqi military losses (while harder to estimate) in the several thousands. The duration of this immediate conflict is yet uncertain, but some of its aspects already suggest that it may inaugurate a much longer conflict lasting for decades.

The war itself was initiated by the United States and Britain without UN endorsement and in the face of opposition stretching far beyond the Middle East to encompass public opinion across most of the world. In these circumstances, a very short war was needed, involving the almost complete collapse of the Saddam Hussein regime. Instead, the regime survived the initial attacks, resistance in most of the towns and cities has been much greater than the US military commanders expected, and there have been few instances of crowds welcoming the liberators.

Many US strategists had anticipated an immediate collapse of the regime. This did not happen yet they still confidently expected US forces to be on the outskirts of Baghdad and ready for occupation of the city within four or five days.

In the event, some US forces are now close to Baghdad, but the extent of the Iraqi resistance so far means that they will either have to establish large forces close to the city, or else almost immediately fight their way through the city using their overwhelming firepower. Already, there are signs of a much more aggressive use of area impact munitions and other forms of firepower, with civilian casualties rising rapidly. This situation is born of two requirements – the need to gain the initiative because of political pressures, and the inevitable response to the risk of suicide bombings.

A Trail of Bitterness

The effect across the region, though, is fundamental in its impact. Across the Arab world as a whole, the picture is of an aggressive superpower, aided and abetted by Britain, invading and occupying one of the major Arab states. Furthermore, Iraq may be a twentieth-century construct, but it represents Islamic and predecessor civilisations dating back many thousands of years.

There remains little affection for Saddam Hussein anywhere in the region, although the Americans are currently achieving the extraordinary feat of making him considerably more popular than he was. Much more significant is the gathering support for Iraq and the Iraqis, based on the firm belief that they are being subjected to a western conquest that will become a long-term subjugation.

Already this is attracting radicals to Iraq; it is also a 'gift' to al-Qaida and its associates. President Mubarak of Egypt, one of the strongest allies of the United States in the region, talked in Suez of the risk of this war giving birth to 'a hundred bin Ladens'.

Unless the regime suddenly collapses, events of the next four weeks will only reinforce the almost visceral opposition to what the Americans and British are now doing. Following their earlier reversals, the US forces can decide to attack the core leadership of the regime almost at once, using their available troops combined with massive use of weaponry. This could well achieve the objective of regime termination, but the human costs would be enormous; thousands of civilians would die and tens of thousands would be injured.

Instead, they could wait for two to three weeks for reinforcements and then move in, again employing massive firepower which would kill many civilians. In either case, the war could still end within six weeks. A higher level of Iraqi resistance might involve a longer siege of Baghdad and continue through the summer heat.

How this war ends, though, is largely irrelevant in the long term. The important point is that it will leave a trail of bitterness and despair that will last for years and even decades. In part, this will be a legacy of the sheer impact of the bloodshed and destruction, and a near-universal perception across the region that the United States and its Israeli ally are in the business of controlling the Arab world.

The perception here is at least as important as the reality, and in any case there are far too many aspects of the war and its probable aftermath that allow this perception to gain some credibility.

A Failure of US Intelligence

Whatever Tony Blair may hope for, it is becoming clear that Washington's initial post-war plan is for the United States to have firm control over the country. The 23 ministries will all be headed by Americans, with appointed Iraqi advisers, and the overall head of the state apparatus will be a US General, Jay Garner, who has close links with Israel as well as being president of an arms contracting company that makes missile guidance systems.

There is abundant evidence that Washington's security neo-conservatives believe it to be absolutely essential for the United States to have effective control of the Gulf. With its massive oil reserves now accounting for nearly 70 per cent of world totals, and most industrial economies increasingly dependent on Gulf oil, controlling the region has become an essential feature of the Republican security paradigm.

This means terminating the Iraqi regime followed by the occupation of the country and the establishment of an acceptable client state secured by a permanent US military presence. It further means deterring Iran from presenting any threats to US security, a process that will be made much easier by control of Iraq.

There seems to be no understanding whatsoever of the effect of this on the region; nor does the US seem to realise that it plays directly into the hands of militant radicals. Instead, there is a naive belief that such a western-dominated order can be sustained, perhaps stemming from apparent past successes in working with local elites.

The US mistake lies in failing to recognise three key trends. The first is the demographic process that has resulted in many millions of young people who are increasingly marginalised from economic participation. This is compounded by the second trend, the effect of secondary and tertiary education on millions of people across the region, giving them a much clearer understanding of what is happening. Such people all too frequently see their ruling elites as benefiting at their expense as well as being inextricably linked with the US and other western states. The third trend is the existence of new channels of communication like al-Jazeera that present the realities in the Middle East in a way that has not hitherto existed.

The end result is a bitterness that will express itself in many different ways in the coming years, not least in the development of further radical and extreme social movements such as al-Qaida. Even in Iraq itself, there may be sustained resistance to US dominance, but this will be marginal compared with the reaction across the region.

A Vital Choice

Gulf oil will be the dominant energy source for the world for upwards of 30 years. If the US neo-conservatives establish a paradigm of clear-cut western control of the region, with Iraq at its centre, then the stage is set for a conflict that lasts just as long.

The Iraq war may be over within three months or it may take longer; in either case, it has the potential to signal the development of a much more sustained conflict. Whether this occurs depends in turn on a key variable: the endurance and success of the Bush administration's conception of international security, the essential requirement for a New American Century.

If this conception does succeed, a 30-year war is in prospect. If, by contrast, a saner approach to international security develops, the beginnings of a peaceful order could be shaped. What happens in Iraq in the next few months may determine which route is taken.

BITTER REACTIONS *8 April 2003*

The pace of events has quickened in the last, intensive days of combat in the Iraq war. The focus of world and media attention is on the fate of the regime in its Baghdad heartland. But a sense of the impact of war on the country and region as a whole is also essential at this crucial stage.

For a few hours on Saturday 5 April, it began to look as though the war was coming to an end. Reports from US military headquarters in Qatar suggested that substantial numbers of tanks and armoured personnel carriers had driven right in to the centre of Baghdad and were taking up positions to occupy significant parts of the city.

The advance built on several days of intense bombing of Iraqi army positions to the south of Baghdad that appeared to have destroyed as many as three Iraqi divisions with the loss of several thousand troops. It also followed the rapid occupation of the main civil airport on 4 April. These developments together seemed to indicate that resistance was crumbling and that the Iraqi regime was on the point of collapse.

By the morning of Sunday 6 April, an imminent end to the war seemed less likely. US forces had certainly been able to use their extraordinary firepower in the open country south of Baghdad, and they had almost certainly killed and injured very many Iraqi soldiers. Even so, their initial attack on Baghdad represented more of a major armoured reconnaissance than the final termination of the regime.

This was followed by the even more substantial US incursion into the centre of Baghdad on 7–8 April. Its aim is clearly to take over and destroy the physical centres of power of the regime; it is being pursued with the use of massive force. This might bring the main phase of the war to a rapid end and would undoubtedly save thousands of lives. It would not necessarily mean an end to all conflict, as other parts of Iraq might still have militia willing to fight on.

Even such an immediate end, though, is by no means assured, and any attempt to assess what is now happening has to take into account three significant factors: American military superiority, Iraqi military and civilian losses, and the responses of regime forces to the invasion of their country.

The US Military in Command

The first factor to register is that the US forces have overwhelming superiority in terms of technology and firepower.

There is complete air supremacy, the weapons capacity of B-52 and B1B planes is enormous and the army and Marine Corps are equipped with weapons that are three or more decades ahead of those of the Iraqis. After twelve years of sanctions, Iraqi forces are nowhere near the level they were in the 1991 war. Moreover, the American forces are able to combine near real-time intelligence gathering with a huge array of precision-guided weapons, and they can also call upon an inventory of area-impact munitions.

It is this category of weapons, combined with the mass use of artillery that has killed so many Iraqi soldiers and also many civilians. There has been some recent controversy over the use of cluster bombs, but it is commonly forgotten that a single MLRS missile launcher can deliver the destructive power of 40 cluster bombs. These weapons are so powerful that they are sometimes referred to as conventional weapons of mass destruction, and are being used repeatedly by US forces in the field.

In the case of the Massive Ordnance Air Burst (MOAB) weapon, *Aviation Week* (17 March 2003) reported that its test launch in Florida on 11 March produced a detonation audible, and 'mushroom cloud' visible, from almost 50 kilometres away; and quoted an air force official that '(a)t least a dozen MOABs are being rushed through production for delivery to units that could use them to bomb Republican Guard troops'.

Iraqi Losses

Although the Saddam Hussein regime has given frequent details of civilian casualties, it has not tried to report on military casualties. In the last few days, US sources have been more explicit, citing the destruction of up to three Republican Guard divisions in addition to 2–3,000 deaths in the fighting at the airport and in the city. Earlier there were reports of 1,000 Iraqi soldiers being killed around Najaf and British sources estimated that up to 500 were killed on the weekend of 5–6 April in the fighting around Basra.

In the light of these figures, and even assuming that only one in five of the soldiers in a 'destroyed' division actually dies, the military losses incurred by Iraqi forces will already run to at least 10,000. In modern war, it is assumed that three people are seriously injured for every person that is killed. This is likely to be the case for the Iraqis, with many of those injured subsequently dying as medical support away from the towns and cities will be extremely limited. Thus, 20 days of war has almost certainly resulted in around 40,000 Iraqi soldiers killed or seriously injured – hardly a clean war.

The civilian losses have been much lower, but are still heading towards 1,000 people killed and perhaps three times as many seriously injured by the end of the second week of war. To take only one major example, the determined US attack on Nasiriya to try and dislodge fedayeen militia involved sustained bombing over several days that killed around 230 civilians as well as many more military.

There is ample recent evidence from independent sources of the intense difficulties faced by the civilian population in Baghdad and elsewhere. According to the Red Cross, at the height of the 5 April fighting, all the hospitals in Baghdad were under pressure. The al-Yarmouk Hospital, for example, was receiving 100 casualties per hour. The hospital at al-Mahmudiya, south of the city, was unable to cope with the number of casualties, and the Red Cross was trying to get urgent help to the hospital at Hilla further to the south.

In short, as many as 10,000 soldiers and 1,000 civilians may have been killed and over 30,000 injured in less than three weeks. Such a toll is recognised only at the margins of the western media, but is much more clearly registered across the Middle East – where it is perceived as the killing of Arabs in their thousands by Americans, in the interests of a policy of conquest and occupation.

Iraqi Responses

This level of loss must surely mean that the regime is near its end, though here again some caution is necessary. At the start of the war, on 19–20 March, there was an initial assumption that 'shock and awe' would bring about immediate regime collapse. Even if that did not happen, Basra was expected to be liberated in two days at most, and US troops were expected to be surrounding Baghdad within five days. Apart from Baghdad, little or no resistance was envisaged.

It has turned out very differently, yet the same kinds of assumptions persist at each phase of the war. While it is obvious that Iraqi forces have no prospect at all of defence against US military power in the field, resistance in towns and cities has been substantial. Basra may now be close to occupation by the British, but this will have taken nearly three weeks instead of two days, and opposition may still lie ahead. Nasiriya and Karbala still have active irregular forces, as do a number of smaller towns; together they are tying down thousands of American troops.

Moreover, the depiction of the Republican Guard is occasionally misleading. In 1991, this eight-division force was the elite group within the Iraqi armed forces, but the regime was concerned about its loyalty in the mid-1990s, reducing it in size and charging it with the perimeter defence of Baghdad and other parts of Iraq. There is little evidence that the Republican Guard was ever assumed to be sufficiently reliable to be allowed into Baghdad in force.

In the period before the war, some experienced analysts were assuming that the Republican Guard would offer virtually no resistance at all, and that the more general components of the Iraqi army would surrender in their tens of thousands. As it turned out, the mass surrenders were far smaller than expected, and the Republican Guard did fight, albeit with huge losses.

The questionable loyalty of these troops in the 1990s meant that the most reliable elements were concentrated in an entirely different set of forces, the Special Republican Guard and other units, including the fedayeen. These together may number as many as 30,000 people, trained especially in urban warfare and assumed to be markedly loyal to the regime. As far as it is possible to say, these groups have played little part in the war and are available in Baghdad for the defence of the regime.

A Hollow Victory

The implication of the foregoing analysis is that it is at least possible that the war has some time to run, and that it will involve substantial further loss of life, both military and civilian. While the regime has been severely weakened and might even be close to collapse, it is also likely that US forces will take time in moving into the whole of Baghdad, attempting to bring in up to 20,000 more troops over the next ten days.

The problem for US military commanders is that they are under political pressure from Donald Rumsfeld and others to terminate the regime and end the war quickly. They have the means to do this, in the shape of their overwhelming firepower in pursuit of the defending forces, but the inevitable consequence of that would be much greater numbers of civilians killed and maimed. The current operations in Baghdad do indicate that this is the military policy now being pursued.

A relevant factor here is the popular mood in the Middle East, which is turning ever more strongly against the United States. A protracted war would allow that to develop further, while a sudden escalation of violence by US forces might end the regime more quickly but at the cost of passionate anger across the region in protest at a higher level of casualties.

In the United States, the dominant perception seems to be that the war is already as good as won, and that peace and tranquility will rapidly follow a stunning victory. In reality, whether the war ends soon or drags on, it is likely to prove a hollow victory with a deeply bitter and unstable peace.

AFGHAN LESSONS, IRAQI FUTURES *11 April 2003*

In an assessment of the development of the Iraq war just under two weeks ago, an analysis of the problems faced by the US forces emphasised the unexpected resistance that they had met. Nonetheless, the overwhelming military capabilities of the US forces were highlighted and it was suggested that they had several options available, including waiting for reinforcements.

In the event, the US launched an immediate attack on Baghdad which (the earlier analysis concluded):

> would be highly risky and could only be achieved by combining a ground offensive with a very heavy use of air power that would result in large numbers of civilian casualties, certainly measured in the thousands rather than the hundreds as at present. If this option was taken, it could start within a week ...

The Price of Victory

Although information from the coalition forces is of variable reliability, it would seem that the attack on the international airport was achieved with the use of just such extraordinary firepower, so much so that the coalition claimed that 2–3,000 Iraqi soldiers were killed within 36 hours. This gives some indication of the fearsome capabilities of the US forces, but also highlights the dangers to civilian life of any use of such methods within Baghdad itself.

In practice, though, this is largely what happened earlier this week – the heavy use of firepower in an urban area, with an inevitable cost in lives of civilians and military. In one incident last Monday, within a few hours of the US advance into the centre of Baghdad, the *International Herald Tribune* reported one incident:

> Caught in the crossfire, according to a chilling account by an Associated Press reporter, were a number of pedestrians, including an old man with a cane, looking confused. When he failed to heed

three warning shots by the Marines, they killed him. A red van and an orange-and-white taxi were also riddled with bullets after they failed to heed warning shots.

Similar incidents were repeated across the city. They stemmed both from the vigorous nature of the US offensive and the risk to its troops of fedayeen and other determined fighters, including possible suicide bombers. Such civilian losses were an almost inevitable result of a decision to move rapidly into the city with forces that were highly mobile but totally insufficient to pacify the whole city.

By going for the centre of the city, the US forces were hoping and intending to destroy the regime in the presumption that resistance would collapse. It did so, but only at a huge cost and with some immediate, and predictable, consequences.

A report from Reuters carried in a few western media outlets reported that most Baghdad hospitals were filled to beyond the point where they could cope, and were running short of anaesthetics, basic equipment and even clean water. The report concluded:

> Iraq's problems have been compounded by international sanctions against the government of President Saddam Hussein, which have made it difficult to stock analgesics and morphine. Aid agencies have long warned that Iraq and its 26 million people were in poor shape after two earlier wars and years of sanctions.

A large part of that responsibility obviously lies with the regime itself, but the nature of the blunt sanctions is also relevant. In any case, by the onset of the recent war the Iraqi population had been severely weakened. In this light, the effects of any attack would be magnified, and urban warfare would be particularly destructive. This is precisely what happened.

A Vacuum of Power

The disorder and anarchy that has developed in Baghdad and elsewhere is a combination of several different factors.

First, obviously, is that a brutal and repressive regime was very effective at maintaining order, right down to the use of a more or less conventional police force. Once the regime had collapsed, its forces of control disappeared within hours, leaving a near-total public order vacuum that has resulted in even hospitals and universities being looted.

A second factor is the paucity of US troops to even attempt to maintain public order, even if they were instructed to do so. The decision to use heavy firepower and relatively small numbers of ground troops means that forces now in Baghdad are actually thin on the ground and largely concerned with countering such armed resistance that continues. In any case, even if they were concerned with public order control, the possible presence of suicide bombers would make their task problematic.

More generally, there is the question of US military culture. US troops have very little experience of peacekeeping or even of post-conflict stabilisation. The common view is that this kind of work is 'not proper soldiering' and should be left to the Scandinavians and others of a similar bent. The United States has had minimal engagement in UN peacekeeping operations in the past 50 years, and its activities in Kosovo and elsewhere have been characterised by the establishment of heavily protected encampments and the use of mobile patrols based on armoured vehicles with a minimal involvement of local populations.

In the chaos of post-war Iraq, it would be possible for the United States to invite the UN to put forces in to ensure stability, but the Bush administration is deeply reluctant to do this, as the clear intention is to secure Iraq under firm American control. The end result is that long-term political control is sought without the commitment to short-term peacekeeping.

In the Afghan Mirror

The lessons from Afghanistan are only too relevant here, not least in what has happened there even while the war in Iraq has been waged. Almost every experienced political figure with knowledge of Afghanistan declared that it would be essential to have some kind of stabilisation force for the whole country to facilitate the development of stable government.

The International Security Assistance Force (ISAF) was indeed set up, but has been restricted to 5,000 troops operating in the Kabul area alone. UN insistence on the need for a 30,000-strong ISAF able to operate throughout the country has been repeatedly resisted by Washington.

As a consequence, the rest of Afghanistan has remained under the control of warlords or even factions allied to the Taliban. Recently, US and Afghan soldiers were involved in serious fighting with suspected Taliban militia that left eight dead and 15 captured; and a week ago, Haji Gilani, one of the closest associates of President Hamid Karzai, was murdered outside his home in Oruzgan province. US action in Afghanistan has been focused on countering a resurgence of Taliban activity and has involved considerable military action largely unreported in the western media. One of the most substantial counter-attacks came three days ago after guerrilla forces had attacked an Afghan military checkpoint that had been providing security for local forces.

An immediate US response came from Marine Corps AV8B aircraft dropping laser-guided bombs on presumed guerrilla forces, but one bomb hit a family compound killing eleven of the twelve civilians in it. Afghan officials later admitted that this tragedy would further inflame anti-American feeling in the region, aiding the Taliban as they regroup for a summer campaign against the Afghan government and American forces.

In short, the war in Afghanistan is far from over, and up to 10,000 US troops are still involved in trying to maintain control of the country. In Iraq, a much larger problem is emerging as Washington remains adamant that it will be in charge after the war is finally over, but is extremely reluctant to counter the current disorder. What appears to be a sudden victory is already taking on a very different mantle, and one that may even cause the more hawkish elements of the Bush administration to restrain their rhetoric of success.

2
Aftermath

INTRODUCTION

This chapter covers the seven-week period from just after the termination of the Saddam Hussein regime through to the beginnings of an insurgency. At the start of the period, many parts of Iraq were in disarray, caused by a combination of looting, lawlessness and a desperate shortage of medical supplies. The police force was largely dysfunctional and coalition forces were quite unable to maintain public order.

Even so, there appeared to be no attempt to seek the deployment of any kind of UN force to oversee post-conflict reconstruction. Instead the United States took control of many aspects of the Iraqi economy and there were even the first of a series of reports that the US was intent on establishing permanent bases. While there were stout denials of any connection between the termination of the Saddam Hussein regime and the long-term value of controlling Iraqi oil supplies, this was becoming a common theme across the Middle East. It was made more plausible by the lack of any evidence of weapons of mass destruction in Iraq, undercutting the supposed core motivation for the war.

Three other factors are relevant in appreciating the long-term significance of some of the developments during this period. One was the information coming to light, primarily from independent non-government sources, about the extent of civilian and military casualties suffered during the first three weeks of the war. This was already beginning to confirm the fears of some of the independent analysts who, before the war, had warned of high civilian casualties but who had had their views summarily dismissed.

A second factor was the growing evidence that Iraq was under the firm control of the coalition, with the United States clearly in overall charge. It was already apparent that US corporations were getting the prime contracts for reconstruction and that Iraqi state industries would be privatised. Furthermore, and in an extraordinary move, the Coalition Provisional Authority took the decision to disband the Iraqi army, throwing several hundred thousand young men into unemployment.

Finally, by the beginning of June, there was evidence that opposition to the coalition military presence was spreading beyond sporadic attacks into something very much more serious – an insurgency was in the early stages of development.

All of these issues were overshadowed by one more general trend. This was the development across much of the Middle East of the belief that a key Arab state was under western occupation. However much opposition there had been to the old regime of Saddam Hussein, this was being sidelined by a more general theme of opposition to US control. While the oil motive was barely discussed in Washington, it was a matter of common acceptance in the Arab world.

TURNING SERIOUS *17 April 2003*

There are three features of the period immediately following the Iraq war that offer an insight into the likely prospects for the country in the weeks and months ahead.

The first is that the extent of the human cost of the war is starting to become apparent. Although some recent newspaper reports have suggested that Iraqi military casualties amount to no more than 2,000 soldiers killed, there is abundant evidence that at least 10,000 were killed and over 20,000 injured.

Among civilians alone, the figures are heading towards 2,000 killed and several thousand injured, and this does not begin to take into account the near-collapse of health provision in many parts of the country. In Basra, there is a critical shortage of drugs and equipment, and operations even on children have been undertaken in recent days without anaesthetics. In Baghdad, several of the main hospitals have been closed or have been able to offer only a limited amount of medical help.

This is impacting on a health system that is already devastated by twelve years of sanctions, with many people experiencing chronic ill health on top of a near-permanent lack of crucial equipment and other medical supplies. Even a week after Basra had come under British control, there remained severe shortages. The absence of medical help is extraordinary, especially given that it had proved possible to move huge supplies of military equipment into the region in the midst of the conflict.

Many of these and other immediate post-war problems had been predicted by medical non-government organisations (NGOs) such as MEDACT, so there is in principle no excuse for the US and British governments consistently failing to deliver aid, even as military forces are withdrawn from the region.

The second feature of the current situation directly follows from this. The frenzy of looting and other manifestations of disorder that followed the overthrow of the old regime indicate a new risk: that ordinary Iraqis will start to turn militantly against the US and allied forces. Indeed, this is already starting to happen. In many parts of Iraq, a mood is developing that remains deeply positive about the end of the Saddam Hussein regime but tempers this with a strong belief that the regime has been replaced not by liberators but by an occupying power.

The latter perception is reinforced by the apparent inability of these occupying forces to maintain order, and is further exacerbated by the fact that the number of Iraqis whose relatives have been killed by US and British forces is now in the hundreds of thousands. It is an extraordinary situation that an occupying force that has eliminated a brutal regime is already beginning to be treated by the people of the country with deep suspicion.

The third relevant feature of the war's aftermath is the evident reluctance of the United States to allow the UN arms inspectors to return to continue their work of disarming Iraq of any chemical or biological weapons, even though UNMOVIC (United Nations Monitoring, Verification and Inspection Commission) still has a mandate to do just that. US and British specialists are now scouring the country looking for these weapons but, in the absence of any kind of independent verification, any 'finds' will be dismissed as fabrications throughout much of the region.

This attitude, and the failure to deliver immediate humanitarian assistance, leads to the obvious questions of whether US motives are concerned with facilitating the development of a genuinely democratic and independent Iraq, or whether the reality is of an occupying power that intends to ensure its long-term influence by 'running' a client regime.

The Oil Factor: Two Scenarios for the US in Iraq

To understand how these elements may help shape Iraq's future, it is necessary to make clear that two quite different things have happened in the last month – one obvious and one much less so. The first is that the Saddam Hussein regime has been deposed; the second is that the United States now controls five times as much oil as it did before the war. This is because Iraq's proven oil reserves are about four times those of the United States – even excluding the possibility that there is much more oil to be discovered, perhaps beneath the western desert.

One month ago, the United States was the world's sole superpower but was rapidly running down its own oil reserves while having to import nearly two-thirds of its requirements to feed an exceptionally profligate oil-based economy. Now, by occupying Iraq, it controls oil reserves of a capacity second only to those of Saudi Arabia.

Many will argue that this is a grossly unfair analysis and reaffirm that the war was fought to depose a wicked Iraqi regime and to rid the region of a military threat that extended to chemical and biological weapons; in this light, the oil issue is seen as strictly irrelevant.

The validity of this argument will be tested by what happens over the next year. If Washington is acting with the best of motives and intends a peaceful, democratic and genuinely independent Iraq to develop, there will be three early indicators. The US will withdraw virtually all its occupation forces and hand over to some kind of transitional, multinational stabilisation force; the UN and other intergovernmental organisations will be heavily involved in the development of democratic governance; and, most significant of all, the US will make no attempt to set up permanent military bases on Iraqi soil.

If, on the other hand, the United States maintains a heavy political influence stemming from its current military occupation, and ensures that an Iraqi administration is essentially a client regime of Washington, then the question of oil will come to the fore. The most telling indicator of all will precisely be the third indicator above: any move to establish a long-term military presence, as has happened recently in Uzbekistan and is probably now happening in Afghanistan.

What will be really significant is if two or three major and well-resourced US military bases begin to be established in the coming months. One would most likely be in the immediate vicinity of Baghdad, a second would be near the northern oilfields between Kirkuk and Mosul, and a third might be close to Basra and the huge southern oilfields.

Such developments could take place even while US occupying troops are being withdrawn from much of the rest of Iraq, and while the US allows UN and other agencies to enter the country to aid its civil reconstruction (albeit under indirect US influence).

If the practice of US occupation bears out this scenario, it will demonstrate that a primary motive for the war, with all its death and destruction, will have been a determination to maintain long-term control of Iraq. By acting thus, the United States will have overcome the most serious impediment to solidifying its global status: it will be a superpower in every sense, including secure access to long-term energy supplies.

Where, in all this, is the declared US commitment to a democratic Iraq? The coming months will also test whether that is reality or mirage.

PERMANENT OCCUPATION? *24 April 2003*

If the prime intention were to ensure a completely independent and democratic Iraq, then the signs would include the early and substantial involvement of the UN and other intergovernmental organisations in reconstruction and in the democratic transition, the rapid withdrawal of military forces and their replacement by an international stabilisation force, and the absence of any intention to maintain a long-term US military presence in the country.

The early indications are that none of this will happen. Instead, all the immediate signs point to long-term US control. Notably, the search for chemical and biological weapons has been taken out of the hands of the UN inspectors, even though the UN mandate is still in force. It is possible that UNMOVIC might be allowed a verifying role, but it is clear that the actual search for chemical and biological weapons is under strict US control, even if it means that any discoveries will be judged by many across the region to be fabricated.

New US Military Bases

A more significant development is the remarkable speed with which the issue of permanent US bases in Iraq has come to the fore. Press reports, particularly in the *New York Times*, suggest four bases are to be established. One is likely to be at Bashur in the Kurdish north of Iraq, another at Tallil near Nasiriya in the south. These two centres will be based on existing Iraqi airfields and will be close to the major northern and southern oilfields. As expected, a third base will be established close to Baghdad itself, probably at the international airport, which has already been mooted as the logistical and command centre for the current US occupying forces.

The surprise has been the report of a fourth planned base at the H1 airfield in the west of Iraq, towards the Syrian border. In its way, though, this should hardly come as a surprise. There are thought to be further large reserves of oil to be discovered in the western desert. Furthermore, the H1 base would lie on the route of the old oil pipeline that, prior to 1948, used to run from the northern oilfields of Iraq across the western desert, through Jordan and on through the old Palestine mandate territory to a terminal at Haifa in what is now Israel.

According to a credible report in the *Observer*, Washington and Jerusalem are drawing up plans to redevelop this pipeline as a major new route for Iraqi oil through to the Mediterranean, under American and Israeli control and with Jordanian acquiescence. This would serve two purposes. First, it would provide the US with an alternative route for oil imports avoiding the shipping lanes of the Persian Gulf. Second, it would provide its close ally Israel with a secure long-term source of oil.

After the reports, there were immediate denials from Washington, not least because of the growth of opposition to US occupation that has been developing in Iraq far faster than was expected.

It may be that these bases will not prove to be the huge facilities such as those in Kuwait or Saudi Arabia. The form there has been for substantial airbases with up to 5,000 personnel, or major logistical bases storing equipment for ground forces that could be deployed rapidly to the region. This may be what happens in Iraq, or the bases may be smaller but allowing ample scope for rapid re-enforcement. The process could even be accompanied by a certain scaling down of military forces in Saudi Arabia and Turkey.

At the same time, the picture that is beginning to emerge is of a much more pervasive US presence across the Middle East, South-West and Central Asia and the Horn of Africa, and an increased involvement in South-East Europe.

The major new developments of the past couple of years have been the basing arrangements in Afghanistan, Uzbekistan and Djibouti, agreement to having US forces in Pakistan, a small but significant US military presence in Georgia and Kazakhstan, a major base in former Yugoslavia and base facilities in Bulgaria. All this is on top of long-established and substantial bases in western Gulf states from Kuwait right down to Oman, together with the large airbase and logistics facility further south at Diego Garcia in the Indian Ocean.

It all adds up to a major military investment in two regions – the Persian Gulf (or South-West Asia) and Central Asia around the Caspian basin – that are the primary and secondary regions of the world for new oil exploration and development.

Caspian basin oil is certainly significant. But the total reserves there are probably barely one-tenth of those of the Persian Gulf, and it is there that the real US focus is concentrated. Iraq is the world's second largest repository for oil reserves. While Saudi Arabia remains way out in front, there are serious doubts in Washington over its stability and also concerns over the degree of domestic support for anti-American actions such as those of 11 September 2001.

On this basis, the successful destruction of Saddam's regime and the subsequent occupation of Iraq by US forces should be a great victory for the neo-conservative security agenda, safeguarding a key country and giving leverage on two other parts of the 'axis of evil' – Iran and Syria.

Dangers Ahead

Why, then, is the US presence in Iraq already looking tarnished and potentially unstable? US forces have been made welcome in Kurdish areas. In other parts of Iraq the reception has been, at best, much less enthusiastic. Many Sunni Arabs have been sullen if not oppositional, and the speed of development of a strident political voice by Shi'ite communities in much of the south of Iraq is said to have been a shock to US military and political planners.

The reasons are many. There is, for a start, the mistaken idea that destroying an unpopular regime is a recipe for friendship. It is mistaken not least because many Iraqis simply do not believe that the United States is in the business of allowing the development of a genuinely independent and democratic Iraq to replace the old regime. The suspicion stems partly from the recent disorder but much more from a recognition that the underlying reason for the US intervention has much more to do with control of oil reserves, not least because the United States was, in the past, closely allied to the Saddam Hussein regime.

It also relates to the numbers of people killed and injured in the war. Civilian deaths are now recorded at over 2,000 – see <www.iraqbodycount.net> – with thousands of injuries, as well as tens of thousands of soldiers killed or injured. Hundreds of thousands of people across Iraq will be related to, or friends of, people killed or injured by the putative liberators.

Further, the awarding of reconstruction contracts almost exclusively to US corporations may cause resentment. The work is likely to be paid for by Iraqi oil revenues. To put it crudely, Iraq seems likely to end up subsidising American companies to repair damage done by American forces in the war – hardly the behaviour of a welcome liberator, much more that of a determined occupier.

Such views may not be entirely fair – Iraqi subcontractors and workers on the ground may be employed to do much of the work – but they are not too easy to counter. In any case, the reality is that the US destruction of the regime and subsequent occupation of Iraq is simply not getting the welcome and support from the population as a whole that was confidently expected in Washington.

Most worryingly for US planners, demands for the establishment of an Islamic regime are coming from numerous people representing the majority religious identity in the country, an identity shared by most Iranians.

This is not to say that Iran intends any direct interference in Iraq, but it has itself been labelled a key player in the 'axis of evil' and will be unlikely to refrain from informal support for the Shi'ite communities so closely connected to it across the open border.

In the United States, the majority opinion sees the Iraq war of 2003 as another great victory. Wiser counsels are more cautious. Controlling the political development of Iraq in a manner that ensures a compliant regime is not going to be nearly as easy as was expected, and this is before one takes into account the wider regional implications of a foreign state, allied to Israel, occupying a major Arab state. When we factor in the likely impact of that on the support for al-Qaida and other radical paramilitary movements, the Iraq war may already have the makings of a deeply hollow victory.

LOSING THE PEACE *1 May 2003*

Donald Rumsfeld's visit to the Middle East involved only the briefest of stops in Iraq, but it was evidently an occasion for celebrating a famous victory. In doing so, he made it clear that destroying the Saddam Hussein regime was only the first example of the US strategy of pre-empting possible threats.

This argument may lose some of its potency as a result of the failure to find the supposedly ready-to-use weapons of mass destruction, but this problem is hardly going to interfere with a triumphal 'good news' story.

After all, a brutal and repressive regime in Iraq has been destroyed and a people liberated. Once again, the irony that in a previous existence, Donald Rumsfeld was leader of a US mission to Baghdad when Saddam Hussein was a valued ally can be conveniently forgotten. It is also best to dismiss the problem that so many Iraqis see the US forces as occupiers rather than liberators. The shootings in Fallujah reinforce this point, but again it is not something that will cause much concern in most of the US media, where the emphasis is on celebration.

France and the US: Diplomatic Fallout

In victory, the United States is already concerned with responding to those who did not offer it the support that was considered to be deserved, and France is the leading culprit in the league table of international bad behaviour. So far, the punishment has been light, but involves some exemplary actions that could foreshadow more serious moves. According to the US weekly *Defense News*, the Pentagon has taken the decision not to allow any US military aircraft to take part in the forthcoming Paris Air Show. Nor will it allow senior officials to attend.

This may seem a small issue, but the Paris show is, along with Farnborough, one of the world's leading air events. It serves, in particular, as one of the main means for the French aerospace industry to demonstrate its products, and a high level of attendance from potential customers is essential. If the

Americans stay away, this might seem to give the French free rein, but the grimmer reality for the latter is that US exhibits fresh from the Iraq war – and with 'combat proven' plastered all over them – would have attracted more visitors who would then have also been exposed to French products.

Another ostensibly minor move was the reported decision by the Pentagon to refuse a French request to extend the tour of duty of its representative at the US Air Force's (USAF) Global Positioning System Program Office in California. Again, this may not appear significant, but GPS is the most widely used space-based navigational system and there is considerable symbolism in denying the request.

The extent of the hostility to France in Washington is hard to exaggerate. Rumsfeld's special assistant for Europe in Brussels, Evan Galbraith, is quoted in *Defense News* as saying that the US and France may remain allies, 'but the rupture is the worst I've seen since the Vichy Government was in power'. Such a phrase is a calculated insult, given that Vichy France was little more than a Nazi puppet regime.

The decision to boycott the Paris Air Show comes at a time when the French aerospace industry is not faring too well and desperately needs a better export record, yet up to a third of all its exports go to the Gulf region which is now more firmly influenced than ever by the United States. As one French official remarked, 'Two years ago, if the Saudis, for example, decided to buy a French tank or fighter, it would have been possible. But today, can you imagine the White House letting the Saudis buy the Rafale for its Air Force? It's just not possible.'

It is issues such as these – seen as early signs of a further move to an aggressive foreign policy – that are concerning France, Germany, Russia and other European states. They help explain this week's meeting involving France, Germany, Belgium, and Luxembourg that discussed the further development of a European defence identity outside of NATO; they also illuminate the decidedly cool reception that Tony Blair received in Moscow.

Leaving Saudi Arabia

Meanwhile, the US decision to pull out most of its forces from Saudi Arabia is more complex than it first appears. It certainly serves the purpose of easing the domestic position of the House of Saud, not least because the US presence has been a powerful recruiting tool for al-Qaida, but the presence of American forces has also been difficult for the Pentagon itself.

In 1998, when the US staged its four-day air campaign against Iraq known as 'Desert Fox', the Saudis not only refused to let the US fly strike missions from its main Saudi base, but even refused to let the USAF re-deploy its advanced F-15E strike aircraft to available bases in neighbouring Gulf states. This time, too, the USAF had to refrain from using Saudi Arabia as a major launch platform for strike aircraft.

Moreover, the US's very presence in Saudi Arabia has been problematic for nearly a decade. There were a number of attacks on US personnel in the early 1990s, and these culminated in the attack in Dharhan in 1996 when a huge truck bomb exploded outside the Khobar Towers barracks block, one of a number that served what was then the main USAF base in Saudi Arabia. Nineteen Americans were killed and hundreds of people were injured. As a result, the US built a new base at a remote site at the heart of Saudi Arabia. The Prince Sultan Air Force Base cost $500 million and has housed up to 4,000 US personnel, with no less than 400 of them devoted entirely to perimeter security even though the base is in the middle of nowhere.

Because of its location, the base has been thoroughly unpopular with USAF personnel who have had to serve tours of duty there. This, combined with the security problems, provides a further reason for evacuating Saudi territory. Much of the relocation will be to facilities in Qatar, which is considered a much safer country for US personnel, but it will also be even more necessary to maintain a substantial presence in Iraq.

It is in Iraq, though, that the United States may find itself in an even worse situation than in Saudi Arabia. Virtually every day sees a deepening of the US security predicament in Iraq. It seems clear that US forces are not remotely interested in the creation of any kind of multinational stabilisation force to provide security for post-conflict peace-building, and it is becoming increasingly apparent that US combat troops are simply not equipped or orientated towards peacekeeping. The shootings in Fallujah come in addition to many smaller incidents over the past three weeks, and they suggest that Iraqi opposition to perceived US occupation is likely to escalate.

It would be a deep and bitter irony if the US forces end up facing in Iraq the kind of insecurity that they have experienced in Saudi Arabia and that is now one of the main motives for their intended withdrawal from the Kingdom.

ABSENCE OF CONTROL *15 May 2003*

A month after the fall of the Saddam Hussein regime and the start of the post-war United States occupation of Iraq, there is disorder and violence in much of the country and widespread antagonism to US influence. Several of the key US officials appointed to administer the country are already being replaced, and unease about post-war developments is shared even within the British government.

Meanwhile, a series of well-planned and carefully executed attacks in Riyadh demonstrate that US interests elsewhere in the Middle East are still vulnerable. The Riyadh bombings, timed to coincide with Colin Powell's visit to Saudi Arabia, constitute the most serious attack on US interests since those of 11 September 2001.

Al-Qaida is Back

The bombings took place amidst a period of high security in the Kingdom, and followed recent discoveries of arms and explosives in Riyadh itself. There had been warnings of possible attacks against US interests, yet the Saudi security forces were evidently unable to prevent their execution. This security failure could owe something to lack of competence, and be complicated by the broad support that exists in Saudi Arabia for anti-American actions, but it also compels recognition of the very many 'soft' targets that exist in this oil-rich country.

Although the US plans to withdraw about 4,000 uniformed troops over the next year or so, they represent only a small if visible part of US involvement in Saudi Arabia. This numbers over 30,000 people, mostly civilians, who work in many different ways to support the Kingdom and its oil industries. Most of this presence will remain, as will the military bases, even if they are now going to be kept on a stand-by rather than an active status.

In any case, al-Qaida's motives in Saudi Arabia have always extended beyond merely the removal of US forces from the Kingdom. Equally significant has been the long-held belief that the House of Saud is a corrupt and highly unacceptable Keeper of the Two Holy Places. That motive, along with a continuing US presence, will go on feeding the resentment that lends support to al-Qaida. The organisation has now shown itself to be far from defeated by the United States in its 'war on terror'.

US Forces in Regional 'Draw-Down'

The Riyadh bombings come at a time of fundamental changes in the distribution of US military forces throughout the Middle East, Europe and South-West Asia. The partial withdrawal from Saudi Arabia has been widely reported, but less well known is the recent downgrading of bases and facilities in Turkey and Jordan and the imminent departure of substantial US forces from Kuwait. These will be followed by withdrawals from Bahrain and the United Arab Emirates.

Some of the US forces are being moved to Qatar, and the basing of a range of aircraft in Oman (including strategic bombers) will continue – both states are considered to be safer environments than their western Gulf neighbours (see *Aviation Week*, 5 May 2003).

This redistribution of US forces is in turn part of a much wider move that involves a steady decrease in maintaining very large overseas airbases, often close to centres of population and therefore more at risk from paramilitary action. This will even mean a 'draw-down' of US forces in Western Europe, but this will be accompanied by an increase in the number of bases that will be available for use when required. Several such bases have already been established in Uzbekistan, Afghanistan and elsewhere in Central Asia, and it is probable that some new bases will be developed in South-East Europe – that is, in countries close to the Middle East that do not have substantial Islamic populations.

Behind these policies lie three considerations. The first and most immediate is the acceptance by the Pentagon that the scale of hostility to the United States in the Middle East requires real restrictions on large-scale deployments on the grounds of the security of American personnel. A second factor is simply the huge cost of keeping the forces overseas; this is reinforced by the frustration among many service-people themselves to being restricted to secure bases in remote places for months on end.

The third consideration is the more general shift by the US military towards the rapid deployment of forces to meet particular security threats, in contrast to the previous approach of having permanent large-scale bases located overseas. A small sign of this trend is the US Air Force's increasing concentration on long-range precision-guided missiles, coupled with reconnaissance drones; these are designed to make it easier to fight wars 'at a distance'.

All of this is, in effect, an admission that the very presence of substantial US military forces in oil-rich regions such as the Persian Gulf and the Caspian basin is fuelling deep and abiding resentments among the people affected, now made even worse by what is perceived as the occupation of Iraq, a major Arab state.

The current discoveries of mass graves in Iraq is further evidence of the brutal character of Saddam Hussein's regime, but in the context of the control of Iraq by Washington, it is not easy for US forces to argue against the widespread view in the Arab world that one form of autocracy is being replaced by another. It is certainly accepted in Washington that US forces will remain in an occupying role in Iraq for many months if not years, but even when they go, some major military facilities are planned to remain, including three or four bases kept on in different parts of the country.

The US Logic, and its Defects

There is, then, a US military trend towards large numbers of stand-by bases and other facilities stretching across South-East Europe, the Middle East and through into Central Asia, whose underlying motive is the long-term security of oil supplies. The US will continue to maintain large bases in countries that are considered sufficiently friendly to its interests. In other cases, bases will be available as and when required, with the US military continuing its acquisition of rapid deployment and expeditionary capabilities.

The core problem is that, whatever the Pentagon thinks, the strategy simply will not work. Al-Qaida is recovering from the disruption caused by the termination of the Taliban regime in Afghanistan. There, some Taliban militia are even reforming, and the Riyadh bombings demonstrate al-Qaida's continuing viability in Saudi Arabia. Moreover, the foreign occupation of Iraq will provide an extra justification for its activities to a list that includes hostility to the House of Saud, opposition to western influence in the Gulf and the running sore of Israeli occupation of the Palestinian territories.

The decrease of the United States' overt military presence across the region does not alter the basis of its strategic policy there: long-term security of oil supplies coupled with enduring support for Israel. Control cannot be achieved solely by cruise missiles fired from hundreds of miles away. The local commercial, political and security interests and connections remain, as will opposition to their presence. The Riyadh bombings indicate a deeper lesson: just as Washington may have thought that it had gained greater control of a strategically crucial region, it may actually be in the process of losing it.

THE IRAQI CALCULUS *29 May 2003*

Towards the end of the intense and chaotic Iraq war, reports began to emerge of large numbers of civilian casualties. While coalition sources played these reports down or ignored them altogether, independent analysts such as Iraq Body Count were beginning to accumulate evidence from multiple sources suggesting that up to 2,000 civilians had been killed and many thousands injured.

In the six weeks since the end of the war, much more information has emerged, and it shows that the number of civilians killed was much higher than the early evidence suggested. In particular, casualty figures began to be made available from hospitals across Baghdad and from elsewhere in Iraq. These suggest that over 6,000 civilians were killed in the three weeks of war, added to whom are the continuing casualties from unexploded cluster munitions and other weapons.

The problem of unexploded ordnance persists, and its very pervasiveness gives some idea of the extensive use by the Americans and the British of area-impact munitions such as cluster bombs. This, in turn, is relevant to the loss of life among the Iraqi military. Figures are difficult to adduce, and are certainly not now available from coalition sources, but some informed calculations measure them at between at least 10,000 and probably 15,000 soldiers killed over the three-week period (see Jonathan Steele's 'Body Counts', *Guardian*, 28 May 2003).

During the war itself, coalition representatives in Qatar did speak readily of the 'destruction' of three Iraqi Republican Guard divisions, in addition to several thousands of other deaths. Since the war, reports from some of the journalists 'embedded' with leading US forces indicate widespread carnage among ill-protected Iraqi troops exposed to the full force of coalition firepower.

From all the different sources it is reasonable to conclude that around 20,000 Iraqi soldiers and civilians were killed in the war. Iraq has a population that is about one-tenth of that of the United States, so an equivalent loss in the United States would be of the order of 200,000 people killed in three weeks. In the eleven years of the US involvement in the Vietnam war, from 1964 to 1975, the US lost over 58,000 of its forces.

In modern warfare it is a common calculus that for every person who dies, three more are seriously injured. On this basis, it is likely that at least 50,000 Iraqis were injured in addition to the 20,000 killed.

Such a number, in such a short space of time and in a country with a relatively small population, means that millions of Iraqis will have personal knowledge of someone killed or injured in a war that has been described repeatedly as a war of liberation. Perhaps this should be recognised as a factor in the subsequent unpopularity of US troops within the country.

Motives for War

It can be argued, of course, that the very brutal and repressive regime of Saddam Hussein could not be terminated without inflicting extensive 'collateral damage'. There are two problems with this approach.

First, the stated aim of the war was to disarm Iraq of weapons of mass destruction (WMD), yet intensive searching has failed to find them and the main US inspection team is now being withdrawn. This aim of WMD destruction is now being downgraded, and more emphasis is being placed on the regime's repeated flouting of UN resolutions; this too is an uneasy argument, given the failure to obtain UN authorisation for war on such a basis.

Second, it is difficult to sustain the argument for regime termination because of its innate brutality, given that Saddam Hussein was on several occasions closely allied to the United States, even at a time when his regime was engaging in systematic repression, including the use of chemical weapons against its own Kurdish population.

Moreover, the stated aim of bringing Iraq to an independent democracy does not seem too plausible. It now appears that occupying forces will remain for up to two years, and that permanent US military bases are already being established. Given Washington's recent experience with Turkish parliamentary democracy, it is unlikely that it will facilitate a democratic Iraq that could well require all US forces to leave the country forthwith.

A suspicion across the region has long been that the Iraq war was essentially about the control of oil and the need to decrease dependence on Saudi Arabia. This belief has been fuelled by the comment of Philip J. Carroll, the US official in charge of Washington's oil policy in Iraq, that Iraq's interests might best be served by ignoring OPEC quotas and exporting all the oil it could. As the *Washington Post* put it on 17 May 2003:

> Flows of Iraqi oil to the world market unconstrained by OPEC quotas could further erode the cartel's already limited ability to set prices and might even trigger a price war, eating into the profits of its member countries. Such an outcome would surely delight the Bush administration as well as buyers of gasoline in the United States.

A cynical analyst might conclude that one function of the war, at least in the short term and from a US perspective, was to break OPEC, damage the economies of countries such as Iran and Venezuela and ensure price cuts at gas stations in the run-up to the 2004 presidential election.

The Condition of Iraq

The UN resolution of 22 May lifting economic sanctions on Iraq does give some semblance of authority for the current foreign occupation of the country, but it will also give a certain authority for UN officials to deliver independent analyses of the state of the country. This has already started with robust warnings from the senior UN humanitarian assistance officer in Iraq, Ramiro Lopes da Silva of a powerful backlash developing against US occupation.

In the weeks since the war ended, progress in stabilisation has been appallingly slow. There are continuing problems with electricity and water supplies, sewage and waste disposal, along with a lack of medical supplies. Criminality is rife, including persistent looting and robbery, made worse by the widespread availability of firearms.

There have been suggestions that the British have handled things much better in and around Basra, but there is little proof of this. One of the major universities of the Arab world in the city has been looted of almost everything moveable, including electricity cables; this is just one example of a pervasive lack of order in a city under the control of armed forces that are supposed to be experienced in peacekeeping.

In the much larger US-controlled areas, the ominous development has been the rise in attacks on US troops. It is apparent that there has been little effort to install an effective policing system, either by Iraqi units or by the occupying forces themselves, but the deep unpopularity of the occupiers means that they are increasingly concerned not with policing public order but with protecting themselves. The risk is that this is becoming a vicious circle. The more attacks there are on US troops, the more they concentrate on defending themselves, including shooting at demonstrators – with this reinforcing their image as repressive occupiers.

In these circumstances, the decision to disband the Iraqi armed forces is extraordinary. By doing so, the United States is putting into circulation over 350,000 unemployed young men, large numbers of whom have access to guns and other munitions. It is a recipe for further violence and runs directly counter to standard practice in post-conflict peace-building.

A far more sensible policy would have been to conscript army units into civil reconstruction, using them as the core elements in a process into which many more people could have been incorporated very rapidly. This would have formed a basis for providing immediate employment on a substantial scale. Instead, the opposite is happening, with increased unemployment precisely when public order is becoming so difficult to maintain.

The wider issue here is that all of these developments support the view that the occupying forces have very little interest in the condition of the ordinary people of Iraq – their concern is seen to be with the control of a major Arab state with all its oil riches, coupled with the possibility of this even leading to some form of action against Iran.

The accuracy or otherwise of such a viewpoint is less significant in the present context than the fact that it is very widespread across the Middle East – and is daily reinforced by the actual behaviour of the occupying forces. Thus, the conclusion has to be drawn that current circumstances are leading to increasing bitterness and opposition within Iraq and a further deepening of the anti-American (and anti-British) mood across the region. A radical change of policy is required. There is little sign of that happening, and the peace – such as it exists – is steadily being lost.

POWER WITHOUT AUTHORITY *4 June 2003*

In the approach to the war in Iraq the US military rapidly expanded its strength across the Gulf region – most notably in Kuwait, Jordan, Qatar, the Emirates and Oman, as well as in the Persian Gulf itself. This process followed the major build-up of forces in the wider region as a consequence of the war in Afghanistan in late 2001.

Thus, with US bases and forces ensconced in Afghanistan, Pakistan and some of the Central Asian republics (such as Uzbekistan), the overall picture was one of a remarkable presence across the Persian Gulf and Caspian basin regions – parts of the world distinguished by their massive oil reserves.

Such a presence contrasted with the view from the civilian leadership at the Pentagon which believed that the United States armed forces, especially the army, could maintain international security without having the need for very large numbers of troops based overseas. There might well be a need for large numbers of bases, but most of these could be maintained on a 'stand-by' basis, ready for use when needed, with the overall trend being towards smaller US forces capable of rapid deployment when required.

To some extent this projection had already gone awry before the Iraq war, as it was already proving necessary to keep over 10,000 troops in Afghanistan because of the risk of a resurgent Taliban, but even these commitments pale almost into insignificance as the true nature of the commitment to Iraq becomes apparent.

A Dangerous Vacuum

At the level of political organisation in Iraq, it is already becoming clear that the setting up of a stable client regime in Baghdad is going to take time, and that the initial stages involve a process of appointment of political advisers that will remain under the strict control of the occupying powers.

A foretaste of this was the sudden political change in Basra last week (see William Booth, 'Chafing at Authority In Iraq', *Washington Post*, 30 May 2003). Immediately after the war, occupation forces pointed to the early appointment of a city council in Basra as an indicator of rapid progress on the political front. This appearance of progress has now been halted, with the British authorities summarily dismissing the council on the grounds that it was unrepresentative and too closely linked to Ba'ath party elements.

Instead, there would be no more than an advisory role for some appointees, an outcome decried by Basra professionals who, according to the *Washington Post*,

> say they are being treated like children by the occupation forces and denied true liberation. They say the Americans and British have spoken often of freedom and democracy, but have failed to find a way to meaningfully integrate Iraqis into decision-making positions.

Basra is only part of the story. In Iraq as a whole there has been an abrupt, significant change in American policy. The original plan of the US occupation authority was to bring together several hundred representatives of the country's religious, ethnic and cultural groups in a major conference in July 2003 to advise on the early establishment of a political authority that could take responsibility for issues such as health and education.

This plan has now been abandoned, to be replaced by an interim advisory political council, with up to 30 members hand-picked by US forces. This move, coming at a time when the US military forces in Iraq are beginning to realise the extent of their predicament, is likely even further to alienate Iraqi opinion against America and its British allies.

Some elements of the US military predicted these developments several months ago. In February 2003, the US army chief of staff, General Eric Shinseki, said that it could take hundreds of thousands of troops to make Iraq secure after a war. This view was roundly criticised by Defense Secretary Donald Rumsfeld and his deputy, Paul Wolfowitz. The civilian leadership at the Pentagon believed that an initial force of around 100,000 would be adequate and could, moreover, be scaled down rapidly in the wake of victory. Indeed, in the immediate aftermath of the war, US Department of Defense sources suggested that there might be fewer than 70,000 US troops in Iraq within five months.

The American Predicament

The current situation and the near-time prognosis form a stark commentary on such projections. Now, seven weeks after the end of the war, there are about 160,000 US and British troops in Iraq; they are supported by around 40,000 other troops in neighbouring countries, especially Kuwait – some 200,000 personnel in all. Such is the state of disarray in Iraq itself that the commander of US ground forces in the country, Lieutenant-General David McKiernan, conceded last week that the war had not ended, a point reinforced by frequent attacks on US troops in Baghdad and elsewhere.

What is now happening is that many of the forces that fought the war and were expecting to be replaced by new army units are being kept on in Iraq, even if some of them have been in the Middle East for nine months. Instead of replacing them, the new units will reinforce them, leading to the maintenance of up to 200,000 troops for the foreseeable future.

The main problem for US troops lies with often-violent opposition to their presence in some parts of Baghdad and in extensive areas to the north and west of the city. It is likely that a substantial part of the 3rd Infantry Division will have to be deployed to Fallujah, to the west of Baghdad. This could involve up to 10,000 troops and support elements in one of Iraq's smaller cities, albeit one that has seen 17 Iraqis killed and scores injured in recent clashes with US troops.

Another US division, the 4th Infantry, is currently in place to try and maintain security in a large area of Iraq between Baghdad and the Kurdish north. This includes Tikrit where support for the old regime is still evident, and the 4th Infantry is now to be reinforced with troops from other units, with a brigade of several thousand more troops to be held in reserve in Baghdad.

What this all adds up to is a very substantial security problem that adds a military dimension to all of the many problems facing the US occupying force. Indeed, the very use of the term 'occupying power' is now in common usage in western political circles, including those in Britain and even the United States. This is a far cry from a belief that a victory would be a matter of liberation, with troops welcomed with open arms across the country.

It would be an exaggeration to portray this as equivalent to the United States getting bogged down in a Vietnam-type morass; but neither is it accurate to downplay the US predicament. The problem – and the opportunity – for Washington is that it could extricate itself with ease if it was properly to internationalise the transition of Iraq to an independent democratic state, by permitting a multinational stabilisation force to help it and encouraging progress towards a new form of governance under UN control.

Why, then, does the Bush administration not take this route? The reason, once more, takes us to the heart of the motive for war. As Paul Wolfowitz benignly pointed out in an already renowned interview with *Vanity Fair* magazine, the focus on disarming Iraq of its weapons of mass destruction as the reason for war was a bureaucratic necessity to ensure a coalition of at least two or three states.

It is also clear that one of the central purposes of the war would be to reduce the US's military presence in Saudi Arabia. Although Paul Wolfowitz did not follow through the oil connection in his recent spate of interviews, it is necessary to recall that, by occupying Iraq, the United States now controls one-eighth of the world's oil reserves, five times as much as three months ago.

That alone is the key reason why Washington will insist on a client regime in Baghdad rather than true political independence for the country, even if that entails a much more intensive military occupation of Iraq than was expected before the war of March–April 2003. The regional consequences of this strategic choice are likely to be with us for many years.

3
The Insurgency Takes Root

INTRODUCTION

By mid-June 2003, nearly three months after the start of the Iraq war, there were early indications that an insurgency was beginning to develop. Five weeks later, the evidence for this was overwhelming. Even so, for much of this period the US political authorities in Iraq and Washington were in denial. There were frequent references to 'remnants' of the old regime that were said to be responsible for the attacks, and there was a persistent belief that the insurgency was little more than a series of sporadic raids.

At the same time, Iraq remained under firm US military control with the ultimate authority being held by the Pentagon, not the State Department. Moreover, there was already some recognition that it was not proving possible to draw down the numbers of US troops stationed in Iraq, and there were early indications of problems with troop numbers, some units having to be kept on in the region far longer than had been anticipated.

By mid-July, it was also being acknowledged that the much-vaunted weapons of mass destruction that had been the stated motivation for the war were nowhere to be found. As a result, a shift was beginning to take place towards arguing that the real reason for the war was a response to the humanitarian disaster that the regime of Saddam Hussein represented. It was not an easy argument to foster, given that the old regime had

had close links with several western countries at the height of its human rights abuses in the late 1980s. Furthermore, the severe shortages of electricity and water, the general level of lawlessness and the shortage of medical supplies after the regime's termination did not bode well for the idea that the US occupation would be a humanitarian success.

Two other issues came to the fore during late June and early July 2003. The first was that the use of the term 'liberation' with regard to the coalition's activities was already in sharp decline, to be replaced in much of the media with 'occupation'. This was almost immediately the case across the Middle East from late March onwards, but it represented a subtle change in the western media that only became apparent three to four months into the war.

The second issue was the refusal of the Indian government to commit a full division of troops to support the coalition in Iraq. While the Bush administration was firmly opposed to major UN involvement in Iraq, it was becoming increasingly anxious to gain more support from those few countries with armed forces large enough to provide troops under coalition authority. India was one of the very few countries in the world that had the capacity to commit a full division of more than 10,000 troops but chose not to do so. In large measure this was due to public opposition to the war, combined with the fact that the Indian government was facing important elections later in the year. In the long process of the evolution of the Iraq war, this decision can now be seen as one of the key moments that dictated that the United States was becoming seriously isolated in its military posture and would have to bear the dominant share of the costs of occupation.

THE PROBLEMS OF OCCUPATION *20 June 2003*

In view of the rise in US tensions with Iran, the tortuous path of the Israeli–Palestinian roadmap and the questions facing the

Tony Blair government in Britain over Iraqi weapons of mass destruction (WMD), it may seem perverse to concentrate yet again on what is happening within Iraq. It is, of course, still at the forefront of public discussion, but much of the current argument concerns the motives for the war – especially the issue of the control of Iraq's oil reserves, rather than the aftermath of the conflict. The former may become more exposed as official enquiries are pursued in London and Washington; if so, they could well tarnish the image of a war whose proclaimed purposes were defensive or humanitarian.

But even if the real motives for war are revealed, it is likely that what is happening now within Iraq will prove to be more important, in the light of earlier assessments that the current situation really may be the beginning of what has been described as a potential 30-year war.

A Gathering Resistance

As June 2003 opened, there had been occasional reports of resistance to American troops, including ambushes and sniper attacks, but these were said to be little more than the actions of remnants of Ba'ath support rather than anything more substantial. By early June, however, it became clear to some of the more perceptive analysts that United States forces had been facing considerable opposition stretching over the whole of the previous month. These involved large numbers of individual attacks leading to over 30 US troops killed and scores more wounded.

In response, a number of counter-insurgency operations were mounted in and around Baghdad, together with much larger military strikes against a 'terrorist camp' to the north-west and an area of strong opposition near the town of Balad, north of Baghdad. US military commanders were now prepared to say that there was an ongoing conflict and that they were taking vigorous yet necessary action to counter opposition to their occupation of the country.

Yet despite this, a plausible picture was sustained during the period of fighting itself of mere 'little local difficulties' facing US troops in the context of an occupation that was otherwise going very well. In military terms, the problem was presented as one of isolated and uncoordinated remnants coupled with small numbers of terrorists moving into the country from elsewhere in the Arab world. In no way were these representative of the mood of Iraqis as a whole; and even the Sunni people of central Iraq were said to be, for the most part, neutral about the US presence.

Peace-Building and Counter-Insurgency

More generally, many media outlets were concerned to convey a picture of rapid civil progress in post-war Iraq. An article typical of the current view in Washington is a recent piece by George Ward, the former US coordinator for humanitarian assistance in Iraq ('So Far, So Good', *International Herald Tribune*, 16 June 2003). This thoroughly positive report cites rapid progress in post-war peace-building and reconstruction:

> ...Iraq is in most respects further along the road to recovery than we could have expected before the war. All major public hospitals in Baghdad are again operating. Sixty per cent of Iraq's schools are open. Nationwide distribution of food supplies has resumed.

Ward does mention some residual problems, not least with the police, but his overall conclusion is one of sound progress, to the extent that 'we Americans may soon look back on the post-war looting as only a bump in a long road'; this is contrasted with pre-war predictions of mass refugee flows, destruction of oilfields, epidemics and food shortages.

So is the process of peace-building really going well and are the current counter-insurgency operations no more than minor problems that will be over in a matter of weeks? A provocative counterpoint to George Ward's optimism was given the next day, 17 June, in a report in the *Daily Telegraph* citing a senior British official in Baghdad as saying that the US reconstruction effort was suffering from 'a complete absence of strategic direction' and that 'This is the single most chaotic organization I have ever worked for.'

There may be an element of 'we Brits could do better' in this view, but it is also relevant that the chief US administrator in Iraq, Paul Bremer, has fewer than 600 staff to run a country that was previously run by a rigid dictatorship whose collapse has entailed a complete absence of functioning infrastructure. It is even more significant here that Bremer's outfit is already the second attempt by Washington to control Iraq, the first having had to be replaced within a month of the end of the war.

Some indication of the extent of the predicament is a report in *The Times* (17 June) from a British defence source that the 17,000-strong British force in south-east Iraq might have to stay as long as four years. The same day, the *Independent* carried a comment from Major-General Freddy Viggers (the British commander attached to US military HQ in Baghdad) to the effect that a long-running struggle would ensue unless the remains of the Ba'ath regime were finally eliminated – and that this must include the death or capture of Saddam Hussein. General Viggers cited the experience of the Balkans, where 1,600 British troops were in Bosnia eleven years after the start of the war.

A New Military Pattern

If the peace-building is fraught with difficulties, what is happening on the military side? In the past week it has become clear that the initial operations in north-west Iraq and around the town of Balad formed part of a much wider offensive by US troops. These were followed by major military operations in at least four Iraqi cities, starting around 14 June and continuing for several days.

These included the use of thousands of troops – backed by tanks, planes and helicopters – in a series of operations in and around the city of Fallujah, and were reported to be part of a plan that had been under development for some time, rather than an immediate response to recent attacks on US soldiers.

It is frankly unlikely that these operations will have the desired effect. Widespread arrests, damage to property and the accidental killing of numerous innocent people are all conspiring to increase antagonism to the US presence. Recent days have seen further attacks on US convoys and the killing of a soldier in a sniper attack in Baghdad. It is a situation made worse by the fatigue and edginess of young US soldiers operating in temperatures of 35–40 degrees centigrade; some of these have been in the region for nine months, and few of them are trained for peacekeeping, still less for urban counter-insurgency operations.

Beyond all these problems lies the key question – where is the opposition coming from? The official answer is that small numbers of Ba'ath party loyalists have combined with some remnants of the fedayeen and some radicals coming in to Iraq from elsewhere in the Arab world.

But this is not enough to explain the extent of the opposition. A more accurate answer probably lies in the way in which the first phase of the war ended in early April. Although the US forces were able to use extraordinary firepower against ordinary Iraqi army units and against several divisions of the general Republican Guard to the south of Baghdad, one of the unanswered questions was what happened to the much more disciplined and better-equipped Special Republican Guard.

This elite force, drawn mainly from Tikrit and other areas north and west of Baghdad, numbered at least 15,000 and was considered to be thoroughly loyal to the old regime. Moreover, it was specifically trained and equipped for urban combat and was expected to offer considerable resistance in Baghdad itself.

That resistance never came, and Baghdad fell in a matter of days. There have been persistent reports, although not yet substantiated in any detail, that some of the key senior officers of the Special Republican Guard were bought off by US agents and intermediaries with substantial cash inducements. They were thus able to escape in return for giving US troops more or less unimpeded entry into Baghdad.

The implied result of this arrangement was that many of the key elements of the guard simply melted away, bereft of their core leadership. The consequence, if this analysis is in any way accurate, is that the middle-ranking officers and their troops would have been left isolated, yet able to regroup, with most of their weapons and munitions intact.

If this argument is factored in to the groundswell of opposition to US occupation in many of the Sunni areas of Iraq, then some indication of the extent of the problem facing United States forces begins to emerge. In brief, the latter may be dealing not with isolated 'remnants' aided by a few foreign elements, but with an opposition that includes well-trained, highly motivated regular forces that can readily organise themselves to operate in guerrilla mode.

In an earlier analysis in this series, when the first part of the war appeared to be nearing an end in the second week of April, the following conclusion was drawn:

> In the United States, it would seem that there is a perception that the war is already as good as won, and peace and tranquility will rapidly follow a stunning victory. In reality, whether the war ends soon or drags on, it is likely to prove a hollow victory with a deeply bitter and unstable peace.

At the time this was a minority view, but is now beginning to look uncomfortably accurate. This week's news that Baghdad is considered insufficiently safe for the UK International Development Minister, Baroness Valerie Amos, to make a visit, coupled with the continuing violence in Baghdad and elsewhere, lends support to the view that the war in Iraq is very far from over.

THE FAILURES OF SUCCESS *26 June 2003*

At the end of the long Cold War, in 1989, the United States suddenly became the world's sole superpower. The then United States president, George Bush, quickly welcomed the onset of a 'new world order' modelled on a western-dominated liberal market economy backed by military power. Instead, the anticipated era of peace and stability was rapidly overturned by the 1991 Gulf war, followed by violent conflict in the Balkans, the Caucasus and Somalia, genocide in Rwanda and enduring Arab-Israeli and Indo-Pakistan tensions and conflicts.

Partly as a result, many aspects of the US armed forces were transformed during the 1990s. It was an incremental process but the overall aim was to tailor forces to protect American interests in a fractured and volatile world. Many of the Cold War excesses were scaled down, including much (but certainly not all) of the nuclear arsenals, the tank armies in Europe and the US Navy's extensive anti-submarine forces. Overall, the number of people in the armed forces was cut back by about a third.

At the same time, other forces were maintained or even enhanced. The US Navy kept almost all its aircraft carrier battle groups and added large numbers of land-attack cruise missiles to its capabilities, and the US Air Force went out of its way to develop long-range strike forces. Even the US Army got in on the act with a greater commitment to special operations forces, and the US Marine Corps, with its unique ability to project power overseas, was preserved at close to its Cold War level of force.

Yet it was not clear from the outset that these incremental changes amounted to an entirely new strategy, and there was sometimes a reluctance to commit troops to particular crises, an attitude accentuated by the experience in Somalia. Indeed, it was only with the unique combination of a neo-conservative security agenda and the aftermath of the 9/11 attacks that that strategy really took shape.

The new and aggressive US security doctrine, focused on pre-emption, is now becoming clear, and is being accompanied by rapid further changes in the make-up and basing of US forces. The irony, however, is that at the very time that the strategy is being developed and applied, circumstances are arising that make its viability highly doubtful.

A Global Ambition

The dominant US doctrine during the Cold War was essentially one of containing the Soviet bloc, not least because the Soviet Union had formidable nuclear arsenals and its leaders believed for much of the time that they could 'wait-out' the United States. At the same time, 'containment' did not rule out aggressive policies, especially during the Ronald Reagan era of 1980–88. These included the widespread use of special forces in South-East Asia and Latin America, a maritime strategy in the 1980s that would take a war to the Soviet Union as soon as any conflict started, and a willingness to use nuclear weapons first.

These elements of Cold War thinking have been hugely amplified by the neo-conservatives, with the Pentagon under Donald Rumsfeld and Paul Wolfowitz (and with the backing of the vice-president, Dick Cheney) making most of the running on foreign and security policy at the expense of the State Department. The core of the strategy is the policy of pre-empting likely threats, whether they be 'rogue' states such as Afghanistan and Iraq, or paramilitary organisations like al-Qaida and its associates.

The policy of 'getting your retaliation in first' can take a number of forms, involving everything from targeted assassinations and clandestine operations through to full-scale pre-emptive war against states. Given the developments now being introduced in the nuclear weapons programme, it could even extend to the use of new generations of small nuclear weapons.

Overall, this policy requires quite different force dispositions from those of the Cold War period, where the main concentrations were in Europe and elsewhere on the periphery of the Soviet bloc. Now, these dispositions stretch over more dispersed global zones of instability that are considered to include the northern parts of the Andes, North Africa, South-West and Central Asia, and parts of the western Pacific.

The United States nowhere faces a single, rival superpower; thus, it does not believe that there is any longer the requirement to have massive forces permanently based overseas. Instead, it is now implementing a plan for a few forward-operating military 'hubs' – large facilities located on US territories such as Guam, and thoroughly reliable allies such as Britain.

Britain is actually important for three reasons. First, it has substantial existing facilities such as the airbase complex at Lakenheath/Mildenhall in Suffolk, the recently activated stand-by base at Fairford in Gloucestershire and the huge surveillance centre at Menwith Hill in North Yorkshire. Second, it provides the US with the major support base at Diego Garcia in the Indian Ocean. Third, and most important of all, the British are regarded as the most acquiescent of allies – least likely to oppose the new US strategy.

Elsewhere, current locations such as the bases in Turkey or Saudi Arabia will be downgraded because they are in politically unreliable states, and the large forces in South Korea will be relocated away from the demilitarised zone to allow them to be more mobile and therefore available for regional contingencies. The large air force base at Ramstein in Germany will probably remain but many of the 60,000 army troops will be withdrawn.

The overall plan is to open a number of bases in many parts of the world but they will not be like the huge facilities of the 40-year Cold War. Instead, they will have small numbers of troops assigned permanently, but with the capability to take very large forces when required.

Many such bases already exist, including those in Kuwait, Oman, Qatar, the Emirates, Djibouti and Bahrain, but much of the concentration of forces in Germany may be redistributed to Bulgaria and Romania, closer to the Middle East. As ever, the Middle East remains key, both because of its immense oil reserves and also the US's close connection with Israel. Whatever happens in Iraq, a permanent military presence there is as good as certain.

Further east, in Central Asia, the US's temporary bases acquired at the time of the Afghan war in Uzbekistan, Tajikistan and Kyrgyzstan are likely to be made permanent, while recent reports of a major expansion programme at the base near Kandahar suggest a long-term presence in Afghanistan.

Another region, South-East Asia and the western Pacific, is viewed by the Pentagon as being of growing importance and there are reports that it may seek to re-establish a US military presence in the Philippines, if the political climate allows. It may also be seeking basing rights and staging areas in northern Australia, a country considered to be much more accommodating to US interests than others in the region.

In mapping this range of ambition, it would seem that the United States intends to maintain even larger forces overseas than it did at the height of the Cold War, but this conclusion would be thoroughly misleading. The aim, rather, is to have the ability, when required, to operate in any of the zones of potential threat, taking vigorous pre-emptive action, mostly by using air power, the Marines and Special Forces. This would enable the US to destroy any threats, whether from unacceptable regimes or paramilitary groups.

A Project with Unexpected Results

The problems with such a strategy are many and diverse, but two particular ones are already emerging. The first is that it is based on the belief that there is only one way for the world to run and that that is the American way. The Project for the New American Century and similar neo-conservative groups are absolutely convinced that there is no alternative to the plans they have articulated. Yet their views are repeatedly rejected in country after country across the world. This generic opposition may take many forms, from the mild to the radical, but it means that everywhere, the environment for US efforts to enforce its global control is potentially dangerous.

The second problem stems from the first and arises when the United States uses its huge military power in what it considers to be its necessary security interests. The assumption is that a 'threat' can be dealt with in a rapid military operation, to be replaced by the early imposition of a benign peace. Already, this assumption is revealed as deeply flawed.

Eighteen months after the defeat of the Taliban, Afghanistan is in deep disarray and the US will be obliged to maintain military forces on the ground, in a hostile environment, for years to come. In Iraq, violence and instability increase by the day, as US forces find it difficult, if not impossible, to control a resistance to occupation that is as deep-seated as it is unexpected.

With as many as a dozen attacks each day on US units, and with foreign attempts at reconstruction being repeatedly hindered by looting and violence, the prospect for an early draw-down of US forces is unlikely. The problems they face extend also to the British forces, and they will make other countries much more reluctant to commit their troops to the many insecure parts of Iraq.

The problem for the neo-conservative strategists, then, is that their belief that vigorous force will be followed by an immediate peace is wrong. Tough military action in pursuit of its own security interests is much more likely to end up with the United States being directly involved on the ground, with its involvement extending to long-term counter-insurgency campaigns.

A number of articles in this series suggested that the war in Iraq might last right through the summer of 2003. Initially, this seemed mistaken, as formal resistance to the US invasion melted away in a matter of days. Now, less than two months after President Bush's declaration that the war was at an end, these earlier assessments may turn out to be more accurate.

A key implication of all this is that the real significance of what is happening in Iraq, and indeed Afghanistan, may relate to the very viability of the pre-emptive strategy of US neo-conservatives. The United States has formulated a military strategy designed to 'keep the violent peace' by the use of short sharp bursts of vigorous military force; but its likely result is to embroil US forces in dangerous, complicated and costly regional occupations – the very opposite of what was intended.

THE GROWING INSURGENCY *3 July 2003*

In a speech on 1 July, President Bush acknowledged that US forces would remain in Iraq as a 'massive and long-term undertaking', facing up to the 'terrorists, extremists and Saddam loyalists' who have been killing and injuring US forces. He also implied that the situation was under control. This view is echoed by the head of administration in Iraq, Paul Bremer. 'Those few remaining individuals who have refused to fit into the new Iraq are becoming more and more desperate,' Bremer said, also on 1 July. 'They are alienating the rest of the population.'

This upbeat assessment contrasts with casualty figures recently released. According to the *Washington Post*, since the war started on 20 March, 195 US military personnel have died in accidents or combat, but nearly one-third of those deaths have happened since President Bush declared the war to be over on 1 May. Putting to one side the casualties suffered in accidents, in the nine weeks since he made his speech on the aircraft carrier USS *Abraham Lincoln*, 31 US and British military personnel have been killed and 178 wounded. The number of deaths may seem high, but it is the second figure, of close to 200 wounded, that is actually the more significant.

In modern warfare, a crude medical calculus is that three people are wounded for every person who dies. In Iraq, currently, the ratio for allied soldiers is six to one. The reason for this is almost certainly that US troops exposed to attacks are commonly patrolling in armoured vehicles and are wearing body armour that provides effective protection against life-threatening injuries from light arms and grenade fragments. As a result, many soldiers have their lives saved but are suffering serious injuries, especially limb injuries.

The reason this is significant is that it lends credence to reports of large numbers of attacks on US units in central Iraq, with as many as a dozen attacks on patrols every day. It is stretching credibility to lay this at the door of the desperate 'few remaining individuals who have refused to fit into the new Iraq'. Rather, it suggests the US and Britain could be getting involved in a very difficult situation that may grow into a full-scale anti-occupation insurgency.

The easy answer is that time will tell, and that we will get a reasonably accurate idea within six months. At the same time, there are several pointers that already give us a sense of the possible direction of events.

Military Control and Iraqi Anger

The first aspect to remember is that Iraq is under a fully-fledged military occupation run from the Pentagon, not the State Department. The ultimate authority in Iraq is General David

McKiernan, with Paul Bremer heading the Pentagon's Office of Reconstruction and Humanitarian Assistance (ORHA) reporting to Defense Secretary Donald Rumsfeld.

Progress at democratisation has been remarkably slow, with very limited Iraqi influence allowed from former exiles or in-country sources. The calling of congresses at national or local levels has been consistently delayed and local administrators, where present, are appointed by the occupying forces.

Baghdad was initially placed under the control of Barbara Bodine, a State Department official, but she was transferred away from the post within a month and, as of 29 June, has not been replaced. Roger 'Buck' Walters, a Texas businessman and former US Army officer, administers southern Iraq. W. Bruce Moore, a career US Army officer with service in Vietnam and Somalia, administers northern Iraq.

The second factor is the impact of the Iraqi war casualties on attitudes to the liberators/occupiers. Civilian casualties were somewhere between 5,500 and 7,000 killed (www.iraqbodycount.com), with military casualties certainly exceeding 10,000 and possibly much higher. Overall, as many as 20,000 Iraqis were killed in three weeks of fighting, and around 50,000 were probably injured.

Although there were significant civilian casualties in the fighting around Basra, Najaf and other southern cities, the main concentration of deaths and injuries was in and around Baghdad. The Republican Guard divisions south of Baghdad sustained most of the military casualties. Much of the ordinary Iraqi army was not heavily engaged in the fighting and melted away or was subsequently disbanded by the US occupying power.

Thus, the great majority of the casualties would have been drawn from the Sunni areas of central Iraq, and most of those 70,000 killed or injured would have had a network of family and friends running to millions of people. The great majority of the Sunni population of Iraq would probably have known someone killed or injured in this war. It is an aspect that appears to be entirely ignored by most analysts but may come to be seen as underlying much of the opposition now in evidence.

Related to this is the third factor – that the Sunni communities of central Iraq were the main beneficiaries of the old regime. Throughout the twelve years of sanctions, Iraq had a system akin to the old Soviet *nomenklatura* – an elite of a million or so, drawn from the security and intelligence forces and *apparatchiks* and their extended families. They survived the sanctions period more or less intact, often at the expense of the majority population of Iraq, and comprise the main focus of opposition to occupation.

Even so, are these not just irrelevant if troublesome 'remnants' as we are repeatedly told? The answer is probably no, and the reason relates to the closing stages of the original three-week war. For whatever reason, whether by the Americans 'buying off' the leadership, or by design, the elite Special Republican Guard and the tens of thousands of people attached to the various security and intelligence organisations all failed to offer serious resistance to the US entry into Baghdad, Fallujah and Tikrit.

Almost all of these forces, numbering at least 40,000, melted away with their arms and ammunition largely preserved. Furthermore, in the aftermath of the original war, there was widespread looting of ordinary army munitions stores and the disbanding of that army of nearly 400,000 troops, most of them released to join the ranks of the unemployed. Looked at this way, a picture emerges of 'remnants' that could number in the many thousands, mostly trained in irregular warfare, well-armed and supported by a public mood that, in many parts of Iraq, has become increasingly anti-American.

There are two further factors to add. One is that the US forces, under severe pressure and with internal problems of morale, are increasingly jittery as the attacks intensify. They are reacting with considerable force, including vigorous house-to-house searches and mass detentions, and these actions are only serving to increase hostility to their presence, as well as support for those attacking them.

The final factor is that the entire effort at reconstruction, including plans to redevelop the Iraqi economy along free market lines, is proving deeply problematic. Even twelve weeks after the end of the war, there are persistent and major problems of electricity and drinking water supply, sewage treatment and even food distribution, with long-term delays in oil exporting now anticipated. On top of this, there is rampant unemployment, not least including the hundreds of thousands of young men 'dispersed' from the disbanded army.

Part of the problem lies with the destruction of a rigid and authoritarian regime that was actually well-organised in terms of the running of infrastructure, even under sanctions. But the very sanctions experience meant that much of the infrastructure was crumbling, making reconstruction in the current administrative vacuum particularly difficult. It is a situation being exacerbated by sabotage in a country where key parts of the economy such as oil pipelines, lend themselves to disruption.

Beyond this, though, is a problem which might best be described as cultural – the Bush administration is simply not into peace-building. This is actually in some contrast to attitudes in the European Union, including Britain, and has been demonstrated powerfully in Afghanistan, where the US has consistently blocked the expansion of the International Security Assistance Force.

As already stated, Iraq is under military occupation in a process run by the Pentagon and under the direct control of Rumsfeld, Wolfowitz and their associates. This neo-conservative group operates principally on the basis of forceful control of security threats, a mindset that is being applied in Iraq with the current consequences.

On the basis of all of these factors, a conclusion can be drawn that, on present trends, and leaving aside the further problem of Shi'ite political developments, opposition to US occupation is likely to grow, with an increasing emphasis on insurgency and guerrilla warfare.

Where Next?

One question remains. Is all of this down to the Saddam Hussein leadership? If the opposition is centrally planned and coordinated, then will the capture or killing of Saddam Hussein and his sons bring this opposition to an end and make the tasks for the United States easier? There is no easy answer to this question, and it may well lie at the heart of current US military efforts to find this core group.

Even so, there is evidence of a resurgence of a form of Iraqi nationalism in opposition to occupation, and this is coupled with support for this opposition that includes radical elements from the wider region. In the short term, the capture or deaths of the core leadership might have little effect on the current violence, but it may make a difference.

The key point is that even if it does, this could be short-lived. It is blindingly obvious that Washington does not envisage allowing a truly independent and democratic Iraq to emerge. After all, one of the first requirements of such a government would be for the US forces to leave forthwith.

If the current violence dies down, it may take a year or more for this realisation to have its full impact within Iraq, leading to a resurgence of a more deep-seated and pervasive opposition. On present trends, though, we may not even experience a temporary easing of violence.

An earlier article in this series, one week into the war, sounded a pessimistic note, suggesting a war that might last many months. With the war ending just two weeks later, it was an analysis that hardly seemed to stand the test of time. On reflection, though, it may have been wrong in detail but right in substance, and what we are now seeing is the development of a substantial, dangerous and long-term confrontation with fundamental implications for US security policy in the Persian Gulf.

THE NATURE OF IRAQI RESISTANCE *10 July 2003*

The previous article in this series sought to analyse the nature of the security problems facing US forces in Iraq with the aim of assessing whether a full-scale insurgency was emerging. It pointed to the obvious fact that Iraq was under a coalition military occupation dominated by the United States, with the head of the civil administration, Paul Bremer, reporting to the Pentagon rather than the State Department.

The article also pointed to the likely impact of at least 20,000 deaths during the three-week war on likely Iraqi attitudes to occupation, especially as those casualties were drawn disproportionately from the Sunni communities who had tended to benefit more from the Saddam Hussein regime.

There are other relevant factors in the current tense and unstable situation in Iraq. These include the survival of tens of thousands of members of the Special Republican Guard and militants from Saddam's various security and intelligence agencies, which probably form the basis for attacks on US forces; the continuing failure to restore public services; problems of morale among US troops; and the slow pace of evolution of democratic instruments of government.

One conclusion that can certainly be drawn is that if major security problems continue for US forces in Iraq, then the aggressive neo-conservative security agenda that is so dominant in Washington could actually be damaged. On this basis, developments in Iraq have implications that are potentially global in their impact.

In Fear of the Old Regime

There was also a note of caution in last week's analysis – especially in relation to the nature of resistance to the US presence in Iraq. In this respect, some of the events of the past few days help to give us a more rounded view of what is happening.

Several experienced western journalists currently in Iraq argue that the recent upsurge of attacks on US forces, especially in Baghdad, is making people fearful of the return of the Saddam Hussein regime. As a result, open criticism of the regime voiced in the immediate aftermath of the war is now often being replaced with silence. This condition is exacerbated by the slow pace of political development. A related problem is the increased tendency of the guerrilla forces to target those associated with the occupying powers; the killing of trainee police officers on 5 July is only one example.

A number of former opposition leaders have offered a proposal to counter this fear. They call for the US to put far greater resources into the immediate development of a strong Iraqi security force. However, this is unlikely to be feasible unless it is accompanied by a parallel move towards an early degree of Iraqi self-governance. The importance of such a move does now seem to be recognised as an issue by Paul Bremer and others, but Washington still seems reluctant to give up any of the levers of power.

A Problem of Morale

It is not only the Iraqi people who are facing difficulty in adapting to new realities. There is also an increase in reports of low morale among US troops, many of whom were expecting to leave Iraq two months ago and most of whom were unprepared for dangerous urban warfare operations. A number have started writing to their Congressional representatives, asking for their units to be repatriated. One recent letter said: 'Most soldiers would empty their bank accounts just for a plane ticket home.'

There are currently 145,000 US soldiers in Iraq. Since the US Army can call on up to a million people, it may seem odd that those who have been there longest cannot be replaced by fresh troops. In fact, the trouble is that the figure of 1 million is thoroughly misleading.

The core US Army strength is actually only around 470,000. These include the approximately 230,000 troops deployed in the Gulf region as a whole, with another 140,000 stationed in other parts of the world outside the United States. Most of the remaining troops that make up the 'million' number are actually reservists or in the army's National Guard, almost all with job commitments and families back home. (It is true that there has been a surge in defence spending since 9/11, but most of this is on equipment and increased salaries rather than additional personnel.)

What this means is that an important side effect of the continuing conflict in Iraq will be on recruitment and retention within the US Army itself. This is an unexpected development after the euphoria of a quick victory, but one that is now recognised as potentially serious within the more thoughtful reaches of the Pentagon.

The Pattern of Guerrilla Warfare

These adjustments of policy and thinking will of course need to attend closely to the unfolding realities on the ground in Iraq itself. Recent days alone have signalled the likely direction of events. For the civilian population, an important issue is that problems of electricity supply have actually worsened, with Baghdad experiencing even greater disruption than in the immediate aftermath of the war. For the US forces on the ground, a far more immediate concern is the increase in armed attacks they are now facing.

These attacks are now running at up to a dozen a day in Baghdad and the surrounding area, and are mirrored by other attacks spread across the country, from Kirkuk in the north to Basra in the south. Well over 200 US troops have now been wounded in addition to the 30 killed in hostile action; the number of incidents is now so great that most are not even reported in the western press.

Two features of this guerrilla warfare are of particular concern to the US military leadership. The first is the apparent ease with which individuals can attack US units and then disappear into crowded city districts with little or no risk of their being identified. This is one reason why a $2,500 reward has been offered for information about attackers.

The second is the opposition's capacity to mount large-scale operations. These are no longer limited to a handful of individuals. Last week's double attack north of Baghdad is an example. It started with a carefully orchestrated mortar attack on a sprawling military base outside the town of Balad, 25 kilometres from Baghdad, which injured 17 US soldiers. This would have required transport and careful positioning of weapons and itself represented an escalation in capabilities.

After the mortar attack, a US Army convoy was ambushed on the main road from Baghdad to Mosul, near Balad. There were no American injuries and a number of Iraqis were killed as the troops returned fire. Later, a small contingent from the attacked convoy headed south and met up with reinforcements four miles away, with the combined force then being attacked by another group of guerrillas. Finally, there was yet another attack when US troops returned to the scene of the original ambush to retrieve the bodies of those they had killed.

It is estimated that around 50 guerrillas were engaged in the three attacks in addition to those responsible for the original mortar attack on the military base. This growing capability is made more potent by the ready availability of arms and munitions. When a former bodyguard of Saddam Hussein was arrested on 26 June, US forces recovered plastic explosives, a machinegun, mortars and 10,000 rounds of ammunition at his home (*Washington Post*, 8 July 2003).

Planned or Provoked?

Even this level of guerrilla activity is not conclusive indication that a full-scale insurgency is now in progress. Yet the problems facing US forces are certainly much more substantial than are commonly realised. The key question this raises is the extent to which this scale and type of activity was pre-planned by the old regime before the war. Some journalists have cited a document of January 2003 suggesting that the regime was indeed preparing for this outcome. If so, then it may be that the level of attacks is already peaking and it may still be possible to bring the situation under control.

But what if the violence was not pre-planned – and instead is based largely on post-war improvisation stemming from a deep-seated opposition to US occupation, the ready availability of armaments and the capabilities of some thousands of potential insurgents coming mainly from supporters of the old regime? In this circumstance, the US forces would be faced with a truly dangerous predicament.

The answer is not yet definitely clear. All one can say for now is that the increased intensity, sophistication and scale of the armed attacks suggests that a serious long-term problem of insecurity now exists in substantial parts of Iraq and is going to be very difficult to resolve.

FAR FROM HOME *17 July 2003*

The security problems in Iraq discussed in recent weeks in this series of articles have shown no sign of easing, and some Pentagon sources are predicting that they will get even worse in the coming weeks. Attacks on US units, especially supply convoys, are continuing daily, with further deaths and injuries to troops. A major bomb attack on a police station occupied by US troops was only avoided when the bomb detonated prematurely. Retaliation by US troops is forceful, and frequent pre-emptive raids are further increasing tensions. Even the recently established national advisory council is widely seen as little more than an adjunct to the occupying power.

The extent of the security problem is such that soldiers of the 3rd Infantry Division have just been informed that they will have to stay in the region indefinitely, having been told only last week by their commanding officer, General Buford C. Blount III, that they would be back in the homeland by late summer.

The Costs of Commitment

The developing problems in Iraq come at a time when the huge expenses entailed by the war and its aftermath are having to be revised upwards. This indeed is one of the issues that is encouraging leading Democrat politicians to become much more forceful in their attitude to George W. Bush and his whole Iraq policy.

Until now, the war has cost the US about $50 billion, adding substantially to already-planned military spending for 2003 (see Jonathan Weisman, 'Iraq cost could mount to $100 billion', *Washington Post*, 13 July 2003), but it is the rising cost of post-war operations that is causing particular disquiet.

When the war started in March, there was already an awareness that there would be continuing costs even after the regime had been deposed. At the time, the Pentagon's chief financial officer, Dov Zakheim, estimated post-combat operations at about $2.2 billion a month, but that had increased to $3 billion by the beginning of June and is now estimated at $3.9 billion – or around $47 billion on an annual basis.

What has to be recognised is that these monthly expenditures are being incurred at a time when many of the US forces have actually left the region. Many of the air force units are now back in the United States and the majority of the naval units, including most of the aircraft carrier battle groups, have long since left the region. This context gives us some idea of the extent of the ground force commitments the US is making in Iraq.

The brunt of these operations is being borne by the army, with substantial movements of supplies necessary to sustain troops that are operating continually under near-combat conditions. For the time being, at least, there is no end in sight, and this means an added overall strain on the US federal budget. The $100 billion estimate for military costs throughout the year comes at a time when the current year's federal budget deficit is being put at $455 billion. This is a huge increase on previous estimates and stems from a combination of slow economic growth, tax cuts and the cost of the war and its aftermath.

Such a deficit is a record for the United States, exceeding the previous (1992) record of $290 billion, although it is relatively smaller in proportion to the total economy than some of those truly massive deficits of the Ronald Reagan era at the height of the Cold War.

Yet deficits at this level, which are expected to rise still further next year, are part of the reason why President Bush's popularity is beginning to slip, and also why there is a much more intense focus on what is happening in Iraq. The extent of the US commitments in Iraq mean that there is now serious talk of reversing some of the personnel cuts of the 1990s and increasing army numbers towards Cold War levels – a very different prospect to that favoured by Donald Rumsfeld with his preference for light and highly mobile forces.

A Force under Pressure

The US Army is essentially organised into ten divisions, subdivided into 33 brigades and made up of about 200,000 troops in all. This is less than half of the total army personnel, but it represents the core of the fighting forces, essentially those capable of combat operations overseas. Of those ten divisions, the 3rd and 4th Infantry Divisions, the 1st Armoured Division and the 101st Airborne Division are all in Iraq, together with elements of other divisions.

The Iraq commitments therefore represent the equivalent of five divisions. Another division is committed to Afghanistan and another to Europe, including the Balkans; only one division is currently being held in reserve in the United States. A further measure of current pressures is that, at present, 19 of the army's 33 brigades are stationed or deployed overseas.

There is, in addition, the large Marine Corps, but that has its own commitments in East Asia and would also be used (if these prove necessary) for operations in Liberia, the Horn of Africa and elsewhere. The US Army can also call on large numbers of reservists and National Guard units, but these are all people in regular employment and the numbers already called up are leading to strains in the system.

Thus, both for budgetary and personnel reasons, there is now a premium on trying to reduce troop levels in Iraq, and it is here that the problem is really developing. Until recently, the US hoped and expected that it could persuade a number of states to make significant troop commitments to garrisoning Iraq. There have been some 'successes', with units from Spain, Italy and Poland taking up duties in some of the quieter parts of Iraq, but what were really needed were division-strength deployments from countries that had large professional armed forces.

The Indian 'No'

It is here that problems have arisen, because most such countries are frankly unwilling to make the commitments. Britain is already fully stretched in south-east Iraq, and France and

Germany have both made it clear that they are not interested, at least at any substantial force levels. Spain is highly unlikely to increase its force levels, given the domestic unpopularity of the war and its aftermath, and Turkey and Russia are politically unacceptable even if they were willing.

The one key country that remains is India, with its sizeable and experienced army. The United States asked the Indian army to commit a full division of 17,000 troops to the northern, Kurdish region of Iraq around Mosul. While this is not a region of high tensions, it would have been a very valuable addition for the Americans, relieving some pressure on their own troops while sending a powerful political signal to other states, especially those in NATO.

There might have been questions about India taking part in operations in what is essentially an Islamic country, but in any case the Indian government this week decided not to accede to the American request.

This decision is highly significant as well as something of a surprise. The Prime Minister, Atal Behari Vajpayee, had been under heavy US pressure to agree the troop movements, and there were some sound political reasons for doing so. One was the perceived need for India to ally itself to the world's only superpower; another was Pakistan's evident strategy of positioning itself alongside Washington in the 'war on terror'. Also, India's ability to sustain a full army division overseas would demonstrate the extent of its military capabilities.

Indian defence analysts believe that Vajpayee's decision is very much the result of domestic politics. Put bluntly, the Iraq war was highly unpopular in India, and opposition to sending troops now is very high; recent opinion polls show around 69–87 per cent against any deployment. To complicate matters for the government, elections are due in five states later this year, four of them in strong Congress Party areas, and the results would help set the scene for the general election that is due in just over a year.

Reaping the Consequences

The Indian government may yet make a much smaller military commitment to Iraq, and would probably do it much more readily if there was a stronger UN influence in the country, but the core fact is that the United States simply cannot get many of its presumed allies to help it out, especially as levels of violence and insecurity in Iraq increase.

In March 2003, Washington went to war in the teeth of strong international opposition, with only Britain and Australia (and to a degree Poland) offering direct military support. Its hope was that Iraq would move rapidly into a post-war state of stability, wartime opposition would recede and other states would then come in on a large scale to help with maintaining security.

That has simply not happened, and a bitter insurgency is still developing. The end result is that states such as India, France and Germany are willing to leave the United States to carry the considerable burdens it now faces. Poland, Spain, Britain and others may help out to a limited extent, but in the regions of major instability and violence in Iraq the US is essentially on its own and is beginning to reap the political as well as the military consequences of the war.

A QUESTION OF MOTIVE *24 July 2003*

The Iraq war continues to dominate the 'domestic' as well as 'foreign' news agenda in the United States and Britain. In America, criticism over the inclusion of dubious intelligence findings in the public statements of President Bush before the war is being voiced; while in Britain, the aftermath of the death of the biological weapons inspector David Kelly has intensified the already bitter arguments between the government and the BBC over alleged manipulation of the military threat posed by the Saddam regime.

Before the war, British government dossiers on the threat from Iraq made much of an immediate risk to Britain and its interests, not least through a claimed Iraqi capability to launch weapons of mass destruction (WMD) within 45 minutes of an order being given. The implied urgency of the threat did much to ensure that the UK government had sufficient support from its own members of parliament; this was a much less significant issue in the United States, where the intended fall of the Saddam Hussein regime was widely represented as a necessary part of the war on terror.

Official: No Immediate Threat from Iraq

While there remains the possibility that some evidence of a limited WMD programme may be uncovered, it is now frankly unlikely that evidence will be found to support any kind of precipitate threat. But in any case, a somewhat obscure yet official document from the British Ministry of Defence (MoD), published since the war, itself casts doubt on the motives for launching it.

Operations in Iraq: First Reflections was published by the MoD in early July, before the media-political firestorm over Andrew Gilligan's claims of government manipulation of intelligence information and the subsequent suicide of David Kelly. The document represents an initial analysis of the war from a UK military perspective. While it argues that there was a need to destroy the Saddam regime, it also emphasises that: 'The Government's overriding political objective was to disarm Saddam of his weapons of mass destruction, *which threatened his neighbours and his people*' (para 1.3, emphasis added).

Note that even at this level, there is not assumed to be any direct threat to Britain, an assessment supported later in the document where it is stated that:

> The UK was engaged in a limited (rather than total) conflict with the Iraqi regime and *there was no tangible Iraqi military threat to*

> *the UK*. However, it has been apparent since 11 September 2001 that the UK itself could be a target for specific hostile attack or disruptive action by terrorists, especially when it is engaged in operations abroad. (para 6.10, emphasis added)

Thus, even on this official account, Iraq did not present a direct threat to Britain, and British interests were more likely to be threatened by terrorists rather than Iraq. On the question of whether Iraq was aiding terrorist organisations, the document has little to say. Certainly, repeated efforts in the past 18 months to link the Saddam Hussein regime to sub-state paramilitary groups have come up with little or no evidence.

Hardly any of the thousands of putative terrorists detained in the US, Guantanamo and elsewhere have been Iraqi citizens or have even had any links at all with Iraq. If anything, the international support for al-Qaida and its many affiliates has stretched across scores of countries, with Iraq being far down at or near the bottom of the list.

Strategies of Concealment

As the intensive WMD search continues to draw a blank, it becomes even more difficult to see why the WMD issue was presented as the official reason for the necessity of the war at the particular moment of late March 2003. It is especially problematic that the UNMOVIC inspectors, led by Hans Blix, were not given much more time. The inspectors argued then that they would need many months to do a competent job, even though they had come to operate at a much higher inspection tempo in the days before they had to withdraw.

Furthermore, one issue in relation to the UNMOVIC process has continuing implications. In the weeks prior to the war, Hans Blix and his colleagues were persistent in their requests for serious intelligence data from the US and UK, so that they could 'marry' such data to their inspections. After the war, Blix acknowledged that such intelligence was indeed forthcoming – but when it was acted on, nothing of significance was found.

The implications of this are clear: that the stated motive for war was questionable at the time the war started. UNMOVIC was at the time checking out intelligence findings on the ground but was finding them to be almost wholly inaccurate.

This does at least suggest that the precise timing of the war had much more to do with two factors. The first was the need to terminate the regime before the onset of the summer heat made combat far more difficult; the second was that the longer UNMOVIC had to demonstrate the paucity of evidence of an immediate Iraqi WMD threat, the more the stated motive for the war was eroded.

Retaliation or Aggression?

The wider issue remains as to whether the motive for war had much more to do with Iraq as a geopolitical threat to oil security. Within the current British political climate this, curiously, remains a side-issue. The current emphasis is on Iraqi WMD and manipulated intelligence, and any discussion of the relevance of oil is strongly denied by officialdom even if it continues to be raised in the media and parliament.

Meanwhile, evidence that the war was planned well in advance of March 2003 has now emerged in relation to a military operation codenamed Southern Focus that began in 2002 and continued for a year, until the spring of 2003. In the run-up to the war, a number of analysts pointed to the increase in air raids by US and UK strike aircraft as, it seemed, part of the process of policing the air exclusion zones. At the time, these raids were said to be in direct retaliation for Iraqi attempts to counter this policing function, but it has since emerged that the process was a carefully planned operation whose 'retaliatory' function was a mere disguise.

Southern Focus was targeted at a number of features of the regime including the fibre-optic cable network that had been established with Chinese aid, together with a range of command centres and air defence systems. It was a substantial military operation that involved the dropping of over 600 weapons, most of them precision-guided bombs, on 391 targets. All of this was undertaken well before the war started, and much of it even preceded the seeking of UN resolutions in support of war.

How was the War Waged?

The continuing refusal of US and British sources to give any assessments of the numbers of Iraqi civilian and military killed in the war has been frequently remarked on in this series. In this context, a further revelation throws light on coalition attitudes during the war. It is now known that military commanders were required to submit for Donald Rumsfeld's approval plans for any air attacks that were thought likely to kill more than 30 civilians. In the event, over 50 such attacks were planned and all of them were approved.

The total civilian casualty rate is now believed to be 6–7,000. This figure may in part be explained by such revelations, and raises the awkward question of culpability for war crimes. It is not known whether UK forces were involved in such operations or whether a similar process existed separately for their own strike operations. It is yet another question that is currently sidelined.

Perhaps what is most significant in all of this is how these issues relate to what is now happening in Iraq. As more details of the preparations for war and its conduct emerge, more hard questions are arising. In reality, though, hardly any of these questions would even have been posed as matters of legitimate political concern if the short-term post-war situation in Iraq had developed as expected. If, that is, the coalition forces had been widely welcomed as liberators, if civilian casualties had been low, and if the country had shown evidence of an instant socio-economic improvement, there would have been little or no concern for the conduct of the war itself, or even its motives.

The Momentum of Conflict

The reality on the ground over much of Iraq is very far from this benign scenario, and it is one that even the killing of Saddam Hussein's sons may not substantially alter. Although the death of Qusay and Uday Hussein has been presented as a major morale boost for US forces, it is already clear that the brothers were effectively in hiding in the Mosul villa, and were not protected by a large number of well-armed bodyguards as might have been expected. Thus, they were unlikely to have been playing a significant role in coordinating the guerrilla warfare now affecting US forces.

The three further attacks on US troops in the two days after the brothers were killed lend credence to this analysis. Its ominous implication for the US military in Iraq is that even Saddam Hussein may not be a crucially significant factor in the current violence, and that even his own death or capture may not bring the conflict to an end.

Thus, it is the very fact of the instability, violence and burgeoning guerrilla war, stemming in part from the coalition's post-war policies, that is beginning to focus attention on the wider issues raised by the war, especially the key question of its essential motive. These issues may well receive increased attention in both London and Washington as current media concerns recede; and in time they may even have serious political implications for the respective governments.

4
Overstretch

INTRODUCTION

During the course of August and September 2003, the insurgency took firm root in Iraq, including attacks on Iraqi police and security forces as well as US troops. More notable in terms of long-term trends were the attacks on the Jordanian diplomatic mission, the headquarters of the Red Cross, and the UN offices in Baghdad. The UN attack was particularly significant, not just because of the considerable loss of life but for two other reasons.

One was that the building had been one of the few places in Iraq where Iraqis and foreign personnel could meet in reasonable safety to share problems. Indeed, the canteen in the building was regarded as one of the few bits of 'safe space' in Baghdad. The bombing destroyed this.

The second factor was the degree of bitterness felt by UN staff, especially at the UN Headquarters in New York. The attack in Baghdad made it abundantly clear that the US military forces were not in control of the situation and demonstrated to UN staff that any work they did in the country was fraught with danger. Moreover, this followed marked antagonism to the UN by the Bush administration in the run-up to the war the previous year.

Beyond the immediate problems in Iraq, a detached analysis showed that two years after the start of the 'global war on terror', the al-Qaida movement remained highly active, security in Afghanistan remained deeply problematic and anti-American sentiments were increasing in many parts of the world. Even so, any fundamental re-assessment of the conduct of the war on terror seemed unlikely, even though the war in Iraq was slowly beginning to attract adverse comment within the United States.

WHERE ARE THE WEAPONS? *31 July 2003*

Nearly four months after the fall of Baghdad, intensive searching across Iraq has failed to uncover any evidence of weapons of mass destruction (WMD). More surprisingly, there has been virtually no evidence of any production capability or even storage facilities. The British government still insists that the elusive 'smoking gun' will be found, but it is now frankly implausible that the regime had, as it alleges, a 45-minute capability to use weapons of mass destruction at the time the war started in March 2003.

The coalition's current fall-back position is that the large Iraq Survey Group will eventually find some evidence, but this conveniently omits a substantial earlier process from view. As soon as the Iraqi regime had fallen in April, the US armed forces put in specialist search groups to visit all the key sites earmarked by previous surveillance and intelligence reports. To their own surprise, and that of the US authorities, they found nothing of substance and were ultimately withdrawn.

Even so, controversy over the existence and condition of Iraqi WMD programmes continues. It is particularly significant in Britain, where a presumed immediate threat from WMD was heavily used to bring sceptical Labour MPs into line in crucial parliamentary votes before the war. It makes sense now to stand back and try to get an overview of what really happened.

The Origins of Iraq's WMD Programmes

The Ba'ath regime was interested in WMD almost from the beginning. It saw Iraq as a major regional player, and one way to consolidate this was a significant deterrent capability, especially in the face of a singularly powerful Israel equipped with a substantial nuclear arsenal. Iraq's own WMD ambitions developed in the 1970s and focused on nuclear and chemical weapons, with biological weapons initially sidelined. However, progress on a plutonium-based nuclear programme came to an abrupt end with the Israeli destruction of the Osiraq nuclear reactor in 1981.

After that, Iraq ceased to concentrate on the development of plutonium-based nuclear weapons, because such a programme is necessarily centralised and thereby vulnerable to attack. Instead it opted for a dispersed programme based on uranium enrichment. It also accelerated its development of crude chemical weapons such as mustard gas, put more effort into developing nerve agents and also started a biological weapons programme. Chemical weapons were used repeatedly against Iranian ground forces during the eight-year Iran–Iraq war and also against Kurdish civilians, both at a time when Iraq was informally allied with the United States and with western Gulf states as a buffer against Iran.

At the time of the 1991 war, the nuclear programme still had some way to go, but Iraq had a range of chemical and biological weapons that it might well have used if the regime had been threatened with destruction. After the 1991 war, the UN inspectorate, in the form of the International Atomic Energy Agency (IAEA) and the UN Special Commission on Iraq (UNSCOM), proceeded to dismantle as much of the Iraqi WMD programme as they could. By all accounts they achieved a great deal. Large quantities of crude chemical weapons and their production facilities were destroyed, along with some nerve agents. UNSCOM also oversaw the destruction of numerous missiles and their production lines. The IAEA was particularly successful in destroying nuclear production facilities, often after protracted searches.

By the time the inspectors withdrew in December 1998, virtually all of Iraq's nuclear and missile facilities had been destroyed, along with most of the chemical weapons facilities. It was not clear whether all of the crude chemical agents had been found, nor was there so much progress in uncovering all of the nerve agent work or the biological weapons.

The Approach to War: Three Views of Iraq's Capability

In the months leading up to the war, there were essentially three views about the extent of the Iraqi WMD programme. The first was that a considerable clandestine programme should be assumed to exist, centred on chemical nerve agents and biological weapons, but also involving programmes to reconstitute a nuclear capability and to extend the range of missiles.

The London-based International Institute of Strategic Studies (IISS) took this view, although with significant notes of caution in its own analysis. The US and UK governments held a similar position but went quite a lot further in their claims, most notably with the British emphasis on the 45-minute capability and the overall view that Iraq was an immediate threat with aggressive intent. Even in the run-up to the war, this stance was beginning to fray around the edges as the UN inspectors moved back into Iraq and could not find anything, even at sites identified by US and UK politicians.

The second view was that Iraq had probably retained a limited capability to use chemical and biological weapons, the aim being to have some kind of deterrent to help ensure regime survival. This appears to have been its aim in 1991, and may have been one of the reasons the US forces did not attempt to destroy the regime then.

The likelihood of such a limited deterrent was argued by a number of analysts and in earlier articles in this series, and there were two implications. One was that such weapons were inadequate to constitute a major threat and hence not sufficient to offer any justification for war; the other was that going to war against a regime with even this limited capability was highly risky, and could lead to the use of such weapons with the possibility of a US nuclear response.

The third view was expressed by some independent specialists in chemical and biological weapons, and is now largely forgotten. This was that it was unlikely that Iraq had any kind of effective capability, not least because its ability to produce stable forms of the weapons was highly limited. In other words, old chemical and biological stocks were in all probability virtually useless, and there was little evidence of a reconstituted programme.

On the evidence now available, it is looking increasingly likely that the third view is the most accurate and that Iraq did not have an active WMD capability by early 2003. Some politicians have suggested that the regime destroyed its own weapons in the immediate run-up to the war, but this makes little sense – after all, if you expect that your regime is on the point of destruction and you have got even a crude deterrent, you hardly set about destroying it!

Who Can be Believed?

It is certainly possible that, in the expectation of an eventual end to sanctions, the regime had decided not even to try to redevelop its WMD programme, while preserving the possibility of going back to WMD at a later stage. If this was the policy, then the main reason that it came unstuck was the election of George W. Bush and the consequent intention of the United States to terminate the regime. This in turn went well beyond the WMD issue and had, as earlier articles in this series have outlined, much more to do with Washington's need to ensure the security of Persian Gulf oil supplies.

The implication of all this is that the stated reason for going to war, the threat of Iraq's WMD, simply does not stand up. The political implications of such a situation have, until now, been far more problematic for Tony Blair than for George W. Bush, but this is now changing as the continuing level of casualties suffered by US forces in Iraq puts pressure on the Bush administration to explain its real motives for war.

Under these circumstances, the political need to find the 'smoking gun' increases. This raises a key issue. It is possible, indeed probable, that the Iraq Survey Group will find some limited evidence of a past Iraqi chemical and biological weapons (CBW) programme, and perhaps even some indications of the ability to redevelop one – but all the signs are that such evidence will be very limited and a long way from that required to indicate a serious threat.

If indeed such limited evidence appears, the political pressure for it to be 'sexed up' (to use a phrase that has become notorious in recent British controversy about the WMD issue) will be extreme, but any attempt to do so is likely to fail. 'Dodgy dossiers' and previous examples of over-hype will then be recalled, to the extent that even legitimate evidence, albeit limited, will not be believed across much of the world.

The obvious way beyond the miasma of political mistrust which surrounds the issue would be for the US and its partners to invite the UN inspectors back, with unlimited powers to conduct a thorough search throughout Iraq. There is no sign of that happening. Indeed, the very unwillingness of the US and its British ally to countenance such a move has the ironic result of leaving them with little chance of convincing the world that, on the basis of Iraqi WMD at least, the war was ever justified.

ENTRAPMENT *28 August 2003*

The pattern of violence and killing in Afghanistan has continued. Four government soldiers were killed in an incident on Friday 22 August, and five more died in an ambush in south-eastern Afghanistan the following day. In response, a major counter-attack was organised involving Afghan and United States troops supported by F-16 and A-10 combat aircraft.

Reports remain rather confused but it appears that up to 600 guerrillas described as Taliban fighters were engaged by 450 Afghan government soldiers and a small number of American troops. According to a US military source at Bagram airbase near Kabul, 14 guerrillas were killed; another source said that 40 had been captured.

If previous experience is a guide, the remaining several hundred guerrillas will have dispersed, some of them over the border into Pakistan, to regroup in due course for further attacks. More generally, these incidents indicate the size of the forces that they can assemble, as well as the extent of the military operations that continue to involve the US forces.

Deployment Amidst Insecurity

Although the situation in much of Afghanistan remains difficult, it is the conflict in Iraq that is central to Pentagon concerns. The number of US troops who perished in the war itself is now exceeded by those killed since President Bush declared major combat operations over on 1 May. Over 60 Americans have died in combat since then, and a larger number have been killed as a result of traffic accidents, unintentional discharge of firearms and other causes.

It is now accepted that the opposition in Iraq is growing, not diminishing, as is the degree of disorganisation in public services. This has been ably reported by experienced journalists returning to Iraq after a month or two away (for example, Rory McCarthy in the *Guardian*, 27 August 2003), but it is the changing nature of the attacks on US troops that is most worrying for the Pentagon.

There has been a steady shift away from any kind of conventional engagement, as was experienced during and immediately after the war, to more skilful guerrilla engagements coupled with the use of remotely-controlled bombs. During the war itself, US casualties were 'clustered' into particular incidents of substantial ambushes or the effects of artillery fire or missile attack. Since the war, there has been a widespread degree of dispersal, with many hundreds of small-scale incidents, frequently leading to injuries and sometimes deaths.

One of the effects of the attacks, and the persistent American losses, is a change in military deployments. There are still occasions when large-scale 'sweeps' are undertaken, as with this week's operation involving 3,000 US troops, but there has also been a trend towards reducing the number of routine patrols.

A pattern is emerging that is not unlike US operations in Kosovo, although on a much larger scale. The main troop deployments in the least stable parts of Iraq take the form of concentrations of forces in heavily guarded encampments located in former palaces or military bases. The irony is that just as the Saddam Hussein regime put a premium on the security of its leadership and elite forces, so US forces are having to do the same for their own troops, often using the old regime's facilities.

At a more general level, the decrease in US military patrols means that 'ordinary' lawlessness is certainly not diminishing and this, combined with guerrilla attacks, goes a long way towards explaining the high levels of insecurity. These, typified by the atrocity at the UN headquarters in Baghdad on 19 August, are now so severe that key aid agencies are now pulling their people out of the country.

A Risky Calculation

An even more dramatic response from the US forces has been the recruitment of former intelligence and security operatives from the Saddam Hussein regime (Anthony Shadid and Daniel Williams, 'U.S. Recruiting Hussein's Spies', *Seattle Times*, 24 August 2003). The main recruiting source has been the *mukhabarat*, or foreign intelligence agency of the old regime, and it is being undertaken in the face of objections from the US-appointed Iraqi Governing Council.

Recruitment such as this is a clear recognition that the United States is engaged in a developing guerrilla war in Iraq, and that major counter-guerrilla operations that inevitably drag in and sometimes even kill innocent bystanders, can be deeply counter-productive. A fundamental requirement in counter-guerrilla warfare is recognised to be high-quality intelligence, and the predicament of the US in Iraq is that it is having to rely on such intelligence from people who have been personally and persistently involved in one of the most repressive and brutal regimes of recent years.

The use of former *mukhabarat* personnel is also relevant because the US military now recognise that there are indeed foreign militants entering Iraq to engage US forces, with many of them coming across borders that are thoroughly porous. The reasons for this are themselves significant. On the Iraqi side, there are simply not the border guards or police available to regulate entry, and, more significantly, countries such as Syria are not bothering to maintain frontier controls at their pre-war levels. While they are probably being very careful not to help the movement of militants into Iraq for fear of US retaliation, they see little reason to support the United States in its occupation of Iraq.

The wider issue is the extent to which the opposition to American occupation is coming from outside elements. Going right back to the origins of the war, and the motives for regime termination, the Bush administration was always anxious to characterise the war as part of a much wider 'war on terror', with Saddam Hussein represented as a supporter of terrorist groups.

This was not the overriding motive cited by the British government, and most independent analysts considered it highly questionable. Their reasoning was that the Saddam Hussein regime seemed persistently cautious in any support for paramilitary movements, possible to avoid giving the United States a pretext for a war. More specifically, al-Qaida and similar Islamic paramilitary groups had little respect for the old Iraqi regime since it was essentially secular rather than religious.

What is now happening, though, is that the probable presence of small numbers of foreign militants is being used by the Bush administration as justification for a much wider process of remaking the political map of the Middle East as a core part of the war on terror. This has the immediate political advantage of tying US military losses not to some mistaken occupation of a distant country but to the wider process of making the US homeland safer from terrorist attacks.

Last Battle or First Shots?

This in turn raises the question of whether a genuine policy development is occurring, or merely a crude and cynical device. Certainly, the rhetoric is there. As Paul Wolfowitz put it on US television at the end of July: '...the battle to secure the peace in Iraq is now the central battle in the global war on terror, and those sacrifices are going to make not just the Middle East more stable, but our country safer'. George W. Bush actually made a similar point even before the war, when he told the American Enterprise Institute on 26 February that 'A liberated Iraq can show the power of freedom to transform that vital region by bringing hope and progress to the lives of millions'

(Dana Milbank and Mike Allen, 'US Shifts Rhetoric On Its Goals in Iraq', *Washington Post*, 1 August 2003).

This rhetoric, though, stems from a genuine belief within administration ranks that the consolidation of post-war Iraq is actually a fundamental part of the creation of the New American Century, setting the scene for the transition to pro-American governments across the region. Moreover, because Iraq is the focus for this transformation, so it will attract the Islamic militants from across the region.

As Thomas Friedman put it this week: '...America's opponents know just what's at stake in the postwar struggle for Iraq, which is why they flock there: Beat America's ideas in Iraq and you beat them out of the whole region; lose to America there, lose everywhere' (Thomas L. Friedman, 'The Wider Stakes in Postwar Iraq', *International Herald Tribune*, 25 August 2003).

The key question, therefore, is whether this battle between US forces and the militants has already been joined. It is here that US policy in post-war Iraq is already problematic, for four reasons.

The first is the conspicuous lack of support from those few states that could commit large numbers of well-trained troops to relieve pressure on the US forces. Second, Kofi Annan will simply not countenance a 'blue helmet' operation in the context of US control of the country. Third, most surrounding states will offer little or no aid, a stance made more resolute by the reaction of their own populations both to the US military presence and to the continuing Israeli–Palestinian confrontation.

The fourth reason is perhaps the most significant of all. There has been an abject failure on the part of the occupying power to restore Iraq to economic and social normality, coupled with continuing resistance stemming almost entirely from elements within Iraq rather than militants entering the country from the wider region. That, in all probability, is still to come, and may actually take many months to develop.

In short, if Friedman and others are right, and if what happens in Iraq is central to US policy not just in the Middle East but to the wider 'war on terror', then we are in the very early stages of a prolonged conflict. Moreover, US policy is already in trouble even before the full extent of the conflict has been recognised – we have yet to see how al-Qaida and its related groups will oppose the US presence.

In the immediate aftermath of the 9/11 attacks, some analysts argued that one of al-Qaida's aims would be to draw the United States more fully into the region. The Bush administration may see that large-scale military intervention as the prelude to success in its war on terror whereas the reality could be that al-Qaida and its associates will welcome the presence of 140,000 targets in their midst. No longer do they have to go to America – America has come to them.

A HARD ROAD

4 September 2003

When Uday and Qusay Hussein were killed on 22 July, there was an assumption that the old regime's influence in Iraq was at last nearing its end, and that violent opposition would decline. In recent weeks, four major attacks within the country have all pointed to a degree of strategy and coordination that counters any idea that the United States is still facing the depleted remnants of Saddam Hussein's supporters.

First, the destruction of the Jordanian diplomatic compound had an effect on a number of neighbouring countries, resulting in considerable caution in dealing with Iraqi diplomats and reminding those states that close contact with the United States would encourage attacks on their own people. Second, the attack on the UN headquarters and the assassination of Sergio Vieira de Mello had an even greater effect, leading to a withdrawal of staff from the UN, World Bank, the IMF and a number of non-governmental development agencies.

This week's attack (and the fourth in chronological sequence) on the Baghdad police headquarters was a further indication of the vulnerability of those police and security forces that are being actively trained and supported by the US. Most damaging of all was the third attack, the appalling car bombing in Najaf on 29 August, killing well over 100 people and assassinating Ayatollah Mohammad Baqr al-Hakim. The impact of this on the Shi'a religious and political leadership is difficult to judge, but it demonstrates a capability to plan attacks that are both sophisticated and deep-rooted.

The Evidence of Combat Injuries

Some analysts have suggested that the significance of these attacks on the Jordanians, the UN and the police, and even the bombing in Najaf, are all indications of an opposite trend. The idea is that the need to attack 'soft' targets may actually show that the US security forces themselves are actually less at risk and may even be gaining the advantage. It is an odd conclusion, considering the impact of these attacks and it is, in any case not supported by recent evidence of US casualties.

As mentioned in earlier articles in this series, one of the features of US soldiering in Iraq in recent months has been the combination of the use of armoured vehicles with soldiers wearing helmets and body armour. A remarkable effect of this has been the way in which a much-reduced death rate has been accompanied by a relative increase in serious but survivable injuries, mostly to limbs. This has resulted in a major programme of medical treatment which, when examined in detail, gives a much clearer idea of the problems facing the US Army in Iraq.

Soldiers injured in combat or through accidents are initially treated and stabilised at medical centres in Iraq or at the regional medical centre at Landstuhl in Germany. From there they are flown in C-17 transport aircraft to the Andrews Air Base outside Washington for treatment either at the Walter Reed Army Medical Center in Washington or the National Naval Medical Center in Bethesda.

The scale of the operation is considerable and largely unrecognised (but see Vernon Loeb: 'Number of Wounded in Action on Rise', *Washington Post*, 2 September 2003). Virtually every night a C-17 arrives at Andrews with more casualties. Last Thursday (28 August), a plane arrived with 44 patients, and the following night another was due with a further 36, twelve of them on stretchers.

On arrival at the base, the most seriously wounded are transferred in a fleet of ambulances to the hospitals and others stay at the base pending transport to their own army and Marine camp medical centres across the country. To cope with the influx, a 'contingency aeromedical staging facility' has even had to be created at Andrews, taking over a community centre and an indoor sports hall.

According to Central Command, 1,325 soldiers and Marines have been injured sufficiently seriously to be airlifted back to the United States, with 1,124 of these being combat injuries and the remaining 301 being hurt in vehicle crashes or other accidents. In addition, more than 4,500 troops have been flown back because of physical or mental illness. There does not appear to be any record of lesser combat injuries in Iraq where people are treated and then return to duty.

In the period since 1 May 2003, when President Bush famously declared, on the deck of the USS *Abraham Lincoln*, that major combat operations in Iraq were over, 574 troops have been wounded, more than in the war itself and its immediate aftermath. Moreover, there has been a sharp increase in combat injuries in recent weeks, with an average of almost ten each day throughout August.

Can America Share the Burden?

One of the main effects of this predicament of a worsening security environment is that the Bush administration is reluctantly having to reconsider its attitude to the United Nations, even to the extent of allowing UN officials a modestly greater role in Iraq in return for peacekeeping commitments from countries such as India, Bangladesh, Turkey and Pakistan. Part of the reason is the pressure beginning to come from Congress as the autumn session commences and members of the Senate and the House return from their constituencies with reports of increasing unease.

Even more relevant is the pressure coming from the military themselves. The current political, military and economic control of Iraq is essentially delegated to the Pentagon, not the State Department, and the civilian leadership in the Pentagon, most notably Donald Rumsfeld and Paul Wolfowitz, continues to maintain control while holding the view that no more troops are required and that an increased role for the UN is an unacceptable complication. What is significant, though, is that this view is simply not shared by the military, with some of the most senior commanders actively seeking a more substantial UN involvement.

According to the *Washington Post* (3 September 2003), the vice-chair of the Joint Chiefs of Staff, Marine Corps General Peter Pace, is lobbying administration figures. According to an official quoted in the paper, the head of Central Command, General John Abizaid, and even the chair of the Joint Chiefs of Staff himself, General Richard Myers have been 'strongly engaged in the internationalisation effort, to include a new U.N. resolution'.

In seeking to 'internationalise' the response, the Bush administration faces four problems. The first is the attitude of Security Council members such as France and Russia, originally opposed to the war and unlikely to support any new resolution unless they benefit themselves. The second is the antagonism to the United States among UN bureaucrats in New York, still angry and bitter at the attack on the Baghdad UN headquarters, especially the killing of the widely-respected Sergio Vieira de Mello.

A third problem is that the United States is currently forced to limit the handover to international troops already in Iraq. Prior to the Najaf atrocity, the United States was due to handover security powers from the Marines in southern Iraq to an international force controlled by the Poles, with further sizeable contingents from Spain and Ukraine. The transfer in Najaf itself has been postponed and the Marines will now remain there for at least two weeks and possibly longer.

Fourth, and perhaps most important of all, is the level of violence towards American troops. The extent of this is demonstrated by the injuries cited above. It may not be widely recognised in the general media but is certainly understood by governments of those countries who would be asked to contribute. Furthermore, the recent killing of soldiers from Britain and Denmark demonstrates that other forces would also be targeted – what may be described as a peacekeeping role could easily turn into a costly counter-insurgency war for the other countries as well as the United States.

In the final analysis, Washington will probably be able to contrive a compromise resolution at the UN Security Council prior to George Bush's speech to the General Assembly later in the month, and it is also likely that some extra international troops will be deployed to the more stable parts of Iraq. Even so, it will most likely be on a scale much smaller than Washington would wish, and it will be US troops who will remain at the centre of the conflict.

Given the extent and persistence of the attacks they are now facing, their predicament will not be seriously diminished by a marginally increased international role. The end result is likely to be the steady rise of the Iraq war up the domestic political agenda just as the 2004 presidential election starts to get under way.

THE 'WAR ON TERROR': TWO YEARS ON

10 September 2003

When this series of Open Democracy articles started, less than one month after the 11 September 2001 attacks on the World Trade Center and the Pentagon, the George W. Bush administration was already responding by announcing a 'war on terror', with every expectation that there would be vigorous military action against al-Qaida and the Taliban regime in Afghanistan. Even at that stage there was also talk of an attack on Iraq to terminate the Saddam Hussein regime.

There was concern over the risk of further attacks on the United States, and an immediate worry over anthrax outbreaks affecting people in several American cities. Yet there was also a confidence that the US, as the world's sole superpower, would not have too much difficulty in reasserting control over an evidently dangerous security environment.

Two years later, it is an appropriate time to try and take a detached view of the results so far of President Bush's war on terror. In doing so, it makes sense to go back to the immediate context of the 9/11 atrocities, and to identify three main factors which determined the response of the US government: military capabilities, neo-conservative political strategy, and the traumatic, 'mediatised' impact of the experience itself.

The Condition of the US Military

The first factor was the nature and capabilities of the US armed forces. In the decade or so after the collapse of the Soviet Union, US military forces had been scaled down substantially, but also relative to what were considered to be the major requirements of the Cold War era. While the US Navy lost much of its anti-submarine capability, its carrier battle-groups were maintained at close to Cold War levels and were enhanced with large numbers of land-attack cruise missiles.

The US Marine Corps, with its global amphibious capabilities, retained almost all of its forces and the US Air Force – while experiencing considerable personnel cutbacks – developed a much greater ability to project air power at the global level. The army was particularly badly affected through the loss of much of its armoured capabilities from the old central front in Europe, but it retained its rapid reaction forces such as the 82nd and 101st Airborne Divisions, and also put much more emphasis on Special Forces and counter-insurgency capabilities.

Thus, the US military had adapted overall to the fractured world scene of the post-Cold War era in which, in the words of former CIA director James Woolsey, the United States had slain the dragon but now lived in a jungle full of poisonous snakes.

At the end of the twentieth century, the US military seemed to be overwhelmingly powerful but was also looking to the future, with the probable development of directed energy weapons and a greater emphasis on 'network-centric' warfare and the control of space. All this was part of a wider concern with 'full spectrum dominance', the ability to dictate military outcomes on land, sea, in the air or in space.

The Ambition of Neo-Conservatism

The second factor influencing the United States' response to 9/11 was the state of its domestic politics. The Bush administration which came to office in early 2001 had, contrary to expectations, made no attempt to develop a consensus administration, despite its exceedingly narrow margin of victory (due in no small way to the famous Florida 'chads' and the US Supreme Court). In international affairs, a unilateralist streak became evident almost at once, with its opposition to the Kyoto Protocols on climate change, the proposed International Criminal Court, the Comprehensive Test Ban Treaty and several other treaties and agreements.

The United States would, it seems, engage with others on a multinational basis only where this was felt to be in its direct national interest, but the global attitudes of the new administration were shaped by its embrace of a neo-conservative vision of the 'New American Century'. A form of free market democracy that was modelled on, and also highly advantageous to, the United States was seen as the only legitimate global system – and the world's only superpower intended to pursue it with vigour.

This was an outlook that went well beyond practical politics to become a matter of intrinsic belief, even faith, and it followed that any alternatives were at the very least misjudged and at most malign.

The Political Opportunity of Trauma

The third factor in helping to shape the US government's reaction to the events of 9/11 was precisely the way the very trauma induced by the atrocities acted upon – both challenging and reinforcing – this much wider neo-conservative worldview.

The fact that the effects of the attacks were seen live on television across the United States was even more devastating; there was a grim symbolism in the destruction of the twin towers as the very symbols of modern US business success. This helped set the scene for a vigorous response that was to stretch across the world.

9/11 was clearly aimed at the heart of US commercial and political power and it was therefore critically important to regain control. The US had the military capabilities to launch such a response. In such circumstances, the neo-conservative vision required the 'war on terror' that was to follow.

From Kabul to Baghdad

The Afghanistan war was fought to terminate the Taliban regime and permanently damage al-Qaida, although it had the wider effect of enabling the United States to develop a military presence across Central Asia. The war itself was fought with sustained air power and small numbers of Special Forces. In addition, a key feature was the use of the Northern Alliance forces as ground troops against the Taliban. This process involved a substantial programme of arming these troops, even though the Northern Alliance had a human rights record little better than the Taliban.

Within three months, by the end of 2001, the Taliban had been evicted from power and the Bush administration was able to claim a major victory in its wider war. The military action in Afghanistan had by then cost about as many civilian lives as were killed in the 9/11 attacks.

The Afghan war was followed almost immediately by Bush's 2002 State of the Union address and other speeches that collectively presented two additional messages. One was that there was an 'axis of evil' encompassing Iraq, Iran and North Korea, together with lesser members such as Syria and Libya; the other was that states and peoples were 'either with us or against us' in the war on terror.

The early part of 2002 was perhaps the highpoint of the new vision, but the situation in Afghanistan was already problematic, with further fighting involving substantial loss of life. This stemmed partly from the nature of the war itself. While the Taliban regime had been destroyed, most of the militia had simply melted away rather than fight superior forces, the most extraordinary example being the overnight withdrawal from Kabul. Furthermore, while al-Qaida facilities in Afghanistan were certainly disrupted, it was becoming clear that al-Qaida was far from being a rigid hierarchical organisation centred on Afghanistan and had supporters, networks and affiliated groups in countries stretching across the world.

Furthermore, the United States was already losing support among many of its allies, especially in Europe, not least through its refusal to rein in the Israeli government in its wide-ranging destruction across the occupied territories. Furthermore, the broader problems of the diminishing of human rights in the war on terror, especially the detention without trial of hundreds of suspects, were being accompanied by the use by many governments of the 'war on terror' as a means of countering legitimate political opposition.

Perhaps the greatest loss of support for the Bush administration resulted from its evident determination to go to war with the regime in Iraq, and, as the crisis with Iraq developed towards the end of 2002 so opposition to the more general aspects of US security policy was also heightened, not just in Europe but across much of the world. This culminated in the largest-ever worldwide anti-war demonstrations in February 2003. Yet despite the unprecedented scale of this opposition, the war went ahead in the third week of March 2003 and the regime was terminated within three weeks.

The Iraq war of March–April 2003 initially appeared to be a further major success for the Bush administration. Almost all of the military action was undertaken by US forces, with some 200,000 troops involved; Britain's overstretched armed forces contributed in a much smaller way and there was minor assistance from other states like Australia and Poland. But this was essentially Washington's war and it became apparent almost immediately that the US forces were, for the most part, being seen as occupiers rather than liberators.

Within a few weeks, the post-war situation had begun to deteriorate, and this at a time when al-Qaida and its associates remained active, and where Afghanistan was again deeply unstable. On the political front, in a less deadly but still significant manner, the British government was becoming embroiled in political controversy over the motivations for war, given that Iraq's much-vaunted weapons of mass destruction were nowhere to be found.

The Current Status of al-Qaida

Although there has been extensive punitive action against al-Qaida and its associates and supporters, including the destruction of the Taliban regime, the killing or capture of some leaders, the indefinite detention of many others, and the closing down of some financial channels, the level of activity that the network has been able to maintain is remarkable.

The level of organisation that al-Qaida has been able to sustain is indicated not simply by the attacks it has carried out in these two years, but the ones it planned which were intercepted and aborted as a result of intelligence and security work by government authorities.

These planned attacks include:

- December 2001: the attempted bombing of a US passenger jet;
- December 2001: a major attack in Singapore, perhaps even on the scale of 9/11, using multiple truck bombs, aimed at embassies, Changi airport and the financial district;
- February 2002: bombings of United States embassies in Rome and Paris;
- May 2002: the development of radiological weapons for use in the US;
- June 2002: an attempt to shoot down a US warplane in Saudi Arabia;
- June 2002: a plan to attack western naval ships in the Straits of Gibraltar.

While these planned attacks have been prevented, many more have gone ahead. Together they show a capability that, despite two years of a 'war on terror', is greater than in the two years before the 9/11 attacks. They include:

- March 2002: an attack on worshippers at a church in the diplomatic compound in Islamabad (Pakistan), killing 5 people and injuring 46;
- May 2002: the killing of 11 French naval technicians and 3 Pakistanis in Karachi, injuring 23 people;
- April 2002: the bombing of a synagogue in Djerba (Tunisia), killing 14 German tourists and 7 local people and injuring 24;
- June 2002: a bomb attack on the US consulate in Karachi (Pakistan), killing 11 people and injuring at least 45;
- October 2002: the killing of a US special forces soldier in the Philippines, and frequent bomb attacks there;
- October 2002: a bomb attack on the *Limburg* tanker off Yemen;
- October 2002: the murder of a US diplomat in Amman (Jordan);
- October 2002 to January 2003: four attacks on US soldiers in Kuwait;
- October 2002: a devastating bomb attack on the Sari nightclub in Bali, killing 202 people including 88 Australians and 38 Indonesians and injuring 300 people;
- November 2002: an attack on a US oil company's helicopter taking off from Sana'a airport in Yemen;
- November 2002: an attempt to shoot down an Israeli tourist jet taking off from Mombasa airport in Kenya;
- November 2002: the bombing of the Paradise Hotel at Kikambala (Kenya), killing 11 people and injuring 50;
- May 2003: the multiple bombing of western targets in Casablanca (Morocco), killing 39 people and injuring 60;

- May 2003: the multiple bombing of western residential compounds in Riyadh (Saudi Arabia), killing 29 people and injuring 200;
- August 2003: the bombing of the Marriott Hotel in Djakarta (Indonesia), 13 dead and 149 injured.

It is evident from this list of incidents that it would be quite wrong to see al-Qaida as a single rigid and hierarchical organisation. While there is evidence of connections between a number of groups, including a degree of coordination, what is much more significant is the extent of trans-national support and the ability of national and regional groups to generate and undertake attacks.

Afghanistan and Iraq: No Victory in Sight

More than 18 months after the supposed end of the war in Afghanistan, there is endemic instability and violence affecting much of the country. Large sectors remain in the hands of warlords and their private armies, opium production has increased and US forces are repeatedly engaged in combat with Taliban and other militia.

Hamid Karzai's government struggles on, and is aided by relative peace in Kabul and some other centres, but the president has had to survive several assassination attempts. Kabul's stability is certainly aided by the small International Security Assistance Force (ISAF) but any attempt to expand this to other parts of the country has been blocked by the US.

A pattern of conflict has emerged in which US forces, often using considerable air power, are able to counter-attack guerrilla groups when caught in the open, but are unable to control substantial regions, especially after dark or when guerrillas operate in small units. Meanwhile it is proving far more difficult to develop an Afghan National Army to help ensure security; recruitment is difficult and there are frequent desertions. The army currently numbers little more than 5,000 troops compared with the 70,000 required.

In Iraq, the situation is deeply problematic, as recent articles in this series have detailed. About 140,000 US troops are tied down in an attempt to maintain security, yet scores of Americans and hundreds of Iraqis are dying and thousands are being injured in continuing violence. The US armed forces have already evacuated some 6,000 troops back to the United States, around a quarter of them as a result of combat injuries and accidents, and the rest due to physical or mental illness.

The war itself is now known to have killed over 6,000 civilians and injured around 20,000 in its three-week span, with Iraqi military casualties of course far higher. Even so, many of the elite elements of the Special Republican Guard and other security militia withdrew during the war without engaging American troops, and these may now be forming the core of a well-armed, well-trained and adaptable opposition.

Popular support for the frequent attacks on US forces is limited. The end of the old regime remains intensely popular in the Kurdish north-east of Iraq in particular. But the persistent failure of the US occupying authorities to deliver public services such as electricity supplies and water, combined with a stagnant economy made worse by the disbanding of the Iraqi army, have added to the unpopularity of the American occupying forces.

The predicament of the Bush administration is now considerable, although it continues to insist that Iraq is now a core part of the 'war on terror' and that the conflict simply must be won. This has resulted in President Bush's blunt warning to the American people on 7 September 2003, and the insistence that the wider international community must share the burden, albeit in a context where the United States must be allowed to maintain political, economic and military control.

In making Iraq part of the 'war on terror', a self-fulfilling prophecy is being enacted as militants do now begin to travel to Iraq from elsewhere across the porous borders, and could well link up with dissident elements within the country. Such a presence is probably still minimal but is virtually certain to build. There is now a widespread regional perception that the United States has taken over one of the historic centres of the Arab world and that its governing motives are control of the region's immensely rich oil reserves and support for the state of Israel. Whatever the reality, this is the perception, and the United States has essentially provided 140,000 targets in the heart of the Arab world. This is a 'gift' to paramilitary groups such as al-Qaida and its many associates.

An Audit of the 'War on Terror'

In the past two years, many members of al-Qaida and its associated movements have been killed or detained, the Taliban and Iraqi regimes have been terminated and some paramilitary attacks have been prevented.

Against this, there have been far more attacks on western interests across the world than in the equivalent period before 9/11, killing or injuring over 1,000 people. In fighting the wars in Afghanistan and Iraq, the US forces have killed at least 9,000 civilians and injured tens of thousands more. Afghanistan is deeply unstable with Taliban forces still present, and the security situation in Iraq is frankly dire. There are near-weekly warnings of terror attacks, which heighten the sense of alert symbolised by the London Underground simulation of a gas attack and the warnings of anti-aircraft missile attacks on British Airways planes in the last few days alone.

In this global context, it is very hard to accept any argument suggesting that a successful military campaign is being prosecuted, and there is every reason to question what is being done. For the moment, there is a singular unwillingness in Washington to face up to the reality of the American predicament. But given the state of affairs in

Iraq and Afghanistan and the beginnings of serious political questioning in the United States, such a dose of reality might be forced on the Bush administration much sooner than might be expected.

THE NEO-CONSERVATIVE LENS *17 September 2003*

More US soldiers are being killed in Iraq and many more Iraqis are dying in exchanges of fire. On both sides the injuries mount, so much so that few incidents are now even reported. One exception was the killing of the police chief in the town of Khaldiya, Colonel Khedeir Mekhalef Ali, this week. His appointment two months ago to run the new 600-strong police force had been supported by community leaders who were increasingly concerned at the common lawlessness becoming endemic in central Iraq; his assassination was probably carried out by criminal elements rather than guerrilla forces.

The significance of this lies in the existence of two simultaneous security problems for the United States: the threat to its troops from guerrilla elements and the much wider problem of lawlessness. The issue is also demonstrated by the thousands of people taken into custody in the last five months. The majority of them are detained under suspicion of a wide range of crimes, but there are currently 4,400 in detention suspected of being linked to guerrilla activity.

The Logistics of Overstretch

Perhaps the most pointed indication of the problems faced by US forces comes not from the figures for casualties but from much more mundane evidence related to the ostensibly simple matter of logistics (see Jonathan Weisman and Renae Merle, 'Wearing Out and Adding Up', *Washington Post*, 13 September 2003). As has been widely reported, the cost of the Iraq occupation and planned reconstruction has escalated alarmingly, and the small print of some of the requests from the military is really quite revealing.

Several examples of this are worth noting. First, the issue of body armour. A full suit costs $5,000 and the US Army wants 60,000 of them at a cost of $300,000,000 to enable it to equip every front-line soldier at risk in Iraq with such protection. The nature of the security problem means that this is now considered essential, as is the need to maintain armoured vehicles at far higher levels of activity than were ever anticipated.

Second, because of the persistent threat from snipers and roadside explosive devices, US troops are making huge use of the Bradley Fighting Vehicle, a tracked armoured vehicle that would normally drive about 1,200 kilometres a year and would have its tracks, costing about $22,000, replaced annually.

There are about 600 of these vehicles in Iraq and their use averages the equivalent of over 22,000 kilometres a year, with their tracks having to be replaced every two months. Replacement and support costs will run to about $230 million in 2003. Just to keep up with the demand, Goodyear is currently running three shifts a day, seven days a week, at the Red River Army Depot in Texas.

A third example of the US's logistical problems is the army's request for an additional 595 heavily-armoured Humvee jeeps at a cost of nearly $250,000 each. Fourth, there is particularly heavy wear and tear on the army's helicopters, especially in terms of the corrosive effect of sand on the rotor blades and engines. Army aviation support in Iraq has already used up $1.3 billion in spare parts in the last six months, more than three times the annual spending for the army's entire aviation force in an ordinary year.

The Elements of a Quagmire

The nature of the attacks, and the constant risk of casualties, mean that US forces are concentrating on highly mobile armoured patrols operating from heavily protected bases. As one army official remarked (quoted in the *Washington Post* piece cited earlier): 'Here's a blinding flash of the obvious, there is no front line out there.' Moreover, the continuing threat of attacks means that the army is scarcely involved in crime control, and with a hopelessly ill-equipped and under-resourced police force, crime remains rampant. Even the rise of warlords is now a distinct possibility.

In the face of this disorder and insecurity, the decision to disband the regular Iraqi army is now seen as a double disaster – not only did it put hundreds of thousands of unemployed ex-soldiers back into the community, damaging the economy, but it meant that at least some of them could be ready recruits for the anti-occupation insurgency now under way.

The US occupation authorities have belatedly started to recruit and train a new, smaller army but progress is extraordinarily slow. The plan is for an army of 40,000 to be available, but this will not be fully formed until at least a year from now. Even the initial components, four battalions of around 3,000 troops, will not be ready until early 2004 (Theola Labbé, 'Iraq's New Military Taking Shape', *Washington Post*, 16 September 2003).

The overall predicament faced by the army goes a long way to explain why some of the most senior officers in the US military have been so vigorous in their insistence that their government goes back to seek support at the United Nations. Their hope is that some kind of Security Council resolution will be agreed that will entice other states to contribute significant military forces. Such action is a measure of the deep concern within the US military, a concern that seems not to be shared by the Pentagon's leadership, Donald Rumsfeld and Paul Wolfowitz.

What has become really significant in Washington in recent weeks has been the divergence between a White House, under pressure from the military, seeking a way out of the Iraq morass through an international sharing of the burden, and the persistent views of the neo-conservative security community. This group sees the problems in Iraq in a markedly different light, and is deeply suspicious of any sharing of control of Iraq, especially with the UN.

Current neo-conservative thinking may best be summarised as 'more of the same', and is strangely reminiscent of the early days of the Vietnam war, when the answer to increasing insurgency by Vietnamese nationalist-communist forces was to call for rapid increases in US troop levels, based on the confidence that enough forces could ensure that the war could be fought and won on American terms.

Security versus Ideology

The current neo-conservative agenda requires that the US administration takes three steps. The first is a substantial increase in spending in Iraq, certainly many tens of billions of dollars to guarantee power supplies, public services and a developing economy. It is recognised that this would be a political 'gift' to the Democrats, but the neo-conservative view is that large sums of money must be spent now to help prevent a further security deterioration over the next six to nine months that could help cost George Bush re-election in late 2004.

The second item on the neo-con agenda is for a substantial increase in US personnel on the ground in Iraq, especially from the State Department. The latter is the target of particular anger which sees its public officials as reluctant to volunteer for service in Iraq; an analogy is even drawn with the early years of the Cold War when the whole culture of government service was redirected towards the need to triumph in the contest with the Soviet Union. The neo-conservatives believe that the 'war on terror' is the Cold War's equivalent and successor, that Iraq is central to this war and that the US government and its officials must evince far higher levels of patriotism.

The third neo-con requirement is for a substantial increase in US forces on the ground in Iraq, as many as two full divisions. With support troops, this might entail an additional 50–60,000 troops in Iraq or the immediate region – far too many for the US Army to sustain for any length of time, given its commitments in Afghanistan and East Asia.

In response, the neo-conservative argument is straightforward: America must expand its military force now, primarily by increasing the size of the army. More use of reservists and National Guard units may help in the short term, but there is no alternative to recruiting far more regular soldiers. The predicament was summed up admirably in a recent editorial of the Washington-based *Weekly Standard* (1 September 2003):

> The simple fact is, right now, there are too few good guys chasing the bad guys – hence the continuing sabotage. There are too few forces to patrol the Syrian and Iranian borders to prevent the infiltration of international terrorists trying to open a new front against the United States in Iraq. There are too few forces to protect vital infrastructure and public buildings. And contrary to what some say, more troops don't mean more casualties. More troops mean fewer casualties – both American and Iraqi.

What lies behind neo-conservative thinking is the belief that it is absolutely essential for the United States to maintain control of Iraq. A significant input of international elements to Iraq would challenge this objective, and carries the risk of unacceptable UN involvement. In this perspective, it is clear that neo-conservative circles recognise the extent of the American predicament in Iraq – and respond by recommending 'more of the same'. That such a response is highly likely to make matters worse, not better, is simply not acknowledged.

IRAQI REALITIES *25 September 2003*

Discussions with foreign leaders about the future of Iraq held this week in Washington and at the United Nations failed to deliver an outcome in line with the requirements of the US administration. As this week's speeches at the UN General Assembly showed, the differences between the parties are considerable, and the end result will most likely be one that has very little effect on what is happening on the ground in Iraq.

President Bush's speech this week made few concessions, but what was significant was the combination of the reception given to his speech by the assembled diplomats and politicians, and the blunt warning from Kofi Annan earlier in the day. It is probably unprecedented for a speech from a US President to the General Assembly to be received with so little enthusiasm, and it is significant that Annan felt able to make a notable if implied criticism of unilateral actions such as that against Iraq last March.

Although Bush's position seems robust and unyielding, the reality is that the position of his administration is being determined by a remarkable array of unexpected and unwelcome factors in striking contrast with what had been anticipated as the likely situation once the Saddam Hussein regime had been terminated. This contrast between the theory and the reality is worth recalling in trying to make sense of the extent of the US predicament and the concerns that it is raising in Washington.

The Theory

When the war was fought and the regime destroyed within the space of just three weeks, there was a firm expectation in Washington that effective control of Iraq would be forthcoming. This would lead in due course to an acceptable client regime in charge of an oil-rich state opened up for international business, no doubt to the particular advantage of US companies.

In the short term Iraq would be managed from the Pentagon, which would also be in a position to develop permanent military bases in the country while rapidly scaling down the number of combat troops. According to the *New York Times*, four bases would be established, focused on airbases or airports originally developed by the Saddam Hussein regime.

One would be close to Baghdad, almost certainly at the international airport, but the other three would be carefully chosen for wider strategic reasons. The Talill airbase near Nasiriyah conveniently near to the huge oilfields of south-east Iraq, would become a second, and another would be centred on the airfield at Bashur in northern Iraq, close to the Kirkuk/Mosul oilfields. The final base was expected to be at the H1 airfield, a sprawling complex close to the Syrian border, although there might also be a small naval facility at Umm Qasr on the Gulf coast. Apart from Baghdad, the bases would not be large in terms of permanent military personnel, but each would have a continuing military presence together with facilities for rapid reinforcement.

Their location would serve three long-term purposes – ensuring the security of the two main clusters of oilfields in Iraq, maintaining a base close to Syria, one of the lesser members of the 'axis of evil', and putting real pressure on Iran, a leading member of that axis.

The situation for Iran would be particularly satisfactory from Washington's point of view. Military bases in Central Asian republics such as Uzbekistan would increase influence over the eastern part of the Caspian basin oil-bearing region, helping to diminish any Iranian involvement. Furthermore, permanent military bases in Afghanistan, at both Bagram and Kandahar, would mean that Iran had a US presence in Afghanistan to the east as well as in Iraq to the west, and would also have to contend with the presence of the US Fifth Fleet in the Persian Gulf and the Indian Ocean.

The political result of all of this would be the long-term control of Iraq together with the ability to put maximum pressure on Iran. More generally, success in Iraq would be a powerful warning to states such as North Korea, Syria and Libya that any attempt either to develop weapons of mass destruction or be seen to foster terrorism would meet a response from a determined, effective and overwhelmingly powerful United States.

In Iraq itself, the intention had been to reduce US forces to no more than 60–70,000 troops. Moreover, a substantial proportion of those would be engineering, logistics and support troops, largely concerned with developing the permanent presence. There would be little need for 'occupation' troops because there would be little opposition to the US presence. The significance of this was that the US Army, in particular, would be able to withdraw at least two divisions, a really valuable outcome given the overstretch that the army was beginning to experience.

The Reality

Contrast this with the actual position, and the wider components of the American predicament. Six months after the war, the United States has close to 140,000 troops in Iraq, with a large proportion of them engaged in a violent and costly urban guerrilla war that is causing substantial casualties, is leading to escalating military costs of occupation and shows no sign of diminishing.

Further deaths and injuries in the past week and the second attack on the UN compound have been accompanied by larger numbers of deaths and injuries to Iraqis, adding to the endemic criminality affecting much of central Iraq. Experienced journalists in Iraq are reporting that the security situation within the country is continuing to deteriorate, and this is before there is any real effect from paramilitary groups from elsewhere in the region establishing themselves there.

In the United States, opposition politicians are now confident enough to make comparisons between the $87 billion that President Bush is seeking for Iraq with lack of domestic spending on issues such as health care, urban security and even power supplies. Opinion polls are registering a significant drop in support for Bush, with much of it due to the ongoing war and its costs.

In Iraq itself, members of Iraq's appointed Governing Council are starting to demonstrate independence, including a planned visit to the US Congress to argue for a more speedy political transformation. This coincides with French insistence on similar moves, with little likelihood of substantial international help for the United States in the absence of major concessions from Washington.

The French position may stem partly from French perceptions of their historic role in the Middle East and the Arab World as well as the long-term suspicion of the United States, but there is a profoundly cynical aspect to this, given that France, together with Russia, was the key military supplier to the Saddam Hussein regime prior to 1991 when it committed its greatest atrocities.

Where Next?

Some aspects of the original US plan are still being carried out. Bases are being established in Iraq and Afghanistan, and the Iraqi economy is going to be opened up to privatisation with particular inducements for favoured international businesses. But this cannot disguise the much more general problems now being faced.

Given that the French do want to gain more influence in the region, there may well be a softening of the differences in the next few days and weeks, but there are three issues that add to the weakness of the US position. One is that almost all of those countries capable of committing either significant military forces or substantial aid to Iraq are deeply reluctant to do so. It will be politically undesirable to put their young soldiers at risk in a burgeoning guerrilla war, and few countries intend to bail out the US of its financial commitments.

The second issue is that the bitterness towards the United States that is felt by United Nations professionals remains, stemming partly from the loss of UN personnel in Baghdad but with this serving to sharpen memories of the near-contempt with which the UN was treated by the Bush administration in the run-up to the war.

Finally, the bottom line remains, as ever, that the United States simply must maintain control of Iraq, and to hand over the transition to independence to a multinational body such as the UN will be unacceptable to the administration. The consequence of all of this is that whatever happens in terms of UN resolutions, and whatever appears to be a compromise, the reality will be that the United States remains very much on its own, and will have little option but to continue fighting a dangerous and messy war.

Moreover, this is a war in which external paramilitary forces have scarcely had any effect. If, as is probable, that is still to come, and may develop over the next six to twelve months, then we should not be too surprised if, apparently against the odds, there is a real change in US policy in the early months of next year. Such a change might well result in many US troops being brought home during next year's election campaign, but it would also signal a fundamental shift in US Middle East policy that would contrast markedly with those confident expectations of just a few months ago.

5
The Israel Factor

INTRODUCTION

Between November 2003 and April 2004 the insurgency in Iraq took firm root, and any pretensions that it was a short-term phenomenon finally disappeared in the wake of considerable violence in the city of Fallujah, west of Baghdad, in April. More generally, although insurgents became more systematic in attacking Iraqi police and security forces and government officials, they also continued their actions against US forces. The detention of Saddam Hussein in December 2003 had no substantive impact on the insurgency.

A frequent response from the US military was to use its overwhelming advantage in firepower to counter the actions of the insurgents. The immediate problem was that since many of the insurgents were operating in urban environments and were often mixed in with broadly sympathetic communities, such responses regularly caused substantial civilian casualties.

In their efforts to contain the insurgency, US forces turned increasingly to the experience of the Israeli Defence Forces (IDF) in the Palestinian occupied territories, and it became clear during this period that two forms of cooperation were developing. One was the application of Israeli tactics to counter-insurgency operations in Iraq, with regular exchanges of personnel between the IDF and the US Army's Training and Doctrine Command (TRADOC). The other was the increasing use of weapons and observation equipment brought from Israeli manufacturers for use in Iraq.

While such developments made sense for the US military, an inevitable effect was for the US operation in Iraq to be seen across the region as essentially a joint US/Israeli programme, further adding to anti-American sentiments.

A more general problem for the United States and its coalition partners was the manner in which the activities of al-Qaida and its loose associates was being maintained at a high pitch in a number of countries. As well as specific instances in Uzbekistan, Southern Thailand and the Philippines, the multiple train bombings in Madrid and the seizure of explosives precursors in London both pointed to a 'war on terror' that was coming directly to Western Europe.

THE BA'ATH RESTORATION PROJECT

19 November 2003

Paul Bremer's hurried return to Washington last week and the resulting changes in United States policy in Iraq make it apparent that the full impact of the developing insurgency is now being registered at the political heart of the Bush administration. This represents a belated acceptance of what some of the military commanders in the region, and the military (as opposed to the civilian) leadership in the Pentagon have been briefing for some time; indeed, the latter were among the strongest lobbyists for a new UN resolution two months ago, when it was already recognised that Iraq was simply not going according to plan.

A Spiral of Violence

Within Iraq itself, the insurgency seems still to be gathering pace. There are increasing numbers of attacks on US patrols, a rising casualty list, the recent destruction of five helicopters, and continuing sabotage. Furthermore, the attack on the Italian compound in Nasiriya has had the intended effect of undermining the commitment of foreign governments, a point demonstrated by immediate 'adjustments' in policy by the re-elected Japanese government in relation to possible peacekeeping commitments.

It now seems that the escalating insurgency in Iraq has reinforced domestic political concerns to make it highly unlikely that Japan will contribute significant numbers of troops to Iraq. This outcome is a setback for Japanese foreign policy as well as a substantial political reversal for the country's prime minister, Junichiro Koizumi. Japan has sought to increase its involvement in the Gulf – partly because of its dependence on the region's oil supplies, and partly as an extension of its competition with China whose own increasing involvement in the area included technical support for the Saddam Hussein regime.

Although not widely reported, another trend within Iraq has been the increase in attacks on presumed collaborators. In recent weeks this has included the murder of judges, a newspaper editor in Mosul, an electricity supply executive and one of Baghdad's deputy mayors. This active intimidation has extended to attacks on other people cooperating with the US, especially in the north of the country.

In the past week, an attempt was made to assassinate the manager in charge of distributing fuel products throughout northern Iraq. He escaped, but his son alongside was killed. On 10 November, an interpreter called Khalid Victor Paul and his teenage son were killed as they drove to the latter's school. Both these murders were in the vicinity of Mosul and seem part of a determined effort by insurgents to bring the disorder and violence of the Baghdad region to the north of Iraq.

The developing problems within Iraq are perhaps most graphically indicated by recent casualty figures from the US Army surgeon-general's office. From the start of the war on 19–20 March to the end of October, there were 397 US service members killed and 1,967 injured in combat. In addition, 6,861 troops were medically evacuated out of Iraq over the same period due to non-combat injuries or mental or physical illness. Of these latter evacuees, 2,464 were for non-combat injuries; 504 of the remaining 4,397 were classified as psychiatric.

All these injuries and illnesses were sufficiently serious for the people concerned to be evacuated from Iraq, with the great majority going to the Landstuhl military hospital in Germany and then on to the Walter Reed Army Hospital in Washington and other US centres. A particular concern is raised by a report that 378 troops have been evacuated for neurological conditions, raising fears among veteran groups that a repeat of 'Gulf war syndrome' may be happening.

The American Rethink

The United States' response to the deteriorating security situation in Iraq has three elements. The first is fairly minor, if still significant – namely, the decision to relocate a substantial part of the headquarters of US Central Command (CENTCOM) from its Florida base to Qatar.

CENTCOM is a unified military command developed in the 1980s that covers an arc of 25 countries across South-West Asia, the Middle East and north-east Africa. Despite the fact that major command locations are in the Gulf, its headquarters have always been at McDill Air Force Base near Tampa. In the coming weeks, several hundred staff will move from Florida to Qatar; it is expected that the head of CENTCOM, General John P. Abizaid, will spend much of his time there.

The second development is a series of assaults by US forces against suspected insurgent safe houses, command centres and other facilities. This goes as far as the use of air strikes and tactical ballistic missiles; some of the weapons used are anti-personnel cluster munitions. The intent behind this demonstration of US firepower is to remind the Iraqi attackers of the overwhelming military force available to the occupiers.

An interesting aspect of the current higher level of military activity is that senior US commanders are now confirming the view recently expressed that almost all the insurgency is coming from within Iraq, with only minimal involvement from foreign paramilitaries. According to Major-General Charles H. Swannack Jr., commander of the 82nd Airborne Division, 90 per cent of the insurgents captured or killed by US forces are Ba'ath loyalists or people described as Iraqi religious militants.

One tactic the Americans are pursuing is to destroy the homes of suspected guerrillas. This follows a style of warfare long used by the Israelis in the occupied Palestinian territories. There, it has proved largely futile, serving instead to increase resentment and further militancy. Indeed, some observers suggest that such recent initiatives are motivated more by a concern to 'show the flag' in the domestic US media than to have any real impact on the insurgents.

Moreover, the deployment of intense force repeats a pattern developed during the summer when the Iraqi insurgency first began to gather pace. At that time, the military response was a combination of heavy firepower and large-scale detentions. Contrary to expectations, the insurgency actually increased and the US tactics were in turn replaced by a softer approach.

The third element in the US response is to develop plans for a more rapid transfer of political and security responsibilities to Iraqis, on the assumption that the resulting regime in Baghdad will both be acceptable to the United States and able to exert control across the country. Moreover, it is now apparent that the Bush administration is preparing to return to the UN Security Council to secure an endorsement for this process, in the hope of encouraging other states to help in reconstruction and peace-enforcement.

These three elements of the US response carry the implication that the Bush administration is considering a military withdrawal from Iraq. Pentagon officials are, however, cautious on this issue – and are, in any case, already in the process of developing a number of permanent US military bases in Iraq. Whatever else happens, the United States intends to maintain huge influence in Iraq, based on the promotion of a client regime backed by a lasting military presence, with the core strategic objective of ensuring long-term access to the country's huge oil reserves.

A Planned Insurgency?

The inevitable question raised by this consideration of recent US policy in Iraq, in the context of the recent escalation of the insurgency, is whether the policy is in any way realistic. More critically, is the United States losing control, despite the pace of economic reconstruction, and is this as a result of a pre-planned tactic by the old regime to respond to US intervention with a guerrilla war?

If there are no clear answers to this latter question at present, there are two uncomfortable indicators – from past and present – suggesting that US and coalition forces are facing a challenge far bigger than they had anticipated.

The first indicator is the clear evidence existing even before the war that the regime was planning to use urban guerrilla warfare in the event of its overthrow (as reported, for example, by one of the best-informed correspondents, Rajiv Chandrasekaran; see 'Iraqis Would Use Urban Warfare to Trap US troops', *Washington Post*, 28 September 2002). He quoted a member of Saddam Hussein's cabinet, Mohammad Mehdi Saleh: 'If they want to change the political system in Iraq, they have to come to Baghdad. We will be waiting for them there.'

Chandrasekaran also reported a prescient comment from a western diplomat in Baghdad on potential Iraqi tactics: 'They believe they have a tactical advantage in the cities because they can mix with the civilian population. If soldiers start sniping from apartments filled with people, what can the Americans do? They can't very well blow them up.' What is now happening is that the Americans are emptying the buildings and then blowing them up, a tactic that does little to control the insurgents and much to increase their own unpopularity.

The second indicator is the current military evidence of preparations to oppose occupation. The nature of the insurgency and the types of military operations being conducted indicate that large numbers of weapons caches were dispersed prior to the US invasion. This must have entailed an extensive organisation, one implying that the regime was surer of the loyalty of its supporters than many western media outlets led their readers to believe.

In this light, the early attacks on coalition troops and their convoys as they moved into Iraq and towards Baghdad in March 2003 seem evidence of the nucleus of a guerrilla capability. It also looks more likely that the opening of the prison gates in October 2002 in a general amnesty was a deliberate attempt to increase lawlessness and anarchy after the United States and its coalition partners entered the country.

The Prospect of Regime Rise

These indicators of an insurgency planned even before the three-week war find echoes in two further of its aspects. In the second week of the war, US forces were able to use extraordinary firepower against the general Republican Guard divisions in their defensive positions south of Baghdad. Notwithstanding their experience of US firepower in the 1991 war, the Iraqi military leaders do not appear to have been ready for these attacks and the Guard divisions suffered massive casualties.

The result of almost a week of intensive attacks was that Baghdad was more open to US occupation than had been anticipated by the regime. Thus, Republican Guard divisions were not able to withdraw towards the city and any original plan to suck US forces into urban guerrilla warfare was forestalled.

At the same time – and this may be the key point of all – what the regime was able to do was ensure that the really elite forces such as the Special Republican Guard, various commando groups and the troops attached to the Ba'ath security services were able to withdraw in time, to disperse and then prepare for a long-term campaign. It then took the best part of three months to develop a guerrilla campaign, and six months for it to have a serious and sustained impact on the US forces.

If this explanation is accurate, then the initial victory for the US in the three-week war of March–April 2003 – right up to the toppling of the statue of Saddam Hussein on 9 April – was, to a significant extent, illusory. The old regime may have had its defensive plans disrupted, but it was not destroyed.

The implication is clear, and chilling: the insurgency may still be in its relatively early stages, and the strategy that guides it may even include a progressive US handover to the security forces of a client regime, which would be followed by a civil war and the return of Ba'athist forces to power. Such a prognosis seems quite extraordinary even to contemplate, but it is worth saying that there were a few analysts around before and during the initial three-week war itself who were saying that a long-term US victory was not necessarily assured.

Eight months on, what can be assumed in the present fraught security circumstances is that the Iraqi insurgents will see the US policy of overwhelming force, coupled with talk of a rapid handover to Iraqi political forces, as a sign that they are beginning to make progress towards the achievement of their own strategic objective. The hugely worrying prospect of a Ba'athist resurgence has to be taken seriously. That is a measure of the predicament now faced by the United States in Iraq.

AFTER SADDAM, NO RESPITE *19 December 2003*

The detention of Saddam Hussein raises many questions, one of the most important being whether it means the beginning of the end of the insurgency. Immediate indications are that it may not, and this doesn't just stem from the high levels of violence since his capture. In the past few days there have been a number of car bombs directed against Iraqi police forces and numerous violent demonstrations against US troops. Seventeen Iraqis were killed in incidents on 16 December and US troops continued to suffer casualties, including one killed in central Baghdad, the 199th to die since President Bush declared the war was over on 1 May.

Perhaps more ominous were two other incidents this week. One was the murder on Wednesday of a senior figure in the Supreme Council for Islamic Revolution in Iraq (SCIRI), Muhannad al-Hakim. Mr al-Hakim was the Head of Security in the Education Ministry and cousin of Abdel-Aziz al-Hakim who is the current President of the Iraqi Governing Council. This was followed two days later by a bomb attack on a building in the al-Jihad district of Baghdad used by local militia linked to SCIRI, killing the aunt of one of the security guards and injuring five people.

The US reaction to the continuing violence has been both immediate and vigorous, including a substantial show of force in Saddam Hussein's home city of Tikrit involving tanks and other armoured vehicles patrolling the city centre, with the US-appointed regional governor announcing that 'Any demonstration against the government or the coalition forces will be fired upon.' In the expectation of increasing violence, 3,500 troops of the 82nd Airborne Division will be kept in Iraq for two months beyond their original return home in February and an additional 2,000 troops will be sent to the country.

Against this there has been a widespread if rather muted welcome for Saddam Hussein's detention, as it removed a deep-seated fear among many Iraqis of the return of the regime. The manner of his capture, and the subsequent televising of his dishevelled states and medical examination was of considerable domestic benefit to President Bush, and gave the lie to any substantial political influence that Saddam Hussein may still have had.

This was not dissimilar to the killing of his two sons, in hiding in Mosul and protected just by a couple of bodyguards. At that time, there was an expectation that the shooting of Uday and Qusay Hussein would have a substantial effect on the insurgency but it did not. The hopes are greater that Saddam Hussein's capture and probable trial will have a great impact, but this is best analysed in the context of much longer-term trends.

The Next Six Months

What has become clear since the end of the first phase of the war is that the termination of the regime was not primarily about weapons of mass destruction, nor was it about destroying a particular brutal and repressive abuser of human rights, it was much more about the long-term control of a key state in the world's richest oil-bearing region.

Within a month of the end of the war, the *New York Times* was reporting the establishment of four permanent military bases in Iraq and Paul Bremer confirmed recently that the US intended to have an agreement with any future Iraqi government over the long-term basing of US troops. To put it more bluntly, the US anticipated a 'friendly' government in Iraq, even if this would be seen in the region as a puppet regime.

On such a basis, it would have been reasonable to conclude last April that the termination of the old regime might have resulted in a period of relative calm lasting months or even 1–2 years, but the longer-term establishment of a US presence in the country would eventually lead to an insurgency developing partly from within Iraq and partly through the entry of paramilitaries from abroad. Such an insurgency would have developed as it became clear that this major Arab state was effectively under the dominance of the United States.

What was frankly surprising was the speed and intensity of the insurgency that developed in the immediate post-regime period. Recent figures indicate that, in addition to over 200 combat deaths, some 10,000 US troops and over 1,000 British troops have been airlifted home with combat or accidental injuries or mental or physical illness. Iraqi civilian deaths have been much higher, with at least 1,500 violent deaths in Baghdad alone.

The implications of the wider picture are straightforward. Iraq will be seen as a client state for the foreseeable future, primarily because it gives the United States secure access to massive 'new' oil reserves. These are nearly five times larger than its domestic reserves at a time when it is increasingly having to import oil to meet domestic demand. In seeking to do this it is facing an insurgency that is substantially greater than it expected and has developed very much earlier than even independent analysts had anticipated.

If, then, the insurgency decreases in the aftermath of Saddam Hussein's capture, it would be wise to assume that this will be little more than a temporary decline, to be replaced by a more deep-seated and longer-term form of violent opposition developing over the next 1–5 years. If, on the other hand, the insurgency does not ebb away over the winter, then US forces face a very difficult situation requiring sustained military commitments that would be hugely greater than were anticipated earlier this year.

In either event, the next six months will be the key period. The early indications on the ground, both in terms of this week's violence and the impending reinforcement of US troops, are that the insurgency is not at an end. Perhaps most significant of all has been the caution evident in the statements of both

George Bush and Tony Blair. That, in its own way, is more indicative than anything happening in Iraq itself.

The Israeli Factor

If this analysis is correct, then US forces will be preparing for a sustained period of urban guerrilla conflict, and evidence for this comes from a remarkable meeting that took place in Israel earlier this month. From 1 to 5 December, the head of the Israeli Ground Forces Command, Major-General Yiftah Ron-Tal, hosted a series of meetings and visits from a senior US team headed by General Kevin Byrnes, Commander of the US Army's Training and Doctrine Command (TRADOC). (*Defense News*, 15 December 2003.)

Among those accompanying General Byrnes were Major-General Robert Mixon, deputy commander of TRADOC's Futures Center and Brigadier-General Benjamin Freakly, commander of the US Army's Infantry School at Fort Benning, Georgia. US and Israeli sources have been deeply reluctant to comment on the meeting but, according to the usually well-informed *Defense News*,

> the goals were twofold: to strengthen cooperation among US and Israeli ground forces in future warfighting and military modernization planning, and to evaluate ways in which the US military can benefit from operational lessons Israel has accrued during the past 38 months in its ongoing urban, low-intensity conflict with Palestinian militants.

Defense News went on to quote a US military source:

> Israel has much to offer in the technological realm, while operationally, there are obvious parallels between Israel's experiences over the past three years in the West Bank and Gaza and our own post-offensive operations in Iraq. We'd be remiss if we didn't make a supreme effort to seek out commonalities and see how we might be able to incorporate some of that Israeli knowledge into our plans.

From a strictly military point of view, such cooperation is to be expected, but what is surprising is the apparent lack of any serious political judgement. There is a view across much of the Arab world that Israeli suppression of Palestinian aspirations is essentially a US–Israeli process, with the F-16 strike aircraft and Apache helicopters being seen as US warplanes in Israeli markings. Now we have the obverse of this, Israelis telling the Americans how to suppress the Iraqi insurgency.

As so often, that may be partly a matter of perception but it is deep-rooted and pervasive. The longer the insurgency persists in Iraq, and the longer there is no resolution of the Israel/Palestine confrontation, the more there is a risk of the occupation of Iraq being seen as a US/Israel operation. That alone is going to further increase the enmity towards the United States both inside Iraq and among the many supporters of al-Qaida and its affiliates.

RETHINKING WAR *22 January 2004*

On Sunday 18 January, barely a day before Paul Bremer was due to meet Kofi Annan to seek greater United Nations involvement in the transition to Iraqi self-rule, a pick-up truck carrying half a ton of explosives and artillery shells exploded at the central entrance to the US headquarters in Baghdad. The bomb killed more than 20 Iraqis and overseas contractors, and injured over 60.

The timing was precise, in two senses: it was a direct reminder to the UN Secretary-General that the United States cannot control security within Iraq, and it emphasised the depth of an insurgency that has now claimed 500 US lives and six times that number of serious injuries, and has killed and injured far more Iraqis.

One result of the insurgency in Iraq, especially when coupled with long-term military involvement in Afghanistan, is that US forces are facing serious 'overstretch'. As analysed in last week's column in this series, the fact that the great majority of active service divisions in the US Army are now committed to international deployments means that there are few reserves left for other crises. The result is that major questions are arising over the future direction of US military strategy.

Taming the Jungle

The problem of overstretch has provoked military and political responses in the United States. The tour of duty of army reservists has been extended, to the extent that such part-time soldiers can be required to spend more than a year on duty in Iraq, and a new 'stop-loss' order that prevents regular troops resigning from active duty while they are deployed overseas.

The direct political impact in Washington includes the effort by the Pentagon to secure a very modest increase of 2,400 in troop levels in the 2004 Defense Authorisation Act. Some in Congress want a much greater expansion. The Tauscher Bill, currently under consideration in the House of Representatives, would add 40,000 to the army, 28,700 to the air force and 15,000 to the marines (*Defense News*, 12 January 2004). This overall increase of 83,700 can be compared with the entire strength of the British Army, namely 114,000.

Behind these measures lies a deep division within US defence circles, one that has been greatly exacerbated by the military's experience in Afghanistan and Iraq. On one side are the civilian defence ideologues, led by Donald Rumsfeld, who envisage a military future of relatively small forces armed with very advanced, 'do-anything' weapons that can operate from a distance and coerce enemies into almost any course of action.

On the other side are many in the military itself, along with some independent analysts, who argue that Afghanistan and Iraq are already showing that foreign and security policy cannot be conducted by remote control. In the real world of 'asymmetric warfare' and paramilitary opponents, the attempt to mould the world into a 'New American Century' by bombing from afar will more likely produce a response that drags US forces into 'on the ground' involvements that are messy, costly and of indeterminate duration.

This entire controversy relates to some much longer-term trends that have shaped US forces since the end of the Cold War. In the early 1990s, Bill Clinton's first CIA director, James Woolsey, characterised the post-cold war world by saying that the United States had slain the dragon but now lived in a jungle full of poisonous snakes. George W. Bush expressed a similar thought in inimitable fashion in a campaign speech four years ago:

> it was a dangerous world and we knew exactly who the 'they' were. It was us versus them and we knew exactly who them was. Today we're not so sure who the 'they' are but we know they're there.

Taming the jungle and fighting 'them' involved a dual approach: substantial cuts in the massive US forces of the Cold War era, coupled with a greater emphasis on rapid deployment, long-range strike, special forces and counter-insurgency support. Behind it lay a belief that technological superiority can provide an edge against just about any enemy. If, the logic went, you are capable of targeting any building in an entire country with highly accurate cruise missiles, and if the military of that country have no way of destroying such missiles – surely that kind of capability will ensure almost total political control?

There was also an economic aspect to a strategy built around a reliance on such military strikes. In its attacks on Serbia and in the disputed territory of Kosovo from March to June 1999, NATO strike aircraft found it very difficult to identify the well-protected and dispersed Serbian military forces, so the campaign was gradually refocused against the infra-structure of the Serbian economy. By attacking power plants, factories, refineries, transmission lines, roads, railways, bridges and tunnels, the NATO forces inflicted some $60 billion of damage on the Serbian economy (*Economist Intelligence Unit*, 21 August 1999). This reduced an already weakened economy to even further dilapidation and helped create the circumstances which led to the overthrow of Slobodan Milosevic the following year.

Lessons in Flexibility

The logic of this post-Cold War thinking, as practised today by those of Donald Rumsfeld's persuasion, is that the realities on the ground are proving to be very resistant. US forces are thoroughly mired in costly and difficult counter-guerrilla warfare in Afghanistan and Iraq, with no end in sight in either country. Indeed, even the long-term aim of maintaining a client state in Iraq is now beginning to be questioned, to the extent that the US appears more ready to permit, with UN assistance, the early emergence of a limited democracy.

Again, the military and political dimensions are linked. The current problems faced by the US in these two theatres are leading to a substantial rethink of military strategy itself. What happened in the 1990s was little more than a series of revisions of pre-existing Cold War doctrine. What is now beginning to be undertaken is a complete review of doctrine, one that starts from scratch and pays serious attention to the many flaws in US military strategy revealed by current conflicts (*Defense News*, 22 December 2003).

This review is being conducted under the leadership of US Joint Forces Command; a series of Joint Operating Concept papers has been developed to try and make sense of the unpredictable and volatile environment. One paper (leaked to *Defense News*) employed classic 'military-speak' to convey the problem:

> Enemies are not 'doctrinally "template-able"', with fixed alliances and obvious political goals.

The broad outlines of the result of the review can be anticipated. US forces must become hugely more adaptable, and the different branches of the armed forces will have to act in much closer cooperation with the intelligence agencies. Furthermore, much greater authority has to be delegated to local commanders, since the sheer unpredictability of paramilitary and guerrilla forces means that standard operating procedures simply do not apply.

The problem for the US military is that in theory such developments may be very seductive, indeed obvious – but they still do not relate to the real world. The military's more sophisticated analysts are beginning to recognise that control from a long distance using overwhelming force does not work if your opponents do not operate according to the same strategies. Even a much more flexible application of military doctrine will not work if the doctrine is, at root, faulty.

This is because the opposing forces can adapt their own strategies to your changing posture, learning on the ground in swift response to the changes you introduce. This has happened repeatedly in Iraq in recent months. For example, the insurgents have directed much of their recent efforts not to attacking heavily-armed and adaptable American military patrols, but to Iraqis considered to be collaborating, as well as key aspects of the economy.

They have been particularly astute in their targeting of energy supplies. A pipeline may be blown up but it will then be left completely alone for the days or weeks that it takes to repair the damage. As soon as it is operating again, another section of the same pipeline is destroyed. The cumulative effect is not to bring Iraq to its economic knees but to make life difficult for most ordinary Iraqis, in the expectation that blame will reside with the Americans and their Coalition Provisional Authority.

Insurgents have blown up electricity pylons, but disruption has been limited and repairs can be undertaken quite quickly. Those same insurgents almost certainly have the capacity to wreck the country's power system, either by attacking one or two of the few power stations currently operating or, more likely, by attacking the more vulnerable switching stations. They have not done so on any scale, most likely because they are waiting for the combination of the hot summer weather and the installation of an Iraqi administration in July, when the impact would be much greater.

A Failure of Imagination

What is true in Iraq may prove true on a wider scale. Thus, George W. Bush's 'war on terror' is likely to entail changes in the US military posture, within the context of rapidly increasing defence budgets. But the paramilitary response may be even less 'military' than in the past. Instead, it could employ a whole range of asymmetric actions against which even the most flexible military forces are inappropriate.

The problem for the Bush administration is that neither in Iraq nor in its wider war is it able to grasp the need to go beyond the immediate conflicts and to address the broader issues – most importantly why and how al-Qaida and its associates are able to gather and maintain such widespread support. The Cold War was sustained, in part, by an implicit belief that the issues at stake could best be understood and managed by military confrontation. It lasted over 40 years. It is not impossible that Bush's 'war on terror' will have a similar timescale.

A WEEK OF VIOLENCE *1 April 2004*

The year since the first phase of the Iraq war ended, and the occupation by United States-led forces began, has seen a recurrent pattern of official optimism about the security situation in Iraq being temporarily punctured, but never quite deflated, by succeeding insurgent attacks. On 1 July 2003, two months after George W. Bush had declared final victory in Iraq, for example, the United States' chief administrator in the country, Paul Bremer, expressed a conviction that: 'Those few remaining individuals who have refused to fit into the new Iraq are becoming more and more desperate. They are alienating the rest of the population.'

Soon afterwards, the killing in Mosul of Saddam Hussein's two sons, Qusay and Uday, produced even greater confidence among the occupiers – though this was temporarily disturbed by a series of attacks on mosques, police stations and the United Nations headquarters in Baghdad. Saddam Hussein's detention in December was a moment of further celebration. The flow of positive statements from the Coalition Provisional Authority (CPA) that ensued was not deterred even by evidence of continuing insurgency over the next two months.

The most recent events suggest that at last the pattern might be changing shape, as events on the ground enforce a more settled, reluctant acceptance of persisting high levels of insecurity. What is significant, moreover, is that this might be occurring not simply in relation to Iraq or even Afghanistan, but against the background of wider concerns with the situation in Uzbekistan, the Philippines, Thailand, Spain and now Britain.

An Iraqi Frenzy

In Iraq itself, insurgency attacks against the police and security forces and on expatriates have continued and intensified. On Friday 26 March, rockets were fired at a civic building in Mosul, killing four people and wounding 19. The same day, several hours of fighting between US Marines and insurgents in Fallujah left eight people dead and many injured; in Kirkuk, a police lieutenant was killed by unidentified assailants, and American troops mistakenly killed an Iraqi working for RTI International, a US organisation contracted to USAID.

These were far from the only incidents of a bloody day. Four Iraqi members of the US-trained Civil Defence Corps were killed near Tikrit, and four members of a wedding party were killed and twelve others injured when their vehicles struck an anti-tank mine.

On Sunday 28 March, a British and a Canadian private security official guarding engineers working for General Electric at a power plant near Mosul were killed. In a separate incident in the same city, a senior official appointed by the CPA to head the Ministry of Public Works was attacked while on her way to a meeting in the Kurdish city of Dahuk, north of Mosul. Nesreen Barwari survived the attack, but her driver and bodyguard were killed and two other people injured. The next day, another high-level target who narrowly avoided assassination was the governor of Diyala province, Abdullah Shahad al-Jaburi, targeted in a bomb attack on 29 March that injured twelve people, including four police officers. Three British troops were injured in a bomb incident in Basra.

This combination of incidents culminated on 31 March in an outburst of intense violence in and around the troubled city of Fallujah, west of Baghdad. Five US Marines were killed when an armoured personnel carrier was blown up, and in a separate incident four US civilian security personnel were killed.

The latter attack, accompanied by fierce expressions of hostility to the occupiers, followed ten days of attempts by newly-arrived US Marines to pacify the city. In its aftermath, the security situation was so bad that neither the Iraqi police nor the Marines attempted to intervene, despite a 4,000-strong Marine contingent being quartered near the city.

There is little sign of the violence abating; most of these incidents are not even reported in the United States or Britain except in the more specialist outlets. Furthermore, while many current attacks are directed against Iraqis and civilian expatriates, the problems facing the US military forces are still considerable. For much of 2003, when US troops were the prime targets, they were typically facing 15–20 attacks every day, with this rising to over 30 a day at times of peak insurgency. US military officials acknowledged last week that, even now, attacks are running at over 20 a day, inflicting frequent serious injuries and several deaths each week.

Thailand and Philippines: Southern Discomfort

While recent events in Iraq are significant, the last few days have also seen important incidents in Thailand, the Philippines and Britain, and by major developments in Pakistan and Uzbekistan.

In Thailand, separatist moves in southern provinces bordering Malaysia – Yala, Pattani, Narathiwat – have in recent months erupted into an insurgency for the first time in nearly 20 years. Insurgents based in the Islamic minority – who form 5 million of the country's 66 million population – have left 55 people dead in the last three months; 28 people alone were injured on 27 March in the bombing of a tourist district. The Thai prime minister, Thaksin Shinawatra, postponed a visit to Europe after the weekend attack to oversee a security review.

In the Philippines, President Gloria Arroyo reported the seizure of 36 kilograms of explosive material and the arrest of militants said to be planning an attack on trains and shopping centres. The Abu Sayyaf group that is fighting for a separate Islamic state in the southern, Muslim-majority islands was held responsible. Arroyo, a consistent supporter of the 'war on terror', is seeking re-election in six weeks' time; it is not yet clear if the news and timing of the detentions was in any way related to the political cycle, or how significant the arrests really are.

In Britain, one of the largest police and security operations ever undertaken involving 700 police in the area around

London, arrested eight suspects and impounded half a ton of ammonium nitrate fertiliser that can, with appropriate technical competence, be used to make a substantial crude explosive charge.

The London arrests seem to involve young British people of Pakistani origin. This does not fit the usual pattern of post-9/11 transnational paramilitary operations, wherein experienced militants – often with direct connections to North Africa or the western Gulf states – oversee the key organisational and technical aspects of an operation, while nationals of a country may be involved only at a subordinate level.

The implication here is that either the key people in this intended operation have not been detained, or else a pattern is emerging of more disparate and possibly self-sustaining groups. Either explanation has implications, although most emphasis within Britain will initially be on the probable prevention of a substantial attack.

A Pakistani Hesitation

In Afghanistan, United States operations against Taliban and other insurgents are continuing. An additional 2,000 US Marines are being sent to the region, based on amphibious warfare ships and ready to be airlifted at short notice to any military operation in Afghanistan or, in principle, Pakistan.

In Pakistan itself, military operations in South Waziristan are slowing after two weeks of fighting; 14 soldiers and government officials captured by local militias early in the conflict have been released. This period was characterised by frequent, combative statements from the Pakistani military. These most recently included the claim that al-Qaida's leading intelligence operative had been killed, but (like the earlier signal that the offensive was close to capturing Ayman al-Zawahiri, Osama bin Laden's deputy) this has now been discounted.

The Pakistani army's operations have failed to kill or capture significant al-Qaida officials, and they have faced a far higher level of resistance to their incursions than expected, in part a result of the intense local antagonism provoked by the accidental killing of many civilians in the early stages. A key worry for the Pakistani leadership was the manner in which its troops were attacked far from the core combat area. In addition to hostage-taking and high levels of resistance, this meant that the army actually had to use local religious leaders to negotiate a truce, leading to its withdrawal from much of the region.

In the retreat, the authorities claimed that al-Qaida operatives had themselves evaded capture by using tunnels of over two kilometres in length, which (by implication) had been dug for this purpose. In fact, these were almost certainly water-supply tunnels used for irrigation, a common feature in agriculture in several parts of South-West and Central Asia. The subsequent destruction of these tunnels by the Pakistani army will not do much to win local 'hearts and minds'.

The Pakistani army's failure in Waziristan has implications for the current US strategy of mounting a major combined offensive on both sides of the Afghanistan/Pakistan border. A lack of success on the Pakistan side might call the whole operation, expected to last several months, in question.

In practice, the likelihood is that the Pakistani army will conduct further operations but face the same difficulties. This, in turn, will encourage the United States to consider deploying forces in Pakistan itself. While the government of General Musharraf may just be persuadable on this point, the popular reaction across Pakistan as a whole could be much more hostile.

An Uzbek Incident

On Monday 29 March, a series of bombings and shootings in two major cities of Uzbekistan, Tashkent and Bukhara, killed 19 people and injured many more. The tight media control in the

Central Asian state makes accurate information hard to obtain, but normally reliable sources indicate that these attacks form part of a wider series of disturbances across the country. These include a bombing on 28 March near one of the residences of the autocratic president, Islam Karimov, and an attack on 30 March on a police checkpoint near Tashkent. Karimov's regime sought to connect the attacks with international Islamic terrorism, although its own severe and long-term repression is likely to have generated widespread internal dissent.

The police seem to have been primary targets of the attacks, although civilians have also been killed and injured. The 29 March attack at the Chorsu market in Tashkent involved two suicide bombers intent on killing police on duty there; the first explosion killed a group of officers as two police shifts were overlapping, the second bomber exploded a device under an hour later when the area had been largely cleared of civilians.

The Uzbek violence has two direct implications for the United States. The first is that the US has worked closely with the Karimov regime, symbolised by its significant military presence at the Khanabad airbase – and has broadly overlooked the regime's poor human rights record in the process. The recent violence has not so far been directed at the American presence, but the sophisticated targeting of Uzbek police units suggests the presence of a paramilitary capability that could well expand to include this.

The second implication is that the attacks challenge the expectation of security analysts that any al-Qaida affiliates in Central Asia would in the initial stages operate more effectively in states with weaker internal security capabilities, such as Tajikistan or Kyrgyzstan – before targeting those, like Uzbekistan itself, with closer American connections. But the immediate problems facing Uzbekistan make it at least possible that a new phase in George W. Bush's 'war on terror' is starting to develop.

A PROBLEM OF STRATEGY *15 April 2004*

In the first twelve days of April, 76 United States troops died in combat in Iraq, making it already the worst month for deaths in action since the fall of the Saddam Hussein regime a year ago. Iraqi casualties are believed to be more than 700, with deep controversy over the number of civilians killed and injured. In Fallujah, local doctors say that about 700 people were killed there alone, most of them civilians. International relief groups put the number at 470, with 1,200 people injured. Those wounded include 243 women and 200 children, giving strong support to the belief that many of those killed were indeed civilians.

While a tenuous ceasefire was negotiated in Fallujah at the weekend, and some Shi'a militias withdrew from areas they occupied, the attitude of the US military leadership has remained aggressive, including a determination to control Fallujah by force if a negotiated conclusion to the conflict fails. Even more robust is the stated intention to kill or capture Muqtada al-Sadr.

Since the 'two-front' fighting developed two weeks ago, against Sunni militia in Fallujah, Ramadi and Baghdad, and against Shi'a militia in Baghdad and across a number of southern cities, copious analysis in the western press has focused on what are now a number of received wisdoms. These include the view that closing al-Sadr's newspaper and detaining one of his deputies was a grave error, given the extent of the militia support he had quietly built up. With the poor economic status and high unemployment of the majority Shi'a communities across Iraq, it was all too easy for these actions to provide a focus for revolt.

Other mistakes include the excessive use of force in Fallujah, even in the light of the previous killing and mutilation of four US private security personnel. Once again, the effect is seen to have been to harden the opposition to occupation. More generally, commentators have focused on the failure to spread the limited rewards of economic growth across Iraqi society, an excessive concern with privatisation and the award of lucrative contracts to US contractors, the disbanding of the Iraqi army last summer and the detention without trial of around 10,000 Iraqis.

The Larger Picture

While all of this may make sense, it is probably more productive to analyse the events of the past two weeks in a wider context, taking in not just the developments in Iraq but also what has happened elsewhere in the region, extending through to Afghanistan and Pakistan, as well as the continuing activism of al-Qaida and its associates.

Since the termination of the Saddam Hussein regime, this series of articles has tried to piece together both the longer-term trends in Bush's 'war on terror' and the consequences of US policy towards Iraq and Israel. In doing so, what might be put forward as realistic analysis has, on occasions, seemed excessively pessimistic. Even at times of apparent progress, it has concluded that substantial problems lie ahead. Are we now entering a period when such an analysis is proving valid? Perhaps the most helpful approach is to go back six weeks, assess how the situation looked to the coalition at that time and then see how circumstances have changed.

At the end of February there was a prospect that the United States would be able to hand over to an appointed client regime in Baghdad by the middle of the year. Violence certainly continued, but substantial effort was being put into building up the Iraqi police, the Civil Defence Force, numerous pipeline and other security organisations, and a new Iraqi army. In addition, many thousands of private security personnel, drawn from scores of countries, were operating in Iraq, and the CPA had privatised many of the functions previously undertaken by the military, right down to the running of supply convoys.

Coalition officials could point to the re-opening of schools, rising oil production and slowly improving electricity supplies – all signs that the Iraqi economy was now developing as a serious entity, in spite of the problems in the months immediately after the fall of the old regime. Moreover, when local elections did take place, it was common for secular politicians to get elected, suggesting that fears of a nascent Islamic radicalism were far from the truth.

It is true that the Pentagon recognised the likelihood of a continuing insurgency and was planning for the possibility of 100,000 troops remaining in the country for up to three years. It was also establishing a network of permanent bases to ensure the long-term security for the United States of this extraordinarily oil-rich country. There were problems ahead, but prospects looked reasonable. At least it was possible that Iraq would not 'blow up' during the US presidential election campaign, that being the dominant political requirement in Washington.

If anything, the concern in US military circles was more with Afghanistan and the persistence there of a Taliban and al-Qaida threat. As a result, the US military in Afghanistan was reinforced and the Musharraf government in Pakistan was persuaded to participate in a major trans-border military operation. Pakistani army troops would move into those parts of the North-West Frontier Province that harboured Taliban and other militias, producing an 'anvil' against which a US military 'hammer' would pound these groups from the Afghanistan side of the border.

The aim was to destroy Taliban and al-Qaida elements in their supposed last refuge, with a real chance of capturing or killing Osama bin Laden himself. This would further cripple al-Qaida at a time when it was demonstrating a diminishing capability in the wake of the already receding attacks in Istanbul the previous year.

A Strategy in Trouble

Look, now, at what has happened in the last six weeks. In Afghanistan, instability continues and the Karzai administration can still not get the support it needs to aid the rebuilding of the country. Warlords remain rampant and Taliban elements have influence across a substantial part of the country. In Pakistan, the army has faced much greater difficulty than anticipated, so much so that results of the first military operations, conducted during March, were minimal.

Meanwhile, a paramilitary group that was at least loosely associated with al-Qaida carried out a devastating attack in Madrid, killing over 190 people and injuring well over 1,000. Warnings of further attacks are a regular feature of the European scene, with multiple arrests in Britain and unprecedented security in Italy. A further issue that has almost been forgotten in western circles is the longer-term impact of the Israeli assassination of the Hamas leader, Sheikh Yassin.

Then there is Iraq, where the security predicament for the United States is potentially more difficult than even the most robust analysis currently indicates. This stems from four factors.

The first is that recent events, especially in Fallujah, have begun to lead to a more general increase in opposition to US occupation that is beginning to take on the form of a new Iraqi nationalism. This is in its early stages, many parts of Iraq remain peaceful and possibly most Iraqis still offer some support to the United States. But current US approaches, with the intent to maintain rigorous control, are highly likely to fuel this nationalism, not diminish it.

Second, the insurgents have become more confident and are demonstrating a greater sophistication in their actions as well as an unexpected degree of coordination. They are proving particularly effective at disrupting supply routes, with frequent attacks on convoys as well as the destruction of bridges. In one sign of their capabilities, insurgents have spotted changes in convoy routes where the US forces are seeking to avoid dangerous roads, and are promptly destroying bridges on those alternate routes.

Third, much of the US policy for stabilising Iraq has depended on the 'domestication' of security – replacing US occupying troops with police, paramilitary forces and the new Iraqi army. This is simply not working. The Iraqi police have lost hundreds of their people to the insurgency in the past year and most are in no mood to lay down their lives at a time of perceived American belligerence. Even more significant has been the refusal of a newly formed and trained battalion of the Iraqi army to support US operations in Fallujah.

What this means is that a fundamental part of the US security policy in Iraq has come apart at the seams, leaving the entire policy in disarray. It is probably the most significant development of the past six weeks and explains the request to Washington from the US military in Iraq for two extra brigades of at least 10,000 combat troops.

What has to be remembered is that a large proportion of the US troops in Iraq are reservists working on a wide range of projects. The core group of perhaps 80,000 combat troops is far too small to secure Iraq even if it were aided by effective Iraqi forces, and these are simply not there.

The fourth factor is that the sudden wave of kidnappings coupled with all the other forms of insecurity means that the pace of reconstruction and economic development has slowed right down, with this likely to get even worse as companies pull out their personnel and countries urge their nationals to leave. If this problem persists, then the entire coalition timetable for Iraqi development comes unhinged.

A Critical Phase

The predicament of the United States in Iraq is serious, verging on the critical, and it is possible that the combination of the

Fallujah violence and the Muqtada al-Sadr phenomenon will come to be seen as the turning point. Bear in mind that the coming months will see the intensely hot summer, and that this may well also see sustained attacks on oil exports and power supplies. Beyond this, the continued reporting by al-Jazeera, al-Arabiya and other TV channels of the civilian costs of the war is leading to much higher levels of anti-Americanism across the region. Furthermore, this is on top of the effects of the Israeli assassination of Sheikh Yassin.

The end result of all of this may be that the United States position in Iraq is actually becoming unsustainable. If so, then is there any alternative that might conceivably be accepted by Washington? One proposal put forward by former senior UN diplomat Marrack Goulding and others calls for a phased US withdrawal followed by a combination of a UN-organised political transition backed by substantial peacekeeping forces provided largely by states from the Islamic world. This might just work if the UN was prepared to take the huge risk involved, and the very fact that it is promoted by such an experienced person as Goulding illustrates how serious the situation has become.

Even now, though, it is a political non-starter in Washington. At its core, the US take-over of Iraq has always been part of a wider policy of ensuring the security of the Persian Gulf, partly in the context of US attitudes towards Israel but much more because of the politics of oil. The lynchpin of this policy is a client regime in Baghdad backed by a substantial and permanent US military presence in Iraq.

If the United States were to withdraw and hand over to the UN, this would be a defeat for its whole regional policy. It is not beyond the bounds of possibility that this could happen, perhaps if John Kerry is elected in November. For the present, though, the security predicament in Iraq would have to get very much worse before such a fundamental reversal of policy could be considered by the Bush administration.

BETWEEN FALLUJAH AND PALESTINE *22 April 2004*

The insurgency in Iraq is on the verge of becoming an uprising. The assault on the Abu Ghraib prison near Baghdad on 20 April and the huge car bombs in Basra a day later, which together killed over 80 people, are evidence that the violence is occurring far beyond the recent epicentre of conflict, the city of Fallujah west of Baghdad.

This spreading campaign is having disastrous effects on United States efforts to engineer the reconstruction efforts. Almost all major work programmes are at a standstill. April 2004 has already been by far the worst month for US casualties, even including the initial three-week war of March–April 2003, and the highly fortified 'green zone' in the centre of Baghdad is now home to thousands of private contractors and their employees who cannot undertake even routine operations because of the lack of security.

How the United States reacts to this new situation will largely determine the further development of the insurgency. The experience at Fallujah suggests that it will play to its strength, that of overwhelming military firepower, even if such a policy ends up being deeply counterproductive.

An Assault in Fallujah

The controversy over the violent confrontation in Fallujah has resulted in sharply contrasting accounts of the fighting and its effects. On one side, numerous reports from medical staff and aid agencies attest to many hundreds of deaths and well over 1,000 injuries. Aid workers present in the city for some of the time confirm evidence of intense levels of violence in the city.

On the other side, senior US military spokespersons say that the Marines used limited force that precisely targeted militants and largely avoided civilians. According to US General Richard B. Myers, for example: 'There has never been a more humane campaign. and that goes for operations in Fallujah.'

Furthermore, military sources have still tried to maintain that the insurgents in Fallujah were relatively small in number and that it would have been possible to gain control of the city if the attackers so determined. The latter argument is called into question by the decision to go for short-term ceasefires with parallel negotiations, the very fact of negotiation suggesting that US control was not feasible without massive costs.

In this context, moreover, two things have now become clear. One is that the level of opposition to US forces was much higher than expected and the second is that there were clear-cut examples of the use of massive firepower by US forces. This is illustrated by a remarkable sequence of events that took place at the height of the conflict last week, on Tuesday 13 April. Although it was just one incident in a long conflict, its significance may turn out to be considerable, not least because details of it are drawn almost entirely from US sources (Pamela Constable, 'A Wrong Turn, Chaos and a Rescue', *Washington Post*, 15 April 2004).

At around 4.30pm on the Tuesday afternoon, a supply convoy of Humvees was moving towards a Marines post on the edge of a US-controlled area when it came under light-arms attack. The convoy turned back and the supplies were shifted to two armoured vehicles that moved forward again. These vehicles were in turn attacked by insurgents using rocket-propelled grenades. One turned back but the engine of the other vehicle caught fire and, in the confusion, the driver took a wrong turn.

It then came under heavy attack and a large rescue column including four tanks was sent to its aid. There then followed a three-hour gun battle between insurgents and Marines, with US Air Force planes brought in for ground attack.

As dusk fell, the Marines fought through several city blocks to reach the point where the 17 Marines in the armoured personnel carrier had taken refuge in a nearby building, their carrier now being burnt out. Eventually, after sustained combat, the Marines were extricated, apparently without any deaths but with several wounded. At least 20 insurgents were reported killed. The rescue operation was hailed as a success. One local commander said: 'This is a story about heroes. It shows the tenacity of the Marines and their fierce loyalty to each other. They were absolutely unwilling to leave their brother Marines behind.'

One immediate implication of this incident was that the level of resistance was very much greater than the Marines had expected. In this light, the evident risk of heavy casualties should any attempt be made to take control of the city may help to explain the calling of a truce.

In any case, though, what happened next was much more significant. To quote the *Washington Post*:

> Just before dawn Wednesday… AC-130 Spectre gunships launched a devastating punitive raid over a six-block area around the spot where the convoy was attacked, firing dozens of artillery shells that shook the city and lit up the sky. Marine officials said the area was virtually destroyed and that no further insurgent activity has been seen there.

The AC-130 Spectre is a development of the Lockheed C-130 military transport in which powerful guns, including a 105mm howitzer, are mounted in the body of the aircraft, pointing out sideways and downwards. In undertaking a ground attack, the aircraft circles the target using a guidance system to ensure that the gunfire is targeted towards specific points on the ground.

Each plane's howitzer can be armed with up to 200 high explosive shells, with the ammunition being used in a matter of minutes. Shells can be targeted to explode over a substantial area, and the action in Fallujah, targeting several city blocks, was equivalent to destroying a small town, even though this was a punitive raid carried out several hours after an attack by insurgents that involved minimal US casualties.

The Israeli Factor

The use of such force in Fallujah is reminiscent of Israeli Defence Force (IDF) tactics in the occupied territories, where substantial airborne firepower has been used repeatedly in urban conflict. An earlier article in this series (11 December 2003) commented on more direct connections between the IDF and the US military. In late 2003, IDF specialists arrived at the home base of US special forces at Fort Bragg in North Carolina, where they were reported to be assisting in the training of US units in counter-insurgency tactics, including the assassination of guerrilla leaders.

Soon after, in early December, a series of meetings was held in Israel, hosted by senior IDF personnel and involving a US team headed by the commander of the US Army's training and doctrine command, General Kevin Byrnes. Reports of that meeting indicate the close relationship between US and Israeli military, with the former keen to learn from the experience of the IDF in the Palestinian territories.

More evidence of that connection is now available, not least in terms of weapons and equipment developed in Israel for the control of the West Bank and Gaza and now being used by US forces in Iraq. On 22–25 March, Israel's ground forces command staged an event in which soldiers and arms technologists spoke openly about systems they had developed to defeat Palestinian militias (Barbara Opall-Rome, 'Israeli Arms, Gear Aid U.S. Troops', *Defense News*, 30 March 2004). Among those present at the event were staff from US Special Operations Command, the US Marine Corps' warfighting laboratory, US Space and Naval Warfare Systems Command and the US Army's National Ground Intelligence Center.

US officials were reluctant to discuss the extent of the collaboration but did indicate that the amount of joint US–Israeli military training had accelerated in the past two or three years. One US defence official said that military-to-military 'cooperation with the Israelis has been going on for decades across all service branches, but it's true that only recently, you've started to see a lot more Israeli systems deployed in different theatres'.

What is clear is that a range of systems developed by the Israeli armaments industry are being purchased for use by the US armed forces, especially for use in Iraq. US forces already use the Israeli aircraft industry's Hunter robotic reconnaissance aircraft; 14 more have just been ordered. They also use the Rafael armament development authority Simon grenade launcher, with a wall-breaching variant now being evaluated by the US Marine Corps. Rafael is also developing a robotic anti-sniper system, once again of interest to the Marines.

Another Israeli company, Tadiran Communications, is providing a pocket-sized combined navigation, satellite radio and digital messaging system, and the Pentagon's Combating Terrorism Technology Support Office (CTTSO) has ordered a number of prototypes of a new Israeli multi-function sensor produced by ODF Optronics of Tel Aviv. This system, termed 'Eyeball', is the size of a tennis ball but contains movement sensors, microphones, speakers and transmitters, enabling it to hear and even communicate with insurgents. As a major from the Marine Corps' warfighting laboratory remarked: 'The Israelis are way ahead of the others in some very interesting, niche fields.'

Through Arab Eyes

From the perspective of a US military commander, anything that improves the US warfighting ability is warranted, but this increasingly close cooperation with Israel has substantial political implications across the Arab world. Whether intentional or not, the signal it sends is that something akin to a combined operation is underway, a reading supported by President Bush's unequivocal support for Ariel Sharon's current unilateral actions.

From a regional perspective, the Israelis are controlling legitimate Palestinian opposition using hard military force, including the employment of a range of new technologies. Now, those same technologies used against the Palestinians are being handed over to the United States for use against the opposition in Iraq, where American forces are already using their preponderance of firepower to try to control an otherwise dangerous insurgency.

This is powerfully demonstrated to Arab audiences by the events in Fallujah, with the 13–14 April ambush and subsequent massive retaliation being just one example. Fallujah is now gaining an almost mythical status with potential long-term consequences that may reach well beyond Iraq.

Similarly, the Israelis kill Hamas leaders – first Sheikh Ahmed Yassin and now Abdel Aziz Rantisi – while the US occupying forces in Iraq talk openly of killing Muqtada al-Sadr. Among the consequences of these and other actions will be an even stronger perception of an Israeli–American war against Islam. It is difficult to imagine a better recruiting sergeant for al-Qaida and its associates.

6
Oil and the War

INTRODUCTION

The end of June 2004 should have marked a major step in the political evolution of Iraq, with the installation of a temporary Iraqi administration led by Iyad Allawi. There was, in particular, an anticipation in the United States that this would be a turning point in the insurgency as evidence developed that Iraq was gaining a degree of independence. In practice, the presence of such an administration made no difference to the insurgency which continued to develop.

In any case, the closing days of the Coalition Provisional Authority under the leadership of Paul Bremer involved a series of moves to ensure that the new administration would be massively influenced by the United States, to the extent that it could be accurately described as a client regime. The new US embassy, which replaced the CPA, was to be the largest embassy of any state anywhere in the world, and its lines of control would stretch to every Iraqi government ministry.

In seeking to maintain this remarkably pervasive influence in Iraq, it became more obvious that the United States had a regional policy that was heavily influenced by the oil resources of the Persian Gulf. For this reason, if for no other, there was little prospect of a wholesale US withdrawal from Iraq, however violent the insurgency might become.

ABU GHRAIB AND ITS IMPACT *13 May 2004*

The graphic images of abused, humiliated and tortured detainees in Abu Ghraib prison near Baghdad have been widely seen across the Middle East in their original uncensored form. These images are considerably worse than the shocking though watered-down versions seen in the western media. Yet the impact is actually likely to be greater in the west because the actions they depict are already widely known in Iraq and throughout the rest of the Arab world.

The International Committee of the Red Cross and US Army reports demonstrate a wider process of abuse than that involving a few 'rotten apples', but the images alone are having a profound effect in the United States, even if they come as less of a surprise to those who have followed the conflict more closely.

For much of the past year there have been persistent reports of widespread ill-treatment from ex-detainees. It has to be remembered that these follow many instances of the killing and injuring of civilians since the first intense weeks of the war. Moreover, they are in addition to the much greater destruction of human life at the start of the war. Overall, the civilian death toll is now at least 9,000 with probably many more than 20,000 seriously injured – many of them maimed for life.

At any one time, up to 10,000 people have been detained without trial, usually with their relatives unable to get any information about them. These elements constitute a ruthless pursuit of war and occupation with continuing human costs. All this was already known across much of Iraq and the Middle East; the recent images serve primarily as confirming evidence, although the aspect of sexual humiliation has had a particularly strong effect within Iraq.

By contrast, virtually none of this previously had an impact in the United States, and the fact that the coalition could say 'we don't do body counts' has been a further indication of the apparent irrelevance of the deaths and injuries of ordinary people.

The effects in the United States are now far greater, especially with the brutal murder of Nick Berg. Support for the war is slipping to the extent that Donald Rumsfeld needs strong words of support from President Bush himself. Moreover, it comes at a time of increased criticism of the civilian leadership in the Pentagon from within the US Army (Thomas E. Ricks, 'Dissension Grows in Senior Ranks on War Strategy', *Washington Post*, 9 May 2004), including demands that Rumsfeld and his deputy, Paul Wolfowitz, be sacked.

Such a substantial change of mood in the space of less than six weeks comes at a time of severe difficulties in Iraq as casualties continue to mount, Fallujah becomes controlled by former Iraqi army personnel and reconstruction is made greatly more difficult. With dissension within the coalition, including the withdrawal of the Spanish, and increased pressure on Tony Blair, prospects for a smooth handover to a client state look dim.

How to Lose a War

In these circumstances, what are the convinced supporters of the New American Century saying? Are they facing up to the need for policy changes or do they believe in a requirement for greater commitment and resilience? Are they still determined to persist with the Greater Middle East Initiative in order to redevelop the region in the American image?

As to the actual treatment of detainees at Abu Ghraib, the reaction is one of concentrating blame directly on the perpetrators so far named. According to the *Army Times* (10 May 2004), in some Pentagon circles they are known as 'the six morons who lost the war'; in the neo-conservative bible, the *Weekly Standard* (17 May 2004) they are 'lowlifes' – people who '...traduced their mission, betrayed their fellow soldiers, and disgraced their country'. While there is an acceptance of the need to identify others in the chain of command, the controversy is seen as evidence of a limited failing that demands a swift response. Richard Starr concludes: 'Bring on the trials, and the punishment.'

What lies below the surface of such a reaction is most probably a deep fear that the Iraq war is starting to spin out of control, threatening the whole vision of the New American Century. As a result, the primary emphasis is on the idea of a few bad apples, the six morons, who are risking the whole project. But the problems in Iraq go way beyond the Abu Ghraib situation, and it is here that the neo-conservative vision has to react.

A key response has been that of Robert Kagan and William Kristol, writing in the current *Weekly Standard* (17 May 2004). They start by expressing huge concern that there is a mood developing in Washington that Iraq is already irrecoverable, that there could be a tipping-point of American public opinion towards a decisively anti-war stance, and that this is not fully recognised within the Bush administration. They worry at the attitudes of 'left-wing Democrats and isolationist Republicans' but are reassured that the administration remains committed to the fight and that there are 'stalwarts' in the Democratic Party such as Joe Biden and Joe Lieberman 'who are fighting against that party's growing clamor for withdrawal'.

These authors' concern with 'isolationist Republicans' is a handy reminder of the split within the Republican movement between neo-conservatives and isolationists; their recognition of the need for Democrat support is an indication of their deep worries over the current US predicament.

In these circumstances, Kagan and Kristol argue for an immediate change of policy in Iraq, the primary focus being on bringing elections forward by several months, to as early as late September. They believe there has been a major policy failure in Iraq, in that the handover to Iraqis has been far too slow. If the entire process was now speeded up, they argue, there would be several positive effects.

Iraqis would be compelled to focus on the coming elections and the insurgents would be seen as attacking the moves to democracy as well as coalition forces – they 'would be antidemocratic rather than anti-American'. This would, for example, focus Sunni opinion on the electoral process rather than the insurgency, with American military actions seen essentially as vital support for the electoral process.

In bringing elections forward, Kagan and Kristol also call for a considerable increase in US troops in Iraq to control the insurgency. They believe the administration should call on European powers such as France and Germany to send troops to Iraq and to provide far greater financial and technical assistance.

They conclude: '...this proposal is not a cure-all. It carries its own risks as well as benefits. If someone has a better idea, we're happy to hear it. But if the administration does not take some dramatic action now, it may be unable to avoid failure.'

The Grip of Unreality

This is a remarkable conclusion from those at the heart of the neo-conservative project, not least because their proposed policy change is so very far from reality. With the United States planning the world's largest embassy in Iraq and with permanent military bases now being established, the idea that the Bush administration is in the business of promoting genuine democracy and independence in Iraq induces nothing more than hollow laughter. It is heard not just in Iraq and across the region, but in Paris and Berlin too.

The remoteness of such views from the realities of Iraq indicates that US policy in the country is indeed in deep trouble, and that those responsible for that policy are doing little more than clutching at straws. A recent article in this series concluded that April 2004 might well come to be seen as the pivotal month in the whole Iraq war. In view of the developments of the last two weeks, that is now looking to be more and more likely.

THE WAR FOR GULF OIL *26 May 2004*

American and British efforts to gain legitimacy and support for their political project in Iraq are entering a new phase, with a draft resolution to the United Nations Security Council being presented and discussed behind closed doors in the UN's New York headquarters. The resolution seeks UN backing for the proposed handover to Iraqi administration on 30 June, with some doubt as to the role and powers of US forces in Iraq after that date.

Meanwhile, as President Bush on 24 May promised 'focused and unrelenting' efforts to 'hold this hard-won ground for the realm of liberty', discussions between his envoy Robert D. Blackwill and the UN's Lakhdar Brahimi continue to address the 'complicated geometry' of Iraqi power relationships after the transfer.

At the same time, the investigation of the affairs of Ahmad Chalabi, the Iraqi figurehead long championed by American agencies to advance their political ambitions in the country, is another indication of the remarkable lack of coherence in United States policy in Iraq, noted in last week's article in this series. While Donald Rumsfeld protested ignorance of the raid on Chalabi's Baghdad residence on 21 May, other sources were circulating evidence to indicate that the Iraqi Governing Council member had been used by Iranian intelligence to tempt the US into its Iraqi adventure.

Behind the diplomacy and the political confusion, the Iraqi insurgency continues. A rocket attack on a US base north of Baghdad on 24 May killed an American soldier and wounded four more; the same day, two British civilians connected to the country's foreign office were killed in an ambush outside the coalition headquarters in Baghdad; two Russian civilian contractors were killed and five wounded in an attack on a bus on 26 May. Most seriously of all, intense fighting around the cities of Najaf and Kufa between coalition troops and forces loyal to the Shi'a radical cleric Muqtada al-Sadr continues, involving controversial damage to the shrine of Imam Ali in Najaf in addition to the deaths of civilians.

Thus, the United States-led coalition remains under severe pressure in Iraq in three areas – political, diplomatic and military. As if they were not enough, a fourth area of concern – economic – has come to the fore in recent weeks, and it is worth examining how the oil factor connects to American strategy in Iraq and the wider Gulf region over the longer term.

Since January 2004, oil prices have risen 25 per cent to reach over $40 a barrel in late May – and as high as $41.80 on 24 May, the highest level since 1983 – awakening fears of a serious oil price shock reminiscent of the early 1970s and late 1980s. The potential impact on United States and British politics could be especially great, not least as there are suggestions that one of the main reasons for the price increases is the anger of some Arab oil producers at recent coalition actions in Iraq.

The actual situation is rather more complex; a continuation of the price trend is not inevitable. But the longer-term prospects are precarious and there is a deeper truth in the assessment of a link between oil and politics: movements in the oil price are indeed intimately bound up with US policy in the Gulf region.

A Mixed Blessing

The first round of oil price rises, from October 1973 to May 1974, was very much a result of the actions of oil producers. Arab members of the Organisation of Petroleum Exporting Countries (OPEC) cartel put up prices and cut production in order to exert influence on western countries to pressurise Israel over the Yom Kippur/Ramadan war. This set in motion decisions by other OPEC members which, along with the activities of speculators, led to a price rise of over 400 per cent within a few months.

The 1979–80 price increases were less extreme and were due mainly to supply interruptions during the Iranian revolution and the start of the Iran–Iraq war. After this, during the 1980s, the power of the oil producers decreased, even though oil-import dependency was spreading to countries such as China. On both occasions, the trans-national oil companies (TNOCs) did very little to curb prices. For them, surging 'bull' markets were very good for business – they could buy oil at one price and sell to the consumer at an inflated price within a few weeks, even though it would take 100 days or more for oil to get from the oilfields to the petrol pump.

'Buy low, sell high' was a good tactic and it was little wonder that many of the TNOCs recorded spectacular profits in 1974 and 1980. This was a lesson that western governments had to learn the hard way – especially those who had persisted in the old-fashioned idea that multinational corporations essentially act in the interests of elite countries rather than their own.

The current price surge does stem partly from some modest OPEC cuts in oil production earlier in the year, and there may indeed be an element of displeasure at US policies, but two other factors are at work. First, a continuing increase in demand, especially in China and the United States; second, speculation fuelled partly by the fear of disruptions of supply due to paramilitary action in Iraq.

Repeated attacks on Iraq's oil infrastructure have caused concern and have added to such speculative pressures. It would normally be possible for the world's largest exporter, Saudi Arabia, to compensate for any shortages by increasing production. This the Saudis are now doing, but only belatedly, so that there are likely to be some further price increases –

especially as demand for gasoline increases with the onset of the summer 'driving season' in the United States with its heavy use of air conditioners, vacation cars and trucks.

Such increases might appear to benefit producer countries like Saudi Arabia by improving their revenue streams. In practice it does not work like this. Many of the western Gulf states such as Kuwait and the Emirates have long since invested many of their oil revenues overseas, principally in Europe and North America. Kuwait gets around half of its governmental income from such investments and the other half from oil exports. This means that if the price of oil surges too much, a recession can ensue in the west and investment income falls.

The consequence of this is a fine balancing act. Many OPEC members would like so see the price remain around $35–40 a barrel – enough for lucrative revenues but not enough to damage investment income. The problem is that this is a difficult if not dangerous balance to achieve, given the current political turmoil in the region.

The end result is that oil prices may hold steady at around current levels, but there is a real risk of a sudden further increase, especially if al-Qaida or one of its affiliates can succeed in disrupting Saudi, Kuwaiti or Emirate exports in addition to the current interruptions in Iraq.

High Stakes, Hard Options

This current volatility may only be a taste of what is to come in the longer-term future. The trend of the past 30 years has been for an increase in dependency of the industrialised world on Gulf oil at the expense of almost every other region. In addition to most of Europe and Japan, with their near-total import dependency, even the United States now needs to buy almost 60 per cent of all the oil it uses, and China and India are rapidly increasing their oil imports as well.

Meanwhile, there are more and more discoveries of oil in the Gulf region. Despite exporting vast quantities of oil throughout the 1990s, Saudi Arabia, Iraq, Kuwait and the Emirates have all seen an increase in the size of their oil reserves. Iraq's estimated reserves actually went up 15 per cent from 1990 to 2002. Only Iran has seen a decrease, and that has been modest. On 2002 figures, these five states, together with the smaller oilfields in Qatar and Oman, collectively have reserves totalling 690 billion barrels – almost 70 per cent of total world oil reserves.

By comparison, the United States has just 3 per cent of world reserves and the UK's North Sea reserves are down to less than 0.5 per cent. Even the combined reserves of the Caspian basin and Siberia are little more than half the size of Iraq's oil. This certainly helps explain why the Bush administration is so attached to the idea of a client government in Baghdad and a nice, friendly, long-term relationship.

This is the current situation, but what also has to be remembered is that this is a snapshot rather than the indicator of a trend. To assess the likely circumstances a generation or two ahead, the signs indicate that Gulf oil reserves will become steadily more important, especially as demand from China and India continues to grow. Put simply, whoever can exert the most influence over the Persian Gulf region, especially if that extends to a capability for military control, will wield quite extraordinary international power.

For that reason alone, if current American policy in Iraq does fail and the result is a disorganised and chaotic withdrawal, the extent of the foreign policy disaster that will unfold will be much greater even than any immediate sense of victory felt by al-Qaida and its affiliated paramilitaries. It could set back US control of the world's richest energy resources for well over a decade. In short, it is no exaggeration to say that what happens in Iraq over the next year could have a defining impact on global security trends well into the third decade of the twenty-first century.

US PLANS FOR MILITARY EXPANSION *1 July 2004*

The combination of two events this week – the precipitous transfer of power in Baghdad, two days ahead of the planned 30 June date, and the NATO summit in Istanbul – presented the American and British governments with an opportunity to claim that events were moving in their direction. The transfer of Saddam Hussein to Iraqi legal authority enhanced the 'good news' mood music.

But even this glimpse of progress for the leading coalition powers was overshadowed by problems. At the NATO summit, the attitude of key member-states meant that the United States did not even try to persuade the alliance to assume command of the multinational division in southern Iraq, still less to commit substantial numbers of troops to the country.

Moreover in relation to Afghanistan, where NATO already commands the International Security Assistance Force (ISAF) based in Kabul, there was a deep reluctance to more than a marginal increase in commitments. This is despite repeated requests from the Hamid Karzai administration, from non-governmental organisations (NGOs) and from the United Nations itself. In brief, what was widely reported as a NATO success was in reality very far from that.

An Endless Insurgency

As the summit gathered, violence in Iraq continued. A single period of 24 hours on 28–29 June is emblematic: three United States Marines were killed by a roadside bomb; two Iraqis were killed in a separate attack on a US military convoy near Baquba; a US soldier, Keith Maupin, was reported murdered after being taken hostage; and a British soldier was killed in southern Iraq, while Britain's foreign office named the security consultant killed the previous week.

There were further attacks against Iraqi targets, including a raid on a police station in Mahmudiya that killed a police officer and a civilian. A roadside bomb in Kirkuk was intended to assassinate Major Ahmed al-Hamawandi, the head of police in Azadi district. He escaped with injuries but one of his bodyguards was killed.

Washington continues to portray all this as little more than routine violence, while US sources emphasise the 'end of occupation' and the beginning of a new era. The truth of these claims will soon become clear; early indications are mostly negative, whatever the short-term 'spin'.

Indeed, it has become clear in recent weeks that Washington has consistently underestimated the insurgency in Iraq. Richard Armitage, Deputy Secretary of State, admitted as much to the Senate Armed Services Committee when he acknowledged that the insurgents' increased effectiveness and coordination reflected their 'central nervous system'. Other administration officials confirmed their inadequate understanding of the insurgency; 'they believe thousands of hidden fighters are more organized than previously thought...' (see Josh White, 'Iraqi Insurgents are Surprisingly Cohesive, Armitage Says', *Washington Post*, 26 June 2004).

The experience of American troops on the ground confirms this. In Baquba last week, more than 100 insurgents overran large parts of the town and maintained control for several hours. One journalist saw them as 'well-equipped and highly coordinated', demonstrating a 'new level of strength and tactical skill that alarmed the soldiers facing them' (see Scott Wilson, 'Adversary's Tactics Leave Troops Surprised, Exhausted', *Washington Post*, 25 June 2004).

Two other aspects of the insurgency are relevant. First, the current situation in Fallujah reveals that the Fallujah Protection Army (FPA), established with US agreement when the Marines failed to establish control of the city, is now working closely with anti-coalition mujahideen insurgents.

An Iraqi journalist reported from the city:

> de facto control of this predominantly Sunni town is exercised by the mujahidin, dressed in their trademark yishmagh headscarfs and armed with Kalashnikov rifles and rocket-propelled grenade launchers. Not only do they stand guard on the street, either with the FPA or by themselves, they also enforce their own brand of religious Puritanism on the town's inhabitants. (Naser Kadhem, Institute of War and Peace Reporting, June 2004)

Thus, a major population centre is now effectively under insurgent control, and it seems that insurgents themselves are progressively embracing more fundamentalist religious attitudes in a country with strong secular traditions.

The second notable aspect of the insurgency is the increase in hostage-taking. US officials believe that the earlier largely opportunistic kidnapping incidents started to coalesce into a pattern around two months ago: 'we have the impression now that there's a loose amalgamation where people can get picked up for any of a number of reasons and then enter an amorphous system that leads them to be handed off from one group to another and then they're evaluated for their value' (see Robin Wright, 'Abductions in Iraq Reflect New Strategy, U.S. Says', *Washington Post*, 30 June 2004).

The kidnappings could be interpreted as a response to the insurgents' tactical failures in other areas, but this is frankly unlikely. They are occurring in the context of an intensifying insurgency and are almost certainly designed (as are comparable attacks in Saudi Arabia) to provoke expatriates into leaving Iraq – further damaging the Iraqi economy just as the new interim government assumes nominal authority.

Iraq's Interim Government

A new Iraqi government is now in office, but the legacy of Paul Bremer's disbanded Coalition Provisional Authority (CPA) remains potent. Bremer's appointee as Iraq's prime minister, Iyad Allawi, has authority over two key posts – national security adviser and head of national intelligence – whose incumbents will serve a five-year term of office, whatever government takes power after any national election. Allawi is already raising the possibility of martial law, curfews and possible election delays, even as his new government would clearly require US troops to enforce such measures.

Furthermore, Paul Bremer's departure was preceded by a series of edicts placing his own nominees as inspectors-general in every Iraqi governmental ministry, again for five-year terms (see Rajiv Chandrasekaran and Walter Pincus, 'U.S. Edicts Curb Power of Iraq's Leadership', *Washington Post*, 27 June 2004). Perhaps the most telling decision is the enactment of an election law establishing a seven-member commission which will have the power to disqualify political parties. In short, a US-appointed prime minister with previous CIA links heads a cabinet that includes several members holding US citizenship, and oversees an administration permeated by a 'shadow' inspectorate secured by the departing CPA chief.

Meanwhile, as Paul Bremer flew out, John Negroponte entered. The new US ambassador takes charge of what is intended to be the largest embassy in any country in the world. Almost 1,000 Americans supported by 700 Iraqis will staff the new Baghdad mission; over $480 million is allocated to construct and protect it and numerous other American diplomatic sites across Iraq.

These missions are being established in Mosul, Kirkuk, Hilla and Basra; there will be five further regional diplomatic teams, in addition to 200 advisers working with Iraqi ministries. All this is highly indicative of the continuing and intensive US involvement in the country. It suggests, to put it in rather less than diplomatic language, that Iraq's 'interim government' is the outward face of a client regime.

Planning for Inflation

The course of the insurgency will help determine Iraq's political future. Perhaps the most interesting indicator here is the United

States' decision this week to prepare for the conscription of members of the individual ready reserve (IRR). This news was reported in only a few media outlets but was covered in much greater detail in papers directly serving the US armed forces (see *Stars and Stripes*, European edition, 30 June 2004).

The thousands of reservists who have already been called up are all best described as 'active' reservists. The army has, in addition, an IRR force of over 117,000 troops – 'servicemembers who have left active duty or active reserve service but still have time left on their obligation to serve'. The terms of the declaration of national emergency issued after the 9/11 attacks allow President Bush to order the activation of these troops, without their consent, for up to two years of consecutive service. On 29 June, one day after the handover in Baghdad, the Pentagon confirmed in an irony-free announcement that an initial cohort of 5,600 IRR members would be considered for 'activation'. More significantly, it is now known that the Pentagon has been pre-screening the entire 117,000-strong force for further troops.

Of all the developments in the past hectic week, this apparently small indicator may turn out to be the most significant of all. Whatever NATO leaders said in Istanbul, whatever Paul Bremer may have said or John Negroponte may yet say, the Pentagon is now preparing to expand the forces available to George W. Bush. United States military planners, at least, are readying for an increase, not a decrease, in the problems the 'war on terror' faces in Iraq – and quite possibly in Afghanistan too.

IRAQ: ECHOES OF VIETNAM *22 July 2004*

The decision by the United States-led coalition to transfer formal authority to a new client regime in Baghdad on 28 June – two days ahead of the pre-announced schedule and in conditions of some secrecy – seems guided by two motives: the desire to pre-empt any major insurgency actions to coincide with the planned date of 30 June, and the need for a 'good news' story at the NATO summit in Istanbul.

For around a week after the installation of Iyad Allawi's government, the intensity of the insurgency indeed abated, with fewer deaths among United States troops and no major bomb attacks on Iraqi security and political organisations. The Bush administration registered some satisfaction that the Allawi regime had been established without major incident.

The relative smoothness of the handover reinforced Washington's view of Allawi as its potential Iraqi 'strongman' who was likely to work closely with its new ambassador, John Negroponte – a career diplomat with extensive experience of working with autocratic regimes in Latin America. The process was not entirely without problems, foremost among them the Allawi regime's alacrity in introducing a range of emergency security measures, including curfews and martial law; there was even a hint that elections for a legitimate government, planned by the end of January 2005, might need to be delayed.

Such decisions hinted at the re-emergence of an authoritarian, even neo-Ba'athist, tendency in the designated Iraqi leadership. This sense was confirmed by persistent if unconfirmed reports of Allawi's severity over prisoners, extending even to summary executions. The emerging overall pattern in the weeks after 28 June was of a client regime adopting some responsibility for security in the context of heavy support by US forces, which included persistent air attacks on presumed insurgent 'safe houses' in Fallujah and other cities.

These indications of a relatively peaceful transition, and the absence of any sharp increase in violence after 28 June, came as a relief for the Bush administration. The Senate Intelligence Security Committee report on the activities of the CIA, and the national commission on terrorist attacks (reporting on 22 July) present problems of political management, but events in

Iraq itself offered a margin of optimism just in time for the run-up to the November 2004 election.

Three and a half weeks after the Allawi regime was inaugurated, the situation in Iraq looks rather bleaker for the United States. This deterioration can be expressed in three ways: casualty, budgetary, and recruitment. There have also been sustained attacks on Iraqi government officials, further economic targeting and – perhaps most significant of all – the consolidation of several areas of Iraq outside of the control of both the Allawi regime and the United States.

A Project Under Strain

At its peak, the military coalition which overthrew the Saddam regime in March–April 2003 and then took charge of Iraq comprised 32 countries. Many contributed only very small numbers of troops, and the numbers are diminishing further.

Spain, Nicaragua, the Dominican Republic and Honduras have already withdrawn their forces. The Philippines, after a hostage crisis involving one of its citizens, is withdrawing its small force ahead of schedule. Thailand does not intend to replace its 450 troops when they complete their deployment in September; the same month, New Zealand is withdrawing its 60 military engineers. In the least publicised move of all, Norway is extracting all but 15 of its 170 troops, and those remaining will be involved in training Iraqi security forces as part of a NATO commitment – the only significant initiative from NATO towards Iraq, whatever the 'spin' of the Istanbul summit. It is true that some countries, including Albania and Ukraine, are increasing their troop numbers in Iraq, but the overall extent of international support (inside and outside NATO) is clearly in decline.

Meanwhile, US military casualties in Iraq continue to rise, even though its forces have decreased their patrolling activity in some areas. The casualties stem mostly from roadside bombs but there has been a notable pattern of substantial mortar and rocket attacks on US bases. This week, US military deaths in Iraq since the start of the war exceeded 900. The number of combat injuries to US troops is now thought to be well over 4,000 (with many thousands more accidental injuries); most of the troops involved are being evacuated to Germany and then the United States.

These problems come at a time when the Pentagon is struggling to meet the costs of the continuing wars in Iraq and Afghanistan. Most of the additional $65 billion approved by Congress for the fiscal year ending in September 2004 has already been spent, and an estimated $12.3 billion is having to be found from within existing defence budgets.

The biggest problem lies with the army, which has overspent by $10.2 billion, mainly because of the very high costs of operations and maintenance, especially in Iraq. For the services as a whole, current cost-cutting includes deferring equipment repair, grounding some air force and navy pilots and limiting training.

At the same time, there has been a decrease in voluntary army recruits, with the pool of future recruits – those who have enlisted but have not yet joined training camps – declining by 23 per cent in the past year. The army expects to be able to meet its enlarged recruitment target for the year, but the inner concern is that recruiting is weak precisely at a time when the US armed forces as a whole are getting daily publicity across the country. The concern, in essence, is that the military involvement in Iraq is becoming unpopular, even among those sectors of society from which recruits would normally come.

This problem, moreover, arrives at a time when estimates of overall Iraqi support for the insurgency are being revised upwards. US officials have commonly talked about a core of 5,000 insurgents spread across the Sunni regions of Iraq, and of Shi'a militias in the south (such as Muqtada al-Sadr's 'Mahdi army') offering intermittent resistance. Officials now concede that insurgent forces are closer to 20,000 in number, and are able to call on wide community support in considerable parts of central Iraq.

A Spreading Insurgency

The casualty, budgetary and recruitment concerns are a serious matter for the US military. For Iraqis themselves, recently increased violence presents equally severe problems. On 14 July, the governor of the northern province of Nineveh, Osama Kashmoula, was assassinated; the same day, ten people died and 40 were injured in a Baghdad car bomb near the fortified 'green zone'. The next day, ten people were killed in the bombing of a police station in Haditha. On 17 July, a failed assassination attempt against the justice minister took the lives of four of his guards.

On 18 July, a senior defence ministry official, Essam al-Dijaili, was murdered in Baghdad. The following days have seen repeated attacks, involving the deaths of four government officials in Baquba and the assassination of a governing council member, Hazim Tawfeek Al-Ainichi, in Basra. This last operation was a further indication of the insurgents' sophistication: according to local sources, insurgents seized a checkpoint near his home during a shift change, dressed in police uniforms, shot their victim, and escaped.

Such assassinations are part of a wider process – six more councillors in Baghdad have been killed in the past few days, bringing the total number of councillors murdered in recent months to over 60 – from a total constituency of councillors in Baghdad of little more than 700.

As the assassinations and car bombs continue, so has economic targeting. In the past two weeks there have been two further pipeline attacks. In northern Iraq, a gas pipeline feeding power stations and a factory producing gas canisters were closed; this was followed by the destruction of another gas pipeline feeding the Baiji power plant. The persistence of the attacks on gas and oil pipelines is having two immediate effects – limiting oil export revenues, so damaging the Allawi administration's revenue base, and further hindering the restoration of power supplies across much of the country.

Beyond even the problems imposed by the American and Iraqi casualties and the economic sabotage, the most significant recent development is the consolidation of Fallujah, a city of 300,000 people, and its surrounding district in the hands of insurgents. Other Sunni towns like Samarra are also effectively no-go areas for US and Allawi forces; much of the Sadr city area of Baghdad, heavily populated by Shi'a, is under the effective control of militias loyal to Muqtada al-Sadr, working by agreement with local police units.

Fallujah, in particular, has taken on the status of a 'liberated' city, but it is also a city in which insurgent forces can plan, train and develop the equipment and tactics for export to other parts of Sunni central Iraq. In this light, the persistent US air raids appear almost entirely counterproductive in that they do not seem to be limiting the insurgency, but rather further antagonising the Iraqi population as a whole.

The Future in the Past

In relation to the repeatedly expressed optimism of the past 15 months, this entire combination of developments suggests an odd sense of history repeating itself.

In the immediate aftermath of the termination of the Saddam Hussein regime in April 2003, the insurgents were described as mere 'remnants' of the old regime that presented little in the way of a long-term problem. Then, in July, the killing of Uday and Qusay Hussein was expected greatly to diminish the insurgency. In the autumn, there were reports that the violence was confined to a handful of extended families that had been identified, were under surveillance, and would be brought under control. In December, the detention of Saddam Hussein himself was greeted with confidence that the resistance to the United States would be fatally damaged. Most recently, the transfer of 'sovereignty' to the Allawi regime was heralded as the prelude to a peaceful conversion from militancy to politics.

It is all, in short, eerily reminiscent of the early years of the Vietnam war. Analysts have been reluctant to draw comparisons between those early Vietnam years and Iraq, not least because of fundamental political differences in the two conflicts. In two respects, though – continuing false optimism and the potential length of the conflict – the similarities are becoming steadily more apparent.

IRAQ BETWEEN INSURGENCY AND UPRISING

12 August 2004

The past two weeks have seen a substantial upsurge in violence across many parts of Iraq, culminating in a major assault on the centre of Najaf on 12 August. The conflict's most visible centres have been Najaf itself, Kut and Baghdad, but the southern city of Basra and a number of towns across central Iraq have also been affected. The intensity of the fighting, at its highest since April 2004, indicates that the Iyad Allawi regime – only six weeks after its appointment in the 28 June handover – is already having to rely heavily on United States forces.

Moreover, some of the US's coalition partners have been unable to maintain security in their particular sectors. Most notably, Polish forces transferred control of two areas to the United States, citing their inability to ensure military stability amidst a deteriorating situation.

The Allawi regime itself has gradually instigated a number of security measures to help keep control of the highly volatile conditions in Iraq. These include a series of curfews, such as a stringent 16-hour per day order applied to the teeming, mainly Shi'a populated Sadr City district of Baghdad; the temporary cessation of oil exports from the southern oilfields because of safety concerns; the closure of the al-Jazeera satellite TV channel's offices in Baghdad on the grounds that it is insufficiently balanced in its news coverage; and (perhaps the regime's toughest move) the restoration of the death penalty, not simply for crimes of murder but including kidnapping and threats to state security within its remit.

It is not clear whether these measures reflect independent decisions of the Allawi regime, or whether they are being done at the behest of the US embassy led by its new ambassador, John Negroponte. Here, two factors are significant: US officials or their appointees operate at a senior level in every Iraqi government ministry, and the regime is dependent on American military forces in Iraq for its very survival.

A Transforming Battlefield

In a longer-term perspective, the past 15 months of conflict in Iraq have allowed the different insurgent groups to learn a wide range of tactics as they become more practised in urban guerrilla warfare. Their proficiency in political and military assassinations, in bomb-making and in the coordinated use of light arms has increased; they have also developed forms of economic targeting and kidnapping that have measurably hindered the pace of reconstruction – and more recently, bringing it almost to a halt. At the same time, the insurgents remain lightly-armed, have no armoured vehicles or body armour and are frequently using ageing equipment.

In response to these challenges, the far better equipped US forces have also adapted their tactics and technology in numerous ways, including increased reliance on Israeli tactics and equipment used to control the Palestinian intifada. In addition to overwhelming air and ground-based firepower, the US is deploying large numbers of the new, highly-mobile Stryker armoured personnel carrier, as well as numerous reconnaissance drones, a wide range of satellite and land-based intelligence equipment and massive quantities of modern ordnance.

Despite this technological superiority, the US forces have been handicapped by severe equipment problems, and these have reinforced their inability to control the insurgent forces in any of the major areas of operations. Two recent examples are illustrative of this. First, the vulnerabilities of the ubiquitous Humvee jeep mean that 3,000 of the Marine Corps Humvees in Iraq have had to be 'up-armoured' with bolt-on 9.52-millimetre steel plates and 12.7-centimetre thick bullet-resistant windows. These typically add more than 25 per cent to the weight of the vehicles, thus decreasing speed and endurance and increasing maintenance costs.

Second, the body armour that is routinely used by US forces has undoubtedly saved many American soldiers' lives, but it has also indirectly resulted in large numbers of severe injuries to arms, legs, faces and throats; many injured soldiers have been maimed for life. In response, a range of more comprehensive body armour is being developed, at the cost of adding further to its weight. An indication of the urgency of this research is the recent move to include protection for the shoulders and underarms; the military is demanding 138,000 sets to be available by January 2005 – sufficient for all soldiers at risk in Iraq and Afghanistan (*Defense News*, 26 July 2004).

If these two indications of how the US military is responding to the problems it is facing in Iraq are combined with a comparison of the situation now with that of a year ago, a wider perspective on the development of the conflict starts to emerge.

A Year of Tumult

In August 2003, it was becoming apparent that a major insurgency was developing. The month was marked by attacks on the Jordanian embassy, the United Nations headquarters in

Baghdad, and the mosque at Najaf; US forces were also taking increasing numbers of casualties.

This column reported a year ago that in the three months after President Bush made his victory speech on 1 May 2003 on the aircraft carrier *Abraham Lincoln*, 52 Americans had been killed in combat, and there had been 112 deaths from other causes – including 'friendly fire' and road accidents caused by speeding to avoid ambushes. Twice-weekly medivac flights were going to the United States, and the Walter Reed Army Hospital in Washington had had to clear non-emergency wards to handle casualties.

Although the intensity of this conflict twelve months ago was far lower than it is now, there was already concern that the Iraq insurgency could prove to be an obstacle to the fulfilment of the neo-conservative 'New American Century' project. Donald Rumsfeld's deputy, Paul Wolfowitz, outlined the stakes at the end of July 2003: '...the battle to secure peace in Iraq is now the central battle in the global war on terror, and those sacrifices are going to make not just the Middle East more stable, but our country safer'.

The astute commentator Thomas Friedman developed the theme in the *Washington Post* (25 August 2003), six days after the bombing of the UN headquarters: '...America's opponents know just what's at stake in the postwar struggle for Iraq, which is why they flock there: beat America's ideas in Iraq and you beat them out of the whole region; lose to America there, lose everywhere'.

What is the position one year on? Since the war started in March 2003, 932 US soldiers have died in combat with many hundreds more killed in accidents; over 750 have died in combat since President Bush's victory address. Accurate figures for injuries are difficult to obtain, but one recent report (*Los Angeles Times*, 8 August 2004) cited an assessment by Pentagon sources: 6,239 troops wounded in action in Afghanistan and Iraq, with over 3,500 of them so severely injured that they have to be retired from active duty. There have, in addition, been at least 10,000 soldiers evacuated to the United States from Iraq because of accidental injuries, and mental and physical illnesses.

These are the American casualties; those borne by the Iraqi people themselves are hugely greater still. Two months after the initial three-week termination of the Saddam Hussein regime, estimates of civilian Iraqi casualties extended to around 3,000 people. This figure now appears to be a serious underestimation. The Iraq Body Count group has carefully monitored civilian casualties in the initial phase of the war and since, offering details of a huge range of recorded incidents, including upper and lower estimates of civilian deaths.

The first three weeks of fighting in March–April 2003 appears to have killed between 7,000 and 9,000 Iraqis, a figure that has inexorably escalated; current estimates suggest an Iraqi death-toll of 11,500–13,500, with up to 500 people being killed each month. In addition, well over 20,000 people seem to have been seriously injured, and the total is rising rapidly.

The western media's capacity to report on the carnage has been restricted by continuing problems of kidnappings and assassinations, which have directly affected journalists. But some Arab stations, especially al-Jazeera, have maintained an effective presence – no doubt one reason for the Allawi regime's antagonism. Another consistently productive source has been the Institute for War & Peace Reporting's programme to train Iraqi journalists; some of them have been able to deliver graphic first-hand accounts of conditions in cities like Fallujah that are essentially under insurgent control.

Elsewhere, the reality of conditions in Iraq is often revealed through apparently marginal statistics. For example, more than a hundred of Iraq's university professors have been assassinated in the past year, adding to the profound crisis facing much of Iraq's higher education system, itself a key potential component in any redevelopment of the country (see 'Academia in Crisis', *Middle East International*, 6 August 2004).

Two other recent developments give an indication of long-term trends that could have substantial significance. First, the establishment in late 2003 of an 'Islamic Resistance Court' in western Iraq; this has extended its remit beyond domestic and other disputes to include cases related to alleged collaborators with US forces and other coalition interests. One case ended in the execution of the defendant and another concluded with the destruction of two trucks after their drivers were accused of working with the Americans. Although the court is clearly without official authority, it has extensive support in this region of Iraq.

Second, the increasing cross-community cooperation in the insurgency; this is revealed in the striking presence in Najaf of considerable numbers of Sunni insurgents from the Fallujah area whose military experience is being used to train members of the Shi'a 'Mahdi army' in Najaf. One group of nine officers and 40 soldiers from Fallujah is under the leadership of Colonel Rifaat al-Janabi, who still dresses openly in his Special Republican Guard uniform and is using his soldiers to instruct local Mahdi army militia in the use of equipment such as mortars and rocket-propelled grenades.

An assumption among many analysts of Iraq has been that different aspects of the insurgency, such as the April 2004 fighting in Fallujah and the current violence in Najaf, are essentially unconnected. Recent evidence suggests that there is such a connection; this implies that a quasi-nationalist cause may be starting to emerge that transcends the confessional communities and is becoming united in common opposition to the United States occupation and the Iyad Allawi regime.

If this is indeed so, then a transition from insurgency to a more general uprising is certainly possible. This would also do much to explain the determination of the US military to suppress the Mahdi army in Najaf, whatever the human and political costs.

From Najaf to Tehran?

In the light of all this evidence, an overview of the current position in Iraq one year after the bombing of the UN headquarters in August 2003 becomes clearer. At that time, the number of US casualties was relatively small though rising, while Paul Bremer (head of the Coalition Provisional Authority) and others were making persistent claims that the US-led coalition was facing merely diehard 'remnants' of the Saddam regime. A year later, the insurgency is still escalating. In response, US forces are operating under extreme pressure, employing large-scale firepower, and taking serious casualties as they support the client regime of Iyad Allawi.

This new Iraqi leadership, even with US military backing, is proving unable to maintain control across wide swathes of the country – including Fallujah, Ramadi, Samarra, Najaf and Baghdad's Sadr City. The experience of the past two weeks of tumult, in the context of a country where reconstruction and economic development is largely stagnant, indicates that the regime and the American military faces a growing insurgency that could develop into a national uprising.

At the same time, and quite extraordinarily, there is increasing talk among neo-conservative elements in Washington of the need to confront Iraq's neighbour, Iran. The use of military force to pre-empt Iran's presumed nuclear ambitions is being openly discussed, and some neo-cons see regime change in Tehran as necessary.

The existing range and depth of problems the US military is encountering in Iraq, and its continuing difficulties in Afghanistan, make it hard to understand how such thinking can survive – yet it does. The remarkable combination of proliferating problems in Iraq and a desire to extend the 'war on terror' to Iran makes one conclusion unavoidable. The assumption among many critics of the Bush administration that the neo-conservatives and their New American Century are thoroughly discredited and in retreat is both premature and singularly dangerous.

FOLLOW THE OIL *30 September 2004*

The leaders of the United States and Iraq, George W. Bush and Iyad Allawi, have declared strongly in recent days that Iraq is on the path to peace, reconstruction is making good progress and a democratic outcome is in sight. These statements are in remarkable contrast with those adopted by the US Secretary of State, Colin Powell, who acknowledges that the insurgency is intensifying, and the Defense Secretary, Donald Rumsfeld, who talks of limiting the January 2005 elections to 'safe' parts of Iraq.

The reality on the ground in Iraq supports Powell not Bush. The violence continues across Iraq to the extent that American military casualties have increased for the third month in a row. US air raids on insurgent strongholds such as Fallujah are now a near-daily occurrence. The predicament facing US troops is radically different from that expected at the onset of war in March 2003, and there is now a real prospect of a protracted conflict that would bear comparison with Vietnam.

In such circumstances it is worth standing back from the immediate problems in order to assess what options might seriously be available from the perspective of the Bush administration. In doing so, it makes sense to recall its expectations of the likely course of events in Iraq 18 months ago; to assess the immediate courses of action available before and after the November presidential election; and to examine a worst-case response if short-term tactics fail to achieve the desired result.

Going Wrong

The United States' prognosis in early 2003 was of the rapid destruction of the Saddam Hussein regime, followed by the establishment of permanent US military bases, the withdrawal of other occupying forces, and the instalment of a client regime. This latter could be achieved by an appropriately orchestrated democracy – perhaps not quite as crude as 'Florida 2000', but still one that achieved the required result.

This strategic calculation, fuelled by the US neo-conservative vision, was founded on a fourfold assessment of Iraq's huge geopolitical significance for the United States. First, the full exploitation of Iraq's undeveloped oil reserves, especially those under its western desert, would be a lucrative target for friendly multinational oil companies. Second, a client regime operating closely with Washington would nurture a fully free-market economy in a country of considerable potential wealth, with US business interests once again set to benefit.

Third, indirect control of an Iraq blessed by substantial oil reserves would enable the United States to exert long-term security influence across the Gulf region as a whole. Fourth, such a redrawing of the regional political map would greatly benefit Israel, and this would ensure the substantial support of evangelical Christian and pro-Israel communities across America's southern states.

Many articles in this series have charted the collision between this neo-conservative dream and the realities of post-Saddam Iraq. There is now a widespread consensus that the insurgency has moved far beyond the capability of US forces to control it. In response, the US administration is engaged in an effort of damage limitation designed to modify its policies in ways that might, from a Republican perspective, still produce valuable outcomes in the region – even if these fall well short of its initial hopes.

But this adjustment cannot possibly extend to a fully-fledged exit strategy, the wholesale withdrawal of US forces and the surrender of political and economic influence. Iraq is far too important for that – indeed such a result would represent a worse policy defeat than Vietnam and could be fatal to the ambition of creating a 'New American Century'.

Thinking Small

What, then, are the immediate and longer-term options for the Bush administration in seeking to retrieve the situation in Iraq? The policy until the election, as last week's article in this series proposed, will be to proclaim progress in Iraq, avoid major military confrontations, yet persist with powerful air raids against centres of insurgency. The assaults on Fallujah and elsewhere may be covered on satellite TV and in the press across the Middle East, but they cause barely a flicker of interest in the American media and are therefore a minimal hindrance in the re-election process.

If the election does guarantee a second term for George W Bush, there will then be a window of opportunity to take much stronger action, even at the cost of heavy civilian casualties. The key period will be the three months between the November election and the scheduled Iraqi elections by the end of January 2005.

During this period, the US could use heavy military force against major conurbations in insurgent hands, especially in the central region of Iraq and in key parts of Baghdad itself. This would involve ground forces as well as airpower and include the kind of intensified, widespread application of force that was employed briefly in Fallujah in April 2004. This would be accompanied by rapidly increased funding to train and equip more Iraqi army and paramilitary forces, with the aim of weakening the insurgency long enough to hold even incomplete elections.

In these circumstances, the Bush administration would again claim (as on 1 May 2003) 'mission accomplished', but with – this time – an elected Iraqi government now in power. It would characterise the many parts of Iraq that might be too insecure for elections as undeserving of the opportunity to vote since they had shown themselves, by their support for the insurgency, to be anti-democratic.

This overall prospectus for early 2005 might be called the United States' 'Plan A'. In it, the insurgency might still be evolving towards a civil war, and the American forces might be playing a less central role; but the US could still ensure the survival of the post-Allawi (or reborn Allawi) regime. This outcome would still allow the US to retain impressive influence in Iraq, even though far less than the neo-cons' 'Greater Middle East Initiative' envisaged.

Looking West

In the present circumstance of relentless violence this would represent an optimistic outcome. But Washington's long-term thinking must go beyond this, and embrace the possibility that any escalation of the use of heavy military force in the coming months would still not contain a growing insurgency. This scenario entails a deeply unstable post-election Iraqi government, and constant attacks on the US forces supporting it – requiring, in turn, reinforcements that might even involve the reintroduction of the US draft.

If US planners judged this to be a more likely outcome, what then might be their 'Plan B'? If a second Bush administration was faced with such an untenable situation in Iraq, its remaining option might be to implement a strategy guided by a sense of its essential requirement: ensuring access not just to Iraq's current oilfields but to potentially lucrative areas of oil exploration in the country's western desert.

It is here that geography is significant. Iraq currently has two major regions of oil production, each outside the 'Sunni triangle' and relatively sparsely-populated: in the south-east (mainly in open country around Basra) and in the north (the Kirkuk–Mosul axis, bordering on areas of Kurdish settlement).

A coherent strategy could establish a degree of security over these oilfields and ease problems of distribution by developing new supply routes – even if the more populous parts of Iraq were suffering from long-term insurgency and civil war.

But a third area of Iraq has a potential for oil production that may equal or even exceed the existing two regions. This is the western desert, and an area of very low population density. Its oil reserves could in principle be exploited with almost no involvement from the people of Iraq, although a client government could help its survival against internal challenge by accruing benefits from export revenues.

This 'Plan B' scenario, unfolding during a second Bush term, would entail the effective disengagement of US military forces from the continuing insurgency/civil war, and a refocus on securing the rich oilfields for the US's immediate and long-term benefit. It is worth remembering here that at least four permanent US military bases are currently being established in Iraq. One is north of Baghdad, two others are close to the northern and southern oilfields, and a fourth is located towards the Syrian border – a gateway, if such were needed, to the western desert.

In this projection of developments, the United States military would be responsible for the security of Iraqi oil (current and future) but have minimal involvement in the main centres of population. It is a far less ambitious vision than the neo-conservatives once embraced, yet it would keep alive one of the essential strategic objectives behind the removal of the Saddam Hussein regime in the first place.

But would it work? This is harder to say. It would still involve a substantial US military presence in the heart of the Arab world, and be seen across the Middle East as a less comprehensive but still vigorous attempt to maintain geopolitical control of a key part of the region. That reality alone would be a remarkable recruiting tool both for Iraqi insurgents and for the wider network of al-Qaida associates and franchises. On present evidence, it would not work, but rather ensure the continuation of bitter, long-lasting war.

But a second Bush administration will have no alternative to staying in Iraq and making the best of its predicament. A fully-fledged withdrawal from Iraq is simply not an option – the country and the wider region are just too important for the current Washington leadership. In the absence of wiser counsel, the Iraq disaster will persist, with all the human costs to ordinary people in Iraq and elsewhere. Without a change of policy, leadership, understanding or heart, it could continue even as Jeb Bush marches into the White House in 2008.

7
Fallujah

INTRODUCTION

The five-week period from 25 October 2004 was notable for three quite separate reasons. One was the re-election of President George W. Bush for a second term, a second was a sweeping statement from Osama bin Laden, and the third was a major assault by US forces on the Iraqi city of Fallujah, seen as the core centre of the insurgency.

President Bush's return to the White House was on a clear if small overall majority of the votes, and this was enough to convince the neo-conservative wing of the Republican Party that there was now a popular mandate to pursue the dream of a New American Century. Although Osama bin Laden's pre-election video was a salutary reminder of the continued vitality of the al-Qaida movement, it had little effect on the US election except, perhaps, to consolidate support for George W. Bush. This might well have been one of the aims, given that al-Qaida was already benefiting from the considerable US military presence in the heart of the Islamic world.

In Iraq itself, there had been indications of an impending US assault on the rebel city of Fallujah, and this commenced within days of the election. After a period of fierce conflict, the city was taken over by US forces, backed up by some Iraqi units, but the insurgency immediately resurfaced in other cities, most notably Mosul. The early indications by the end of November were that the taking of Fallujah was doing little to stem the insurgency, in spite of the most protracted and intensive use of US military power since the start of the war.

IRAQ'S SPIRAL OF VIOLENCE *21 October 2004*

The last week in Iraq has seen the continuation of a pattern that has lasted for some months: persistent violence combined with only limited reporting of events. There have been attacks within the Baghdad 'green zone', repeated assaults on Iraqi police and national guard centres, further kidnappings and regular mortar, small arms and bomb attacks on United States personnel. But only a small part of the insurgency is now covered in detail, mainly by media outlets in the Middle East and some specialist western sources, although the main BBC news website is proving unusually comprehensive in its coverage of attacks.

In the past three months alone, over 200 American troops have been killed and considerably over 1,000 injured. The Iraqi casualties are far greater. Iraq's Ministry of Health published casualty figures until the start of October 2004, but – possibly to avoid political embarrassment – it has now stopped. The 22 weeks up to 6 September revealed a death toll of 3,040 Iraqis in war-related incidents, including 159 women and 128 children. The figures include deaths from insurgent action as well as coalition air and ground strikes; they average 138 a week across this period (*International Herald Tribune*, 20 October 2004).

After the suspension of the Ministry of Health publication, the *New York Times* has attempted to gather its own record of casualties from numerous sources, including hospitals. For the week up to 17 October, it calculated that 208 Iraqis were killed. At the very least, this suggests that the earlier ministry figures were not in any sense overestimates. It also suggests that the ongoing war in Iraq, even at its current intensity, is killing over 7,000 civilians each year.

The Solution is Force

In its Iraq campaign, the US military has sustained a regular level of air strikes on the city of Fallujah, while also continuing ground bombardments there and in Ramadi. It is determined to use particularly heavy military force to disrupt the insurgency, and the forthcoming centrepiece of its actions is likely to be a major assault on Fallujah, probably just after the presidential election on 2 November.

The lead force in this operation will be elements of the United States Marine Corps, the branch of the American armed forces that in the past has taken an especially hard line in urban warfare. This, moreover, comes at a time of sustained US military casualties, with troop units throughout central Iraq being targeted in frequent attacks. In these uncertain and dangerous conditions, where troops will be primarily concerned to minimise their own casualties, the inevitable result is the use of concentrated firepower and the likelihood of substantial civilian casualties.

The return to this strategy of concentrated force is the product of a perception that has been spreading through US military intelligence and leadership circles in the past three months. This sees the insurgency as focused on a few geographical locations such as Fallujah, but with effects that permeate across central Iraq and are becoming steadily more dangerous. It also emphasises the importance of external, non-Iraqi fighters; here, the current notoriety accorded to Abu Musab al-Zarqawi replicates the targeting of earlier public enemies like the Taliban's Mullah Omar and Osama bin Laden himself. In this context, Fallujah is seen as particularly significant because Zarqawi and other foreign paramilitaries are said to be hugely influential there.

This developing mindset among the US elite is challenged by a number of analysts, as well as by the few journalists who have recently worked in Fallujah. One report by a local journalist relayed through the BBC's Arabic service offers a relevant insight into current conditions (18 October 2004). It seems that different clans in Fallujah have their own militias, but they are working together against US forces; relations between the police and militias are good. The reporter was not aware of any foreign fighters in the city and said that any who are present 'have blended in very well with the locals'.

Despite such testimony, and given the timetable to planned Iraqi elections by the end of January 2005, the US seems fixated on the idea that the insurgency can be curbed by 'taking out' such centres as Fallujah. This assessment is reminiscent of the approach taken during the Vietnam war, as well as earlier phases of the Iraqi campaign itself.

It also suggests that, to put it no more strongly, the US leadership is completely misreading a developing insurgency that is much more deep-seated than it thinks, may not actually have important 'centres', and may simply not be controllable by the application of superior military force. In addition, the human and physical damage that will ensue from the use of force may in the longer term further strengthen Iraqi opposition to the US presence.

The strength and persistence of that opposition is demonstrated by another factor that has received surprisingly little attention – the presence of substantial numbers of people prepared for 'martyr' or suicide operations. A recent calculation has found at least 125 suicide bomb attacks on Iraqi and US forces in the past 16 months, many of them directed against the Iraqi police force, which has had over 750 officers killed in the period (*International Herald Tribune*, 10 October 2004).

Very little is known about the people prepared to take this action but there is no indication of any decrease in the numbers willing to do so. Moreover, the attacks are spread across much of Iraq, extending to the north of the country, and may not be coordinated by any one group. This presents huge intelligence difficulties for the US military, who may be dealing with a phenomenon that is even more amorphous than the traditional, and already often impenetrable, guerrilla 'cell' structure.

The significance of this trend is that it has already evolved to a higher degree than among Palestinian groups in Gaza and the West Bank, and militants in Afghanistan. Its intensity in Iraq is perhaps matched only by the Liberation Tigers of Tamil Eelam (LTTE) in Sri Lanka – and the phenomenon there was established only in the course of many years of conflict. If US forces now opt for the massive use of military power against Fallujah and other centres of resistance, an almost certain response will be an increase in popular radicalisation that will include many more candidates for suicide attacks.

This response is also unlikely to be short-term. Overwhelming American firepower may well give the appearance of 'success' against the insurgency – possibly enough to assist the staging of elections in January. But the underlying reality is that such a United States strategy will be deeply flawed, and incapable of achieving its central objective: controlling the Iraqi insurgency.

Britain's Crucial Decision

In this context, the political dispute in Britain about a US invitation to redeploy British troops in southern Iraq to aid the US forces in central Iraq is significant. Whether or not the request is related to the presidential election, British government compliance – although initially involving a battalion of around 850 troops – would represent a significant change in the nature of British operations.

The redeployment would entail a coalition partner committing troops to US command just ahead of a specific intensification of US military operations in the heartland of the Sunni insurgency. If these operations do succeed in their immediate aim of securing central Iraq for the planned Iraqi elections, then the impact on this change in British policy may not be felt for some months. If they fail, the implications for the UK position could be fundamental. If the Tony Blair government does accept the United States request, the result will be that Britain will be much more heavily involved in a Washington-designed military strategy that shows every sign of being deeply counter-productive.

FOUR MORE YEARS FOR AL-QAIDA *4 November 2004*

As the Bush administration moves towards its second term following the election of 2 November, the period between now and the presidential inauguration in January 2005 will be significant for two quite different reasons: political and military.

The first is the composition of the new cabinet, and especially whether Colin Powell and Donald Rumsfeld retain their positions. The new appointments will give a good indication of the power of the neo-conservatives; the likelihood is that Dick Cheney, the vice-president, will retain sufficient power to ensure a cabinet this is markedly to the liking of Washington's neo-con community.

The second is the determined effort that United States forces will certainly make to contain the Iraq insurgency in the run-up to the planned elections by the end of January 2005. The past few days alone have seen a number of serious incidents: the assassination of the Deputy Governor of Baghdad and of a senior oil ministry official; major attacks on oil facilities; the bombing of the Education Ministry, killing eight people; and numerous kidnappings. All this is in addition to frequent attacks on US troops and the Iraqi police and security forces.

In response, the cities of Fallujah, Ramadi and Samarra are expected to be subject to intense military action. The assault on Fallujah may now be imminent, with the heaviest US bombardment for several weeks reported the day after Bush's re-election. The most recent attacks have included artillery bombardments as well as the use of the AC-130 gunship.

Beyond Iraq, there have been three developments in the broader al-Qaida-linked insurgencies. In southern Thailand, a deputy village leader was murdered on 2 November in retaliation for the suffocating to death of 78 Muslim detainees in army custody (and the killing of seven others). The next day, two police officers, a government official and four civilians were killed in four separate attacks. In the Philippines, fighting has erupted between government troops and militias of the Moro Islamic Liberation Front (MILF), just before planned peace talks designed to consolidate a two-year-old truce.

But perhaps the most significant development has been the release of the full transcript of Osama bin Laden's video address. The shortened version shown on al-Jazeera on the weekend before the United States election attracted fervid publicity and may have favoured George W. Bush. But behind the headlines, the extended version is notable for several more subtle elements.

A Political Sermon

In the broadcast, Osama bin Laden appears in an almost authoritative light, using a lectern and avoiding camouflage gear or any display of armaments. Alongside direct condemnation of President Bush and castigation of Arab elites, bin Laden makes pointed references to the 1982 Israeli invasion of Lebanon and siege of West Beirut. This last reference in particular would resonate with Arab audiences by connecting the Israeli destruction of high-rise buildings in Beirut, part of a protracted military action in July–August 1982 that killed well over 10,000 people, with the 2001 destruction of the World Trade Center towers.

This rhetorical connection is skilful in two ways. First is its retrospective linkage of the United States to Israel's 1982 operation in Lebanon, which the US had tacitly backed. By making this connection, bin Laden seeks to establish that the much-vaunted American–Zionist axis has existed for decades, and that the 9/11 attacks were little more than reasonable responses to an alliance that was already evident more than 20 years ago.

The second skilful element is that both the United States and Israel suffered 'defeats' in the months and years after the 1982 campaign. In 1983, the United States Marine Corps lost 241 troops in a suicide-bomb attack on its barracks at Beirut airport, leading to the US's subsequent withdrawal from Lebanon; by 1985, the Israeli armed forces had encountered such difficulty in controlling southern Lebanon in the face of Hezbollah guerrilla action that they withdrew from most of the territory they had occupied.

Beyond the United States–Israel linkage, the full transcript of Osama bin Laden's speech contains a wide-ranging presentation of al-Qaida thinking and policy. Bin Laden's determined effort to sound almost reasonable, if not actually statesmanlike, is reflected in his reference to interviews he gave to CNN and *Time* magazine in the mid-1990s.

More substantially, he relates the 1991 and 2003 wars with Iraq, conjoining the current President Bush's actions with those of his father, and describing the termination of the Saddam Hussein regime as the installation of 'a new puppet to assist in the pilfering of Iraq's oil'.

Here as elsewhere, the transcript relates closely to events and activities across the western world. He quotes from lectures given at the Royal Institute of International Affairs (RIIA); quotes casualty figures in Iraq gathered by Iraq Body Count; and even reminds his audience that many people in the west argued that Bush could have achieved the removal of Iraqi weapons of mass destruction by using the inspection process, 'but the darkness of the black gold blurred his vision and insight, and he gave priority to private interests over the public interests of America'.

The theme of a war for oil is repeated later in the text and linked to the human costs of the Iraq war:

> So I say to you, over 15,000 of our people have been killed and tens of thousands injured, while more than 1,000 of you have been killed and more than 10,000 injured. And Bush's hands are stained with the blood of all those killed from both sides, all for the sake of oil and keeping their private companies in business.

There are other aspects of note in the address, not least its emphasis on the punishing monetary costs of the war to the United States. The conflict may be greatly profitable to private corporations but bin Laden points acidly to the rapidly rising federal deficit, seeming to argue that one aim of al-Qaida is to cripple the United States through inflicting inordinate costs on its war on terror.

In one of the most interesting parts of the entire statement, he seems almost to toy with Washington, presenting the Bush administration and the US military with imaginary targets to drain their resources.

> All that we have mentioned has made it easy for us to provoke and bait this administration. All that we have to do is to send two mujahideen to the furthest point east to raise a piece of cloth on which is written al-Qaida, in order to make the generals race there to cause America to suffer human, economic and political losses without their achieving for it anything of note other than some benefits for their private companies.

Al-Qaida's Brand Extension

Although bin Laden's statement has much to say directly about the United States, perhaps its most significant aspects are those revealing a desire, and perhaps a need, for al-Qaida to embrace new causes. The emphasis on Israel and Lebanon, for example, implies tacit if indirect support for the Palestinian cause and for

Hezbollah in southern Lebanon. Neither of those constituencies has had much regard for al-Qaida, but bin Laden continues to try to suggest the connection to his wider Islamic audience.

It is also significant that bin Laden is now putting so much emphasis on Iraq, and making a connection between the Iraq war and the control of oil resources. This is a mirror image of the Bush administration's own periodic efforts to emphasise the involvement of foreign militias in the Iraq insurgency, even in the absence of much substantial evidence; bin Laden evidently wants to do exactly the same because it demonstrates the involvement of al-Qaida in the foreign policy issue that is impacting most on the United States media.

Al-Qaida may be more a loose network of affiliates motivated by an evolving religious ideology than a coherently-structured organisation with a precise hierarchy and close day-to-day coordination. Such an entity is extraordinarily difficult to counter by traditional counter-terrorism tactics. Instead it requires an understanding of the factors underpinning the support for its ideas – ideas that are becoming increasingly pervasive across the Middle East, and even beyond.

For different reasons, though, both 'sides' need to present an image of al-Qaida as a powerful, unified and effective organisation. Osama bin Laden needs it to demonstrate his strength and authority, George W. Bush needs it as a focus for his occupation of Iraq. In a sense, each needs the other. President Bush's re-election on 2 November 2004 is undoubtedly important for international relations in the next four years. So, in its own way, is bin Laden's videotaped message.

FALLUJAH FALLOUT *11 November 2004*

The United States military assault on the city of Fallujah has lasted four days and is still underway. American sources indicate that it may take several more days for their side to secure control of the city. The extensive reporting of the fighting in the western media relies heavily on reports from journalists embedded with US troops and operating under restrictions, with only a few outlets able to send reliable information from inside the city. Far more such information is available to regional news channels like al-Jazeera.

Amidst the battle, three developments are clear which in combination are likely to have significant effects within Iraq and beyond. First, the US military has gathered together forces massively greater than in April 2004 when the Marines were unable to gain control of the city. It now has up to 15,000 troops available, compared with 3,000 seven months ago. This points to an absolute determination to take control of the city and recalls the doctrine of massive force applied in the 1991 Iraq war.

Second, the US's primary tactic is to make steady advances into the urban environment, deploying large-scale force to saturate and destroy any elements of resistance. Tanks, cannon, howitzers, helicopters, strike aircraft and the powerful AC-130 gunships are all in repeated, systematic use in a dense urban environment in this 'city of the mosques'. Sources within the city suggest that as many as a tenth of its buildings are destroyed and half of its mosques damaged.

Third, Fallujah has acquired an almost iconic significance for the Bush administration, which seems fixated on the belief that controlling the city will curb the Iraqi insurgency. President Bush's re-election reinforces the determination to conquer this centre of resistance.

The Lesson of Samarra

There is no doubt that, even if it takes several days to complete the operation, the United States has the military capability to subdue Fallujah. Already, though, there are many indications that such an outcome will have a minimal impact on the insurgency – and may even be deeply counterproductive.

The last week has seen an intensity of violence and attacks across Iraq that compares with any similar period since the termination of the Saddam Hussein regime.

A single day, 6 November, is illustrative. In Haditha, up to 200 insurgents attacked a police station, killing 21 officers. Another police officer was killed in Baquba, and an attack on a police post in Haqlaniya killed Brigadier Shaher al-Jughaifi, the security chief for western Iraq.

Perhaps the most significant of the day's events was the multiple, coordinated bombings in Samarra, 100 kilometres north of Baghdad. These killed 30 people, more than half of them police officers; it was later reported that the commander of the Iraqi National Guard in the city, Abdek Razeq Shaker Garmali, was among them.

The relevance of Samarra is that it was the site of a US military operation at the end of September that, on a smaller scale, was remarkably similar to the current assault on Fallujah. Its occasion was the presence of several hundred insurgents in the city, to be targeted by a force of 3,000 American and 2,000 Iraqi troops. The operation to take over Samarra lasted three days, by which time the US forces claimed to control 70 per cent of the city, before handing authority to the Iraqis.

The achievement was short-lived. The insurgents filtered back into the city and, just as the current assault on Fallujah was being finalised, were able to demonstrate their continued presence with formidable force. Even after the Fallujah operation had started, reports suggested that several hundred insurgents had assumed control of large parts of the nearby city of Ramadi; there were strong indications that some of the militias active in Fallujah had simply moved to other localities.

A Clash of Perspectives

Notwithstanding the events in Samarra and Ramadi, the Bush administration's focus clearly remains on Fallujah. But independently of immediate events there, the wider significance of the battle for the city may lie in the very different ways it is framed in the west and in the Arab world.

From a US military perspective, the enemy in Fallujah are 'terrorists'. Both senior military officers, and ordinary soldiers and Marines, regularly employ the term in military briefings and media interviews. The implication is that any form of opposition to US forces in Iraq is, by definition, terrorist in nature, and that all counter-insurgency operations are part of the 'war on terror'.

This linguistic shift allows all insurgents to be considered on a par with those extreme elements that kidnap and decapitate foreigners. It has a dual effect: eliminating the idea that any insurgents can be seen as resisting an occupation of their country, and making it easier to justify the use of massive force against them.

This mindset may be shared by some sectors of the domestic audiences in the United States and some European countries who see vivid television images of the firepower deployed by US troops as they move into Fallujah. But across the Middle East and in much of the 'majority world', the message of such images is totally different. In the Arab world, in particular, Fallujah is seen as a foreign army of occupation using massive force to suppress legitimate opposition to that occupation. If to one audience Iraq appears very much a case of 'might is right', to the other it is graphic evidence of the determination of the United States to control a major Arab state in the heart of its region.

The longer-term implication of this divergence of views is clear. Within Iraq, the evidence indicates that the act of subordinating Fallujah will do virtually nothing to curb the insurgency but is more likely to enhance it. More generally, in much of the Arab and Islamic world it will be seen as yet another example of foreign control, further increasing bitterness and frustration towards the United States.

Fallujah, in short, will help create the next generation of militants and a new wave of recruits for al-Qaida and its affiliates. If, at some time in the next decade, the United States loses a whole city rather than two high-rise office blocks, the origins of that tragedy may well be traced back to the impact of what is now happening in Iraq.

DREAMS AND REALITIES *18 November 2004*

After the termination of the Saddam Hussein regime, United States policy in Iraq as seen by the more neo-conservative thinkers in Washington had three features. The first was the development of a regime in Baghdad that would embrace elements of democracy but would essentially be a client regime of Washington, increasing United States influence in the region and serving as a potent warning to neighbouring Iran.

The second was the reorganisation of Iraq as a model free-market economy with an absolute minimum of trade, investment and employment restrictions. What could not be achieved in the United States because of all the limitations of a federal system, trade unions and legal protection, could certainly be achieved in Iraq. This would serve as a beacon for a wider free-market economy across the Middle East operating under strong American influence.

The third was the establishment of at least four permanent military bases in Iraq that would ensure that the whole endeavour had an adequate security foundation. These would be designed, in part, as 'stand-by' facilities, into which very powerful military forces could be deployed if required. This US presence in the heart of the region would make it possible partially to sideline a potentially unstable Saudi Arabia while having the capability to influence regime change in states such as Syria and Iran.

The context in which these objectives were expected to be advanced was that Iraq itself would rapidly be restored to stability, allowing the great majority of US troops to be withdrawn from Iraq within a year, leaving only a few thousand at the newly-established bases.

A Prison of Self-Belief

Twenty months after the start of the war, the evident failure of this plan intersects with political developments in Washington – the re-election of George W. Bush on a secure mandate, the retirement of Colin Powell, the proposed appointment of Condoleezza Rice as Secretary of State, and what amounts to a purge of people in the intelligence agencies who are not in tune with the neo-conservative outlook.

The result is a reinforced determination by the Bush administration to preserve elements of the original plan, in which 'retrieving' the position in Iraq is the dominant component. Fallujah is a central element of its thinking, so what has happened there and its likely aftermath will clarify whether the neo-con dream of a 'Greater Middle East Initiative' can be rescued from its current deep predicament.

The clear-cut American strategy in Iraq has four elements: first, to destroy the insurgency, or at least cripple it to the point where it has little consequence for security in Iraq; second, to build up Iraqi security forces to the point where they can take over most security functions; third, to develop local government administrations preparing the way for elections (*Washington Post*, 17 November 2004); fourth, to withdraw most US forces, but leaving the permanent military bases and US officials deeply embedded in Iraqi governance, while returning to the 'original' plans for Iraq. In current circumstances all this may seem far-fetched, but there is a surge of exuberant self-belief in post-election Washington – a feeling of 'let's roll' that can easily ignore or dismiss difficult realities.

After the Siege

In seeking to achieve these four steps, Fallujah acquired an almost mythical status as an apparently undefeatable rebel stronghold. United States planners calculated that destroying this base of thousands of terrorists would cripple the insurgency and allow US troops to gain military ascendancy across much of the country. The insurgency might not be finished, but the loss of Fallujah would be a blow from which it could not recover.

This plan seemed to be proceeding as expected for the first two days of the latest Fallujah operation. By 11 November, it was reported that 'American forces cornered insurgents in a small section of Fallujah after a stunningly swift advance in which they seized control of 70 percent of the military stronghold...' (*International Herald Tribune*, 11 November 2004).

Even then, it seemed that insurgent forces in the city numbered fewer than 2,000, against up to 15,000 American and Iraqi troops. Most insurgents had apparently already left, yet it still took more than a week for the city to be subdued in spite of overwhelming firepower available to the US forces. There are claims that more than 1,000 insurgents have been killed in the past nine days. There is no way of corroborating this but three aspects of the Fallujah attack are already evident.

First, the insurgents fought with near-suicidal commitment, armed only with light weapons and facing the most modern and best-equipped military forces in the world while vastly outnumbered. The ability of the US forces to take control of Fallujah was never in doubt, but the level of resistance they faced shows that a committed insurgency operating in an urban environment can only be countered with very powerful weapons.

The second is that the US military has suffered serious casualties in Fallujah and elsewhere in Iraq. In the first sixteen days of November, US forces have had eighty-two soldiers killed, the worst rate of loss since March 2003, exceeding even the intensity of April 2004's bitter fighting. In Fallujah itself, there have been well over 200 seriously-injured soldiers, and from Iraq as a whole over 400 were airlifted out of Iraq to the medical receiving centre in Germany.

These injuries may be small compared with the number of insurgents killed, but the availability of body armour and expert battlefield medicine means that most wounded US soldiers survive whereas wounded insurgents die. A consequence of US capabilities is that very many of the American wounded have lost limbs, or have severe face, neck or groin injuries.

While this ongoing toll of injured soldiery – now approaching 10,000 overall – gets little media coverage, it is well known to the military and is one of the reasons why the Pentagon is experiencing increasing difficulty in calling up reserves. In recent months, 1,800 out of 4,000 reservists recalled to duty have sought exemption or delay; of those due to report for duty by 7 November, nearly one-third simply did not turn up (*International Herald Tribune*, 17 November 2004).

The third aspect of the Fallujah siege is that it has been accompanied by an upsurge of violence across the Sunni areas of Iraq that reveals the predominantly indigenous character of the insurgency. The relocation of many insurgents from Fallujah before the US assault started may be linked to the sustained attacks in Mosul, Baquba, Suweira and elsewhere. Mosul has been the most significant centre, with up to 2,000 insurgents taking control of many parts of Iraq's third city.

United States forces have had to be diverted to subdue this upsurge, but it is doubtful that they have the military capability to bring other cities under control using the methods they used in Fallujah. The intensity of the urban fighting means that the resources required are too great. The result is an increased reliance on crude firepower, and an increased number of air strikes against targets in other urban areas across central Iraq.

Fallujah's Legacy

The intense violence of the past few days presents an insight into the accelerating insurgency. American sources have often stressed the existence of foreign paramilitaries in Iraq, in some cases even suggesting that they now dominate the insurgency, making Iraq the core battleground of the 'war on terror'. The last few days show a very different picture – as few as one in 20 prisoners captured are non-Iraqis.

The implications of this are twofold. It means that the insurgency in Iraq is still largely internal, but also that any significant involvement of foreign, Islamic paramilitaries may be yet to come. The impact of the destruction of Fallujah and the effects of occupation on the Arab world makes it probable that their presence will indeed become progressively more significant.

In the longer term – and this means years rather than months – it is likely that Iraq will indeed become a focus of paramilitary resistance. The second Bush administration may hold on to its dream of a stable client state in Iraq forming the centrepiece of US influence in the Middle East. The reality is likely to be a bitter and costly war that could well define the entire eight-year presidency of George W. Bush. Within that legacy, the taking of Fallujah in November 2004 may have an enduring significance.

NO DIRECTION HOME *25 November 2004*

The major United States assault on the Iraqi city of Fallujah has still not quelled all resistance after more than two weeks. As fighting continues in some parts of the city, it is clear that large numbers of Marines will need to be kept there to prevent a rapid return of the insurgents. Meanwhile, other operations involving several thousand American, Iraqi and British troops are underway south of Baghdad. All this takes place amidst claims by senior military commanders in Iraq that Fallujah was a 'success' and the insurgents are now in retreat.

This assessment is even being used to justify an increase in US military forces in Iraq of up to 5,000 more troops (*Washington Post*, 22 November 2004). One senior military officer says: 'What's important is to keep the pressure on these guys now that we've taken Fallujah from them... We're in the pursuit phase. We have to stay after these guys so they don't get their feet set.'

The issue of troop reinforcements is deeply sensitive, especially so soon after President Bush's re-election. The extraordinary idea that Fallujah is a 'success' may well be linked to a wider need to portray the demand for more troops as a signal of the US's determination in Iraq, rather than its dire problems. In any case, the situation on the ground – especially in the largely Sunni areas of central Iraq extending northwards to Mosul – is anything but stable.

The recent experience of Mosul is illustrative of the predicament of the US military forces. At the height of the Fallujah assault, insurgents occupied parts of the city and the US military had to move 2,400 additional troops to counter the sudden upsurge. Thus, rather than being able to go on the offensive in the wake of the Fallujah attacks, the troops needed to respond to the unexpected initiative of insurgents.

Indeed, early indications are that the assault on Fallujah has done little to restrict the insurgency. Before the operation, there were up to 80 insurgent attacks each day on US, Iraqi and other coalition forces; during it, the number surged to 130; now, it has declined to the preceding level. US losses in Fallujah so far are 51 killed and 425 injured, most of the latter serious.

An Army in Overload

This is only one example of the continuing attrition of United States forces in Iraq. Over 1,200 troops have been killed and 8,500 wounded in action since March 2003, with over 15,000 more troops evacuated to the United States because of non-combat injuries and physical or mental health problems, only a fifth of whom return to their units in Iraq (CBS News, 21 November 2004). Thus, total US casualties number 25,000 people.

The effects of the war on the mental health of US soldiers are now being recognised as a serious crisis:

> A study by the Walter Reed Army Institute of Research found that 15.6% of Marines and 17.1% of soldiers surveyed after they returned from Iraq suffered major depression, generalized anxiety or post-traumatic stress disorder – a debilitating sometimes lifelong change in the brain's chemistry that can include flashbacks, sleep disorders, panic attacks, violent outbursts, acute anxiety and emotional numbness. (*Los Angeles Times*, 14 November 2004)

The actual effects are likely to be even greater than this survey indicates; the research involved only those troops willing to come forward and was conducted only among troops serving in Iraq early in the war, before the insurgency escalated.

Meanwhile, further indications of military overstretch are revealed in hearings of the House Armed Services Committee (18 November 2004). The Pentagon alone is spending $5.8 billion a month on its forces in Iraq but testimony from service chiefs indicates that much more money would be needed. The army's chief of staff, General Peter J. Schoomaker, testified that intense efforts to upgrade the armour on its fleet of 8,000 Humvees are less than half complete. The sheer corrosion of equipment in use is much higher than anticipated; the army is currently seeking a further 41,600 radios, 25,000 machine guns and 33,500 M-4 carbines.

The Human Costs of War

The number of civilian casualties in Fallujah is still unclear. An unconfirmed report suggests that 73 women and children killed during the fighting were buried by villagers from a settlement close to Fallujah; a separate, unofficial estimate from Red Cross sources in Iraq estimate that 800 civilians have been killed.

The US military has persistently said that Fallujah was, insurgents aside, virtually deserted at the start of the assault. A significant statistic cast doubt on this. By 21 November, US forces had detained around 1,450 suspected insurgents in the city, but 400 were quickly released as non-combatants and 100 more were due for release soon after. Since almost all those detained were young men of military age, and at least a third of those were clearly regarded even by the Americans as innocent of insurgent activity, it seems certain that there were much larger numbers of older men, women and children in the city right through the fighting.

The numbers of civilian losses remain hard to verify. But the human costs of the economic damage experienced in Iraq since the termination of the Saddam Hussein regime in 2003 are becoming apparent. A deterioration in basic services has led to a substantial increase in acute child malnutrition; research by the Iraqi Health Ministry in cooperation with the United Nations Development Programme (UNDP) and the Fafo Institute for Applied International Studies in Norway shows an increase from 4 per cent to 7.7 per cent of the child population – meaning that approximately 400,000 Iraqi children experience a 'wasting' condition which involves chronic diarrhoea and dangerous protein deficiency.

The Neo-Con Rethink

The official American line of an insurgency in retreat is belied by three factors: continuing attacks across Iraq, high US casualties, and problems of military overstretch. As revealing are indications that some analysts and think tanks which strongly supported the war, even including neo-conservatives, are now urging a fundamental rethink of US policy in Iraq (*Boston Globe*, 22 November 2004).

There is now a growing acceptance in Washington that the strategy of maintaining large numbers of US troops in Iraq who routinely use overwhelming force only serves to exacerbate the insurgency, and has negative effects on the wider 'war on terror'. The Cato Institute study, *Exiting Iraq* (June 2004), concludes: 'The occupation is counterproductive in the fight against radical Islamic terrorists and actually increases support for Osama bin Laden in Muslim communities not previously disposed to support his radical interpretation of Islam.'

An emerging thread among right-wing thinkers is that the Iraqi elections of January 2005 are crucial, and that the US should start withdrawing troops as soon afterwards as possible. As long as some kind of Iraqi government is in power, the opportunity must be seized; otherwise, the argument goes, the continuing US presence around major population centres will demonstrate that a supposedly independent Iraq remains under occupation.

The problem with this line of thinking is that it depends on an Iraqi government capable of maintaining security. Most current indications are that this will simply not happen. The rate of training of Iraqi security forces is far lower than required; only small numbers of elite forces are proving effective alongside US troops in counter-insurgency operations; police and defence forces are under constant attack; there is widespread evidence of persistent infiltration by insurgents.

The central dilemma for the Bush administration is: continue to occupy Iraq to ensure US influence, or begin progressive withdrawals early in 2005 and risk endemic instability. A number of analysts are indeed now advocating this latter course – and almost the only time that a Republican administration could get away with such a fundamental policy shift would be early in a second presidential term.

Why is the US in Iraq?

The key factor to remember here is that the United States is not in Iraq to ensure a transition to peace and stability prior to a complete withdrawal; it is there because of Iraq's immense geopolitical (including oil-related) importance to US security. The United States, as earlier articles in this series have argued, has always intended to build a number of permanent military bases, quite apart from its much larger numbers of occupation forces. This has not changed.

In this light, a reasonably clear plan of action may emerge from current US difficulties – one that represents a significant tactical shift. If even partial elections are held in January, US troops will quickly reduce high-profile counter-insurgency operations and withdraw from Iraq in numbers. The remainder – still likely to be tens of thousands of troops – will be located at a few large, well-protected bases far from major urban centres but conveniently close to current oilfields and areas of future exploration. The cities will be virtually abandoned in the hope that the diminished US presence will undercut the motivation of, and support for, the insurgents.

This would be far from the original proselytising expectations of the United States in Iraq, yet would do nothing to check the view across the region that the US is determined to implant itself in the heart of the Arab world for the long term. The presence of US bases would continue to serve the interests of radical Islamists and insurgency campaigns.

A radically different policy, such as a full US military retreat from Iraq, is unthinkable. For a re-elected George W. Bush in particular, it would represent the collapse of the whole neo-conservative Middle East project. We are still a long way from that.

8
Next: Iran?

INTRODUCTION

The re-election of President Bush in November 2004 resulted in a conviction that there was now a clear mandate to continue with the robust pursuit of the 'global war on terror'. As there was evidence that North Korea had already 'jumped' to nuclear status, with a limited supply of crude nuclear weapons, there was some frustration with the inability to constrain this member of the 'axis of evil', recourse having to be made to extensive negotiations involving six countries including China.

Although North Korea was considered a significant problem, though, it was far less important that Iran, and the months after the election saw an increase in rhetoric from the Bush administration directed towards the government in Tehran. If the occupation of Iraq had been a success from an American perspective, with a stable and peaceful client state acting as host to substantial US forces, then there was an assumption that Iran would present few problems.

In the event, Iraq was in disarray, any kind of political evolution would involve significant power for the Shi'a majority and the influence of Iran was likely to increase. Furthermore, the government in Tehran may have agreed a voluntary declaration with the UK, France and Germany to cease nuclear fuel cycle activities, but this was not guaranteed to last, leading to the unacceptable risk of Iran being able to develop nuclear weapons. Meanwhile, the United States itself was embarking on its own nuclear weapons modernisation programme.

The risk of a future crisis with Iran was increased by two other more general factors. One was that Israel had long seen Iran as the really important threat to its security in the region, and support for Israel was steadily increasing in the United States as a result of a relatively new political phenomenon – the growth in influence of the Christian Zionists. The second factor was, once again, the issue of energy resources, since Iran's success at reaching long-term oil and gas export agreements with China and India was likely to circumscribe the US capacity for action against this founder member of the 'axis of evil'.

IRAN'S NUCLEAR POLITICS *2 December 2004*

The nuclear politics of Iran have recently returned to centre-stage as hurried diplomatic contact between several European governments and Tehran, under the auspices of the International Atomic Energy Agency (IAEA), averted the possible referral of Iran's nuclear activities to the United Nations Security Council. An immediate crisis has been forestalled, but the possibility of such an event remains in the background. Indeed, the nature of the relationship between Iran, Israel and the United States means that it is highly likely.

The View from Washington

The reinvigorated Bush administration feels an absolute requirement to ensure the security of the United States and its international interests by any means necessary. This is evident in its pursuit of the 'war on terror' and regime termination in Afghanistan and Iraq, its substantial increase in defence spending, its move towards national missile defence, and its rigorous intention to prevent the proliferation of weapons of mass destruction. As if this were not enough, two additional factors conspire to shape a particularly severe US policy towards Iran: historic experience of American entanglements with Iran, and the attitude of Israel.

The Iranian revolution of 1979 was a profound shock to the United States, especially in the context of its close alliance with the Shah's Iran during much of the Cold War. The immediate aftermath of the revolution, dominated by the 444-day hostage crisis at the American Embassy in Tehran, meant that Republicans in particular were vigorously opposed to the Islamic regime from the start. This was a factor in the US's tacit support for Saddam Hussein's Iraq during the Iran–Iraq war of 1980–88, when Iraq was seen as a 'buffer' against Tehran's perceived extremism and expansionism.

Throughout the 1990s, the US's oppositional stance towards Iran continued. By contrast, several European states (including Britain) developed extensive diplomatic contacts with Iran in this period. This underlines the significance for Washington of Israel's perception that Iran is the greatest long-term threat to its security.

Israel's policy is rooted in a desire to prevent any other state in the region acquiring nuclear weapons, but it is also concerned by Iran's support for Hezbollah guerrillas in southern Lebanon. Just as US attitudes were hardened by the hostage crisis in 1979–80, the Israeli Defence Forces' (IDF) experience in southern Lebanon was seminal in shaping its attitude to Iran. During 1982–85 especially, Hezbollah actions made it impossible for the IDF to maintain its occupation of large parts of southern Lebanon. Israel's withdrawal in the mid-1980s is recognised (internally if not internationally) as the hardest reversal in IDF history. Hezbollah, presumably backed by Tehran, remains a dominant force in southern Lebanon today.

This experience, which the pro-Israel lobby in Washington is not slow to invoke, reinforces the Bush administration's belief (and its neo-conservative component in particular) that Iran is a core threat to US interests in the region.

The View from Tehran

The forces within the Iranian political system prepared to work for better relations with western states do not stretch to those theocratic elements that wield most power. Yet two aspects of these hardliners' worldview are more widely shared across the country.

The first is intense national pride: Iran's self-perception as a historically great country that is heir to 3,000 years of civilisation dovetails with a belief that it is essentially the keeper of true (Shi'a) Islam, site of the world's finest resource of Islamic learning and believers. Here, Iran (Persia) is rivalled only by China in an innate belief in its global significance; this is also a factor that survives changes of political regime.

The second is an enduring belief that Iran has been subject to systematic and insidious western influence – most recently in Britain's and the United States' interference in the 1950s and their sustenance of the Shah's regime in the 1960s and 1970s.

Today, there is palpable unease that Iran appears virtually surrounded by a potential enemy – the United States. The US has terminated two regimes on either side of Iran in the past three years, the Taliban's Afghanistan and Saddam's Iraq. It retains military forces in Afghanistan and massive numbers of troops in Iraq, with the intention to develop a number of permanent bases in the latter country. It also has a military presence in Pakistan (a nuclear power) and has recently established a series of bases in Central Asia that give it greater leverage over Caspian basin oil reserves.

Iran's unease extends to a private acceptance that the US has near-total superiority in military power: evidenced by the very powerful Fifth Fleet controlling the Persian Gulf and the Arabian Sea, and bases in western Gulf states and in Iran's north-western neighbour, Turkey. Within this already insecure regional context, Iran sees itself illicitly labelled as part of an 'axis of evil' by the world's only superpower – which has declared itself ready to pre-empt perceived threats to its security.

Iran's economy and society indicate the country's potential. Its population of 74 million is expected to grow to over 87 million by 2015; it has the world's fourth-largest oil reserves and second-largest gas reserves. But this potential is shadowed by an ever-present sense of vulnerability at the political level. In this circumstance, there are undoubtedly strong pressures within Iran for the development of some kind of nuclear deterrent. In the 1970s, the Shah saw nuclear weapons as an indicator of regional great-power status; now, they are viewed as a necessary, direct response to an imminent strategic threat. Furthermore, the manner in which North Korea has 'jumped' to a limited nuclear status will have been watched with considerable interest in Tehran.

US Attitudes and Iranian Politics

The process of political decision-making in Iran is complex; ultimate power still tends to lie with the religious leadership, which is particularly strong in the judiciary. There are profound tensions between a conservative theocracy and a diffuse yet vigorous reform movement; the latter seeks inspiration not in the 1979 revolution but in the 1906 constitutional revolution that set Iran on a more democratic path.

Many ordinary Iranians, especially the very large numbers of younger people, hoped that the president elected in 1997, Mohammad Khatami, and the civil government, would pursue a more reformist course. That this has not happened may be attributed to the innate power of the religious elites, or to incompetence; in any case, its consequence is widespread disillusion and stinging criticism (from students, young people, and elements of civil society) of the government.

The United States has supported such criticism, and the limited movements for change (like student demonstrations) that express it. The problem is that Washington's partisanship is unlikely to advance its goal of regime change, for the more conservative religious leadership can find a popular echo by identifying any 'progressive' tendency in Iran as a vehicle for US interference. In its bellicose approach, the United States may actually be circumscribing the ability of the Tehran government, which is not in complete control of the political environment, to find a reformist path.

The Nuclear Trigger

The United States and Israel remain set on precluding Iran's manufacture of its own nuclear 'deterrent' – if necessary, using military action. Three complications of this approach are evident: attitudes in much of western Europe, where there is an even greater difference of opinion with Washington than over Iraq; the close links between Russia and Iran; and – perhaps most important of all – China's increasing interest in developing a solid economic relationship with Iran.

China's interest stems from the need to ensure future supplies of oil and gas for its rapidly industrialising economy. The diplomatic exchanges between China and Iran in recent months have included the visit to Tehran by China's foreign minister, Li Zhaoxing, in November 2004. China has signed a liquefied natural-gas import deal worth over $70 billion over 25 years, and it may seek to help develop the huge Yadavaran field (*Asia Times*, 30 November 2004).

Beijing sees Iran – even more than the Caspian basin – as the best prospect for maintaining large supplies of fossil fuels over the next generation. In Tehran, a closer relationship with Beijing means a degree of security in the face of potential interference from Israel or the United States. Indeed, senior politicians in Tehran now welcome the prospect that China may soon replace Japan as the largest single market for Iranian oil and gas.

This evolving partnership, along with Iran's friendship with Russia and its milder associations with European Union states, does not presage any policy change in Washington, which still views Iran as the main threat to US interests in the Middle East. The risk of a crisis therefore remains. But this complex international picture does mean that any such crisis would generate strained relationships between the United States and Europe, with the possibility too of an uncompromising reaction from China. Once more, the politics of energy, especially oil, emerges as the most potent hidden factor in regional political insecurity.

TIDES OF VICTORY *20 January 2005*

As the most opulent presidential inauguration in United States history takes place, a principal effect of George W. Bush's election victory in November 2004 has become clear: confirming his administration's sense of the rightness of its course of action in Iraq. Bush's clear majority of the popular vote, and the Republicans' success in Congress, gives Bush and his advisers a sense of vindication over Iraq (see 'Bush Says Election Ratified Iraq Policy', *Washington Post*, 16 January 2005). This attitude combines with three other factors to give a clearer picture of the US administration's current thinking towards the Middle East – and especially the prospects of military action against Iran or Syria.

The first is the series of changes instigated within the CIA that will cumulatively lead to a long-term loss of independence for that agency. The administration now sees the role of the CIA and other intelligence agencies as much more of a supportive one – helping it to implement its policies rather than providing independent analyses.

The second is the growing importance of the Pentagon, which is acquiring a much louder voice in US security policy – effectively sidelining not just the CIA and other agencies, but the State Department. It is significant here that serious planning to expand the war in the Gulf beyond Iraq appears to have predated the November election. Whether or not the neo-conservatives were confident of victory, they were certainly prepared to plan for military outreach in a second term (see Seymour Hersh, 'The Coming Wars: What the Pentagon Can Now Do in Secret', *New Yorker*, 17 January 2005).

The third factor is the growing determination and confidence of the neo-conservatives, who now see an opportunity to implant their own worldview even further into US politics. The next two to three years are crucial for them. If they can ensure that US security policy follows the vision of a New American Century in a manner which makes it difficult for a future administration to reverse, they believe that their success could be measured in decades rather than years.

Will the Neo-Con Vision Prevail?

For this to happen, the success of current US policy in the Middle East will be pivotal. If, at the end of the second Bush administration, Iraq is still in disarray and tying down tens of thousands of US troops, if Iran is even closer to having nuclear weapons, and if the Syrian regime survives as one of the lesser members of the 'axis of evil', then a key part of the neo-conservative vision will have been found wanting – and this will affect the viability of the entire venture.

In this context, Seymour Hersh's recent account of Pentagon planning for the Middle East – particularly action against Iran – has the ring of truth. A Pentagon led by Donald Rumsfeld, Paul Wolfowitz and Douglas Feith is very much at the core of the neo-conservative worldview. Its influence is extended by a close working relationship with Dick Cheney and his advisers, while the administration as a whole is now freed from the modestly restraining influence of former Secretary of State, Colin Powell.

But however much preparation may now be underway for action against Iran, any plan for further military strikes in the Middle East faces serious problems. Iraq itself remains deeply unstable, and there is no pretence that the 30 January elections will make much difference. All indications are that the insurgency is deeply embedded, has a vigorous life of its own, and that its sustained attacks on the energy infrastructure are particularly effective in damaging any kind of lasting reconstruction.

In such circumstances, to initiate military action against Iraq's neighbouring countries might have some limited military effect on the insurgency, but it would be greatly outweighed by a further increase in antagonism to the United States across the region. If Syria is a major potential target, the implication of Hersh's *New Yorker* article is that the Pentagon civilian leadership more clearly have Iran in their sights. The huge range of difficulties facing any US military action against the regime in Tehran makes this judgement especially significant.

The Tehran Conundrum

These difficulties are highlighted by the impressive way that Iran is rapidly forging links with other major global players. In November 2004, Iran concluded a deal worth $70 billion over 25 years to export liquefied natural gas to China, a country that will soon be second only to the United States in its demand for imported oil.

More recently, the National Iranian Oil Company concluded an agreement with India worth $40 billion over a similar timescale. This also involves exports of liquefied natural gas, but in addition Indian contractors will be involved in developing two new natural gas fields in Iran and one new oilfield.

These agreements supplement existing close cooperation between Iran and Russia. They demonstrate how Iran's political leadership is systematically developing long-term links with key states. The economic benefits are evident but the political implications, given Iran's current tense relationship with the US, may be even more important.

These benefits make it well nigh impossible for the US to organise effective economic sanctions against Iran, should it try to do so. Iran has significant oil reserves, around 10 per cent of the world total. Its share of world gas reserves is even higher, second only to Russia in the world league. India, China and others recognise this only too well. The natural gas deals are clear examples of a planning outlook that is measured in decades.

In one sense, this reduces the options for the US and might appear to make a military alternative more likely. If it occurs such action would be targeted against a state with increasingly close links with the two emerging Asian great powers, not an isolated pariah state such as the Iraq of Saddam Hussein. Yet none of this means that the neo-cons are going to be distracted from seeking regime change in Tehran. Indeed, the real significance of Hersh's *New Yorker* piece, along with many other recent indications from Washington, is that their vision is very largely unaffected by realities in Iraq, or indeed across the Middle East as a whole.

The near-messianic view of the New American Century is not just still in place: it has been reinvigorated by the November election. The implications for the Middle East, for Europe and the wider world are profound and dangerous.

CHRISTIAN ZIONISTS AND NEO-CONS: A HEAVENLY MARRIAGE *3 February 2005*

The effects of the Iraq war are reverberating across the United States defence establishment. One of its consequences is a major rethink of military budget planning, including a decision to postpone some high-tech projects in favour of increasing the size and capability of the US Army. It is becoming clear that this is happening in the context of increasing civilian influence over defence planning within the Pentagon, as well as a more powerful role for the Pentagon itself within the George W. Bush administration.

US military leaders, according to a well-informed source,

> are worried the upcoming Quadrennial Defense Review (QDR) is being hijacked by a small cadre of civilians, and they believe they will be kept out of the loop, just as they were when budget cuts were decided only a few weeks ago. (*Aviation Week*, 24 January 2005)

The key player in this 'cadre' is probably Stephen Cambone, Under-Secretary of Defense for Intelligence. But the overall trend seems further evidence that Donald Rumsfeld and Paul Wolfowitz (the Defense Secretary and his deputy) are able to maintain much greater control of military force planning than their predecessors.

The senior military are naturally reluctant to cede the control of such planning to civilians. They also have a wider concern that the current hawkish security policy of the Bush administration, including its liking for pre-emption, simply doesn't take military realities into account. A well-rehearsed example is the refusal of the civilian leadership in 2002–03 to listen to voices from within the Pentagon and the US Army War College about the likely consequences of regime termination in Iraq.

Many departments of the United States government – state, commerce, justice and the treasury, as well as agencies such as the CIA – have historically made a contribution to developing United States security policy, in a context where the Pentagon plays the major role. But in the post-9/11 era, as US military forces moved to the forefront of the US response, 'national security' concerns have come to overshadow other influences in policy formulation. In particular, the administration has come to regard the intelligence agencies much more as arms of government policy than as providers of independent assessments. This has been encouraged by, and in turn enhanced, the influence within the administration of neo-conservative security ideologues who are determined to ensure that the dream of the New American Century becomes a reality.

Many commentators have concentrated on the increasing influence of this neo-conservative thinking, especially in the light of the convincing electoral victory of President Bush in November 2004. But a quite different source of influence on US foreign and security policy, often neglected or underestimated, is also becoming significant – the constituency known most commonly as the 'Christian Zionists'.

Towards the 'End Days'

Christian Zionism, also known as dispensationalism or dispensation theology, has been around for over a century and a half but it has only acquired real political significance in the past decade. Its current importance stems from three factors: the voting power of a significant proportion of evangelical Christians in the United States, its visceral support for the State of Israel, and its links with neo-conservatism.

The essence of 'dispensation theology', allowing for internal variations, is that God has given a dispensation to the Jews to prepare the way for the Second Coming. The literal fulfilment of Old Testament promises to biblical Israel is approaching, 'end days' that will involve a millennium of earthly rule centred on Jerusalem. Thus, the State of Israel is a fundamental part of God's plan, and it is essential for it to survive and thrive.

Dispensationalists would argue that this has always been a core part of the Christian message, but most historians of theology trace the doctrine to the thoughts and preachings of John Nelson Darby (1800–1882), a minister of the Plymouth

Brethren active in promoting it in the 1820s. It attracted particular attention in the United States as part of the Biblical Conference Movement in the 1870s, and flourished in the first decades of the twentieth century.

The evangelist Cyrus Scofield was central to this process. His *Scofield Reference Bible* (1909) was the first book published by the new US offices of the Oxford University Press. Its prolific theological interpretations helped make it perhaps the most renowned version of the Bible in North American evangelism.

Michael Vlach describes how many Bible schools teaching dispensationalism were formed in the 1920s, the most significant being the Dallas Theological Seminary in 1924. The *Scofield Bible* became a standard source in these institutions, helping the phenomenon of 'Christian Zionism' to lay down firm roots in the inter-war years.

Many dispensationalists saw the establishment of Israel in 1948 as the beginning of a fulfilment of biblical prophecies. Later moments in the country's history – especially the six-day war in 1967 – gave a further impetus to the idea.

The Bill Clinton years (1992–2000) were more difficult for dispensationalists, partly because they followed the preacher scandals of the late 1980s, and because Clinton was more favourable to the more secular elements of the Israeli political system, not least with its Labour Party. But during his presidency, the main Israel lobbies in Washington – particularly the American Israel Public Affairs Committee (AIPAC) – sought to build close links with the Christian Zionists. In this, AIPAC and similar organisations were recognising the increasing demographic and political power of the Christian Zionists, and also securing a wider base of support at a time when American Jewish communities were scarred by deep divisions that threatened to reduce support for Israel.

A recent, succinct history of Christian Zionism by Donald Wagner of Chicago's North Park University tracks the remarkable coming together of the movement with neo-conservatism during the George W. Bush era, and quotes the leading evangelical preacher Jerry Falwell: 'The Bible Belt is Israel's safety net in the United States.'

Wagner remarks:

> By 2000, a shift had taken place in the Republican Party. It began embracing the doctrines of neoconservative ideologues who advocated US unilateralism and favored military solutions over diplomacy. The more aggressive approach was put into action after Sept. 11, and to no one's surprise, Israel's war against the Palestinians and its other enemies was soon linked to the US 'war on terrorism'. (www.informationclearinghouse.info/article4959.htm)

A number of groups now connect evangelical Christian churches in the United States with support for Israel, many of them making specific reference to Jerusalem. *Stand for Israel*, for example, talks of the need 'to mobilise Christians and people of faith to support the State of Israel...' and declares on its home page that 'Anti-Israel = Anti-Zionism = Anti-Semitism'.

A New Dispensation

This growth in Christian Zionism in recent years forms just one part of the wider increase in the conservative evangelism movement, the fastest-growing sector within American Christian churches. Donald Wagner estimates that it numbers 100–130 million adherents (the population of the United States is 293 million). The proportion of Christian Zionists among this figure is harder to assess, but perhaps 20–25 per cent of US evangelicals could be described as sympathetic to the doctrine's fundamentalist views. At the same time, larger numbers may be inclined to support Israel because of broader dispensationalist sympathies; and the fact that evangelical Christians seem particularly disposed to vote, and to be more likely to support the Republican Party, has allowed them to secure a power even greater than their numbers.

The political consequence is that both Israel and US neo-conservatives have come to benefit from ideological and electoral support from an unexpected and growing source. This has wider strategic implications too: for many adherents seriously believe that we may be approaching the end of the world, that salvation can arrive only through a Christian message linked decisively to the success of the state of Israel, and that Islam is necessarily a false faith that must be combated.

The fusion of religion and politics that Christian Zionism represents remains a largely unrecognised force in American politics. Its alliance with neo-conservatism may yet do much to influence the Middle East policies of the second administration of the born-again George W. Bush.

US NUCLEAR PLANS *10 February 2005*

The visit of Condoleezza Rice to Europe in the past week was accompanied by notably hardline rhetoric towards Iran. In describing Iran (at a meeting with French intellectuals) as not merely an 'authoritarian' but a 'totalitarian' state, the new United States Secretary of State was also underlining the George W. Bush administration's absolute opposition to Tehran's nuclear weapons programme. In this context, recent revelations about the US's own nuclear weapons development plans are particularly significant.

When President Bush was re-elected in November 2004, many arms-control specialists feared that his administration would make rapid progress towards a national missile defence system and modernisation of the US nuclear arsenal. To their surprise, both developments appeared to receive setbacks in the election aftermath.

First, and in light of the rising costs of the war in Iraq, there were indications that a number of high-tech military projects would be scaled back or even cancelled – including programmes connected with missile defence, such as the airborne laser. Second, and more remarkable, was Congress's decision to cut all funding for four nuclear-weapons programmes. These, in turn, were aimed at making it easier to start nuclear tests; developing a new production plant for nuclear warheads; creating advanced design concepts for new kinds of nuclear weapons; and designing and developing a highly specialised nuclear weapon for destroying deeply-buried underground targets.

Bunker-Buster Bluster

The decision over the last of these programmes, known as the Robust Nuclear Earth Penetrator (RNEP), was particularly surprising, given the claims made by Bush administration officials about North Korea's and Iran's plans to situate nuclear weapons in deep underground bunkers. Several factors influenced Congress's decision, including the belief that more 'boots on the ground' rather than new nuclear weapons were needed, as well as traditional horse-trading between people representing different electoral districts.

More thoughtful was the concern of some representatives that the United States could not simultaneously be seen to be investing heavily in new nuclear weapons like the RNEP while condemning other countries for merely initiating such a process. They pointed to the fact that the United States still possesses more than enough nuclear weapons to satisfy the most unlikely needs, and had already modified one of its older nuclear warhead designs to produce a rather crude earth-penetrating device.

Even though the US nuclear arsenal is a lot smaller than at the height of the Cold War, the most recent estimate is that its current deployment still stands at approximately 5,300 operational nuclear warheads, with nearly 5,000 more placed in what is termed a 'responsive reserve force' or else only partially dismantled (*Bulletin of the Atomic Scientists*, January/

February 2005). Many of these weapons contain enormous destructive force; the nearly 400 W88 warheads for the Trident submarine missile fleet are each about 30 times as powerful as the Hiroshima bomb.

The early earth-penetrating warhead was the B61–11, a variant of the standard B61 tactical nuclear bomb, with heavily modified casing and fusing. This was put together in the mid-1990s and can be deployed on the B-2A stealth bomber. At the time it was produced, strenuous efforts were made to say that it wasn't a new weapon but merely a modification of an old one. This was true in the sense that the new weapon recycled the core of the nuclear warhead or 'physics package', but to claim there is little difference is equivalent to taking the engine out of a Chevrolet, using it to power a boat, and then claiming that the boat is still a car.

A Shadowy Strategy

When George W. Bush succeeded Bill Clinton in 2001, most people assumed that the latter's cautious attitude to wholesale nuclear modernisation would be discarded. The nuclear weapons laboratories certainly exerted systematic pressure in arguing for new programmes. Such pressure makes Congress's decision to cut funding even more unexpected – even, to many in the arms-control community, too good to be true. This week it became clear that it was just that, as the Bush administration decided to present Congress with a new funding request (*Washington Post*, 9 February 2005).

Moreover, it turns out that programmes are already underway to design new nuclear warheads using completely different budget lines (*International Herald Tribune*, 8 February 2005). Around 100 specialists at the three US nuclear weapons laboratories – Lawrence Livermore in California, Los Alamos in New Mexico and Sandia in Texas – are involved in an initial $9 million project, one that is planned to develop into a full-scale programme capable of producing designs for completely new weapons within the next five to ten years.

An immediate question arises: given the attitude of Congress, how is it possible that the anodyne-sounding, science-based Stockpile Stewardship Program contains an element focused on producing new weapons? For the advocates of the programme, the answer is straightforward – the United States stopped producing entirely new nuclear weapons at least 15 years ago, many of the warheads in its current stockpile are far older than that, and there is no guarantee that they will work if they have to be used.

In such circumstances, these proponents say, a programme overseeing the maintenance and reliability of the nuclear arsenal has an obligation to produce new designs capable of replacing the ageing arsenal. They also argue that producing new, robust and reliable weapons means that the United States will be able to manage with fewer weapons.

Arms-control experts, by contrast, claim that the US's nuclear stockpile is sufficiently up-to-date in design terms, could be reduced much further, and has no need of a new bout of modernisation. Daryl G. Kimball, executive director of prominent Washington-based group the Arms Control Association, comments: 'The existing stockpile is safe and reliable by all standards, so to design a new warhead that is even more robust is a redundant activity that could be a pretext for designing a weapon that has a new military mission.'

This is the crux of the matter – that the Bush administration seems to have found a way of circumventing Congress's decision to cut funding for what were clearly intended to be major new nuclear weapons programmes.

It is now only three months until the next review conference for the Non-Proliferation Treaty (NPT), which meets in New York in May. Yet even as it approaches, the United States is insisting that Iran cannot even begin the process of developing a nuclear infrastructure, let alone produce small numbers of weapons. For George W. Bush, who says that a nuclear-armed Iran would be 'a very destabilising force in the world', this is a sensible policy; many citizens in the United States and other countries will question whether the same characterisation may equally be applied to current American nuclear policy. Iranians, too, may see things very differently, not least given the size and reach of the Israeli nuclear arsenal.

The Bush administration wants to build a coalition for countering Iranian nuclear ambitions. This means it needs to avoid giving the impression of furthering its own nuclear developments. The Congressional decision in November helped serve that purpose. The more recent reports on what is actually happening in terms of US nuclear developments do not. They lend support to those analysts who believe that the United States will take a singularly hardline stance at the NPT Review Conference. This may be typical of the unilateralist tendencies of the Bush administration, but will certainly not further the control of nuclear proliferation through international cooperation.

IRANIAN OPTIONS *24 February 2005*

This week's visit to several European cities by President Bush has been widely welcomed as an opportunity to improve transatlantic relations in the light of the many policy divisions between the United States and leading European Union states. But in one area – Iran – his comments were the opposite of reassuring to those concerned about the possibility of a new and dangerous military confrontation.

It was widely reported that Bush, in his press conference on 22 February, described suggestions that the United States might attack Iran as 'ridiculous'. This is one occasion when the full quotation is worth recording:

> After all, Great Britain, Germany and France are negotiating with the Ayatollahs to achieve a common objective, something that we

> all want, and that is for them not to have a nuclear weapon. It's in our interests for them not to have a nuclear weapon. And finally, this notion that the United States is getting ready to attack Iran is simply ridiculous. And having said that, all options are on the table. (Laughter.)

At the next day's joint press conference with Germany's Chancellor Schröder, a combination of agreement (Iran should not develop nuclear weapons) and disagreement (over what should be done to prevent this) was apparent. The European view – embodied in the 'European Union 3' (Germany, France, Britain) that has conducted intensive consultation with Tehran – is that diplomacy is the best means of achieving the preferred outcome. In European eyes, this would be to allow Iran to develop a relatively small nuclear power programme, but one that lacks an indigenous capacity for uranium enrichment (given that this can, under certain circumstances, form the basis for enriching uranium to weapons grade). In exchange, Iran would be granted progressive improvements in trade and other aspects of interstate relations.

Within Iran, even this more flexible European policy is deeply unpopular across a wide range of political and religious circles. Iranian leaders are aware that United States policy presents to them a menu of five pressing strategic challenges. First, the world's sole superpower has labelled their country part of an 'axis of evil'. Second, in pursuit of its clear strategy of pre-empting perceived threats, the US has already terminated regimes on either side of Iran (the Taliban in Afghanistan and the Saddam Hussein regime in Iraq). The US may be facing formidable problems in Iraq, but it retains 150,000 troops there, is building permanent bases – and is about to construct a large new military installation near Herat in western Afghanistan, close to Iran's eastern border. Third, it sanctions an Israeli military presence in the Kurdish region of Iraq close to Iran's western border. Fourth, the United States Navy has almost total control of the Persian Gulf and the Arabian Sea.

The fifth challenge goes to the heart of the Iranians' sense of strategic encirclement: the possession of formidable nuclear forces by the United States and Israel combined with their adamant opposition to any prospect of Iran itself possessing such weapons.

This Iranian perspective cuts no ice in the United States or Israel, which regard Iran as a far more significant threat than Saddam Hussein's Iraq ever was, and which are deeply suspicious of such a populous, oil-rich country even wanting to consider a civil nuclear-power programme.

The Music of the Drones

In this tense strategic climate, two issues are of particular concern: the significance of the recent US deployment of surveillance drones into Iranian air space, and the chances of the US accepting a tougher version of the European proposals (in the unlikely event that they were agreed by Tehran).

There is now reliable evidence that the US has been using bases in Iraq for nearly a year to undertake extensive surveillance missions across Iran. This recent information fills in some of the detail of Seymour Hersh's *New Yorker* article (17 January 2005) on moves towards a confrontation with Iran.

The drone missions have two distinct purposes: to probe Iranian air defences and to collect information on nuclear sites (*Washington Post*, 13 February 2005). The US seeks to provoke the use of Iranian air-defence radars in order to gauge their effectiveness. An Iranian attempt to destroy some of the drones would have been useful to the US military in this respect; instead, the Iranians tried neither to intercept nor (except on rare occasions) even to illuminate the drones with radar, thereby limiting US attempts to probe any weaknesses.

At the same time, the effect of this activity is to convince the Iranian military that the United States is indeed preparing for the option of military attacks. This raises the question of whether there could be sufficient changes in Iranian nuclear programmes to satisfy Washington.

To date, negotiations with the EU3 have resulted in the Paris agreement of November 2004, which required Iran to freeze uranium enrichment in return for possible economic, trade and technology concessions. The agreement is voluntary rather than legally binding under current international agreements; Iran could still, if it wishes, embark on uranium enrichment for civil nuclear-power purposes within the terms of the non-proliferation treaty and under the inspection processes of the International Atomic Energy Agency (IAEA).

If Iran did resume enrichment, it is also possible (though not legally necessary) that the IAEA and Iran could agree even tighter verification procedures that would make it very difficult to switch to the rapid development of a nuclear-weapons programme. Iran's response in such circumstances is difficult to measure: there is substantial expertise in the country on nuclear issues, some of it dating back to the Shah's ambitious nuclear programme of the 1970s, and it may even be possible for Iran to embark on the more efficient plutonium route to nuclear weapons. There are, however, economic reasons for Iran to pursue its own uranium-enrichment programme. Producing reactor-grade uranium for the Bushehr nuclear-power plant, for example, would probably be substantially cheaper than buying it from Russia (*Asia Times*, 23 February 2005).

At present, Iran seems prepared to negotiate with the EU3 on the uranium-enrichment issue, and may be prepared to accept a long-term pause in its programme if the rewards were big enough. But these would have to include not just further trade and technology-transfer concessions, but some kind of security guarantee that would simply have to involve Washington.

Will America Invade Iran?

This is the crux of the matter: what will really determine whether the United States, or indeed Israel, will target Iran's nuclear facilities in the coming months. Put bluntly, what must Iran do to make it certain that the Bush administration will not attack it?

This question is posed in starkly practical terms to policy-makers and opinion-formers in Iran. They ask: would it be enough for Iran to return to enriching uranium for civil purposes but under an extremely stringent IAEA verification regime (far tougher than anything imposed on other countries)? Almost certainly, this would not satisfy Washington. So would it therefore become necessary for Iran to abandon all indigenous enrichment programmes, maintaining its relatively small nuclear-power programme solely with imported fuel?

Many in Tehran think that even this would not be enough. The more hardline, neo-conservative rhetoric emanating from Washington, and the recent military surveillance of Iran, convince them that the United States will be satisfied only if Iran abandons all civil nuclear activities, including any substantive research programmes. Indeed, the more intransigent leaders in Tehran believe that the sum total of US attitudes is to present a front behind which is a defined plan for regime termination.

A number of Washington's many voices certainly do advocate regime change, but the more influential view there is probably that a total Iranian abandonment of all its civil nuclear programmes might be enough. This is still far more then the EU3 are asking for, and certainly far more than Iran will concede. Thus, whatever gloss George W. Bush's visit has put on transatlantic relations, there really is a major gap between the United States and the European Union.

It is just possible that the EU3 will be able to exert sufficient pressure on Washington to persuade it to hold back from military action against Iran. Against a mood in influential circles in Washington that sees Iran as 'unfinished business', this would require formidable diplomatic persistence. In brief, whatever the massive dangers of embarking on military action against Iran – which could be far greater even than those created by the Iraq war – it is by no means certain that even a united commitment from Germany, France and Britain can deter the George W. Bush administration.

CONFIDENT IRAN *9 March 2005*

A striking theme emerged from an international conference last week at the Institute for Political and International Studies in Tehran, the Iranian Foreign Ministry's think tank: confidence. The conference was addressed by the Foreign and Defence ministers and by the head of the Expediency Council, Hashemi Rafsanjani. Their outlook was backed up by presentations from a range of Iranian analysts, as well as through many informal discussions on the fringes of the conference.

Rafsanjani, in particular, was significant, given his previous role as Speaker of the Majlis (parliament), past President and possible candidate in the June 2005 presidential election. What came across, from him and others, was a quiet satisfaction combined, surprisingly, with a sense that the leadership is not necessarily convinced that the United States would actually go as far as attacking Iranian nuclear facilities. They may well be wrong on this, but it does appear to be their view.

From the perspective of Tehran, what has happened in Iraq has been broadly useful for the country. It is true that the United States has 150,000 troops in a neighbouring state, has many more in Afghanistan to the east and controls the waters of the Persian Gulf and the Arabian Sea, but it is also thoroughly enmeshed in a bitter and continuing insurgency in Iraq, and the political evolution now under way does indicate that a core aim of Washington's entire Iraq policy – a client government with permanent military bases in this immensely oil-rich state, may eventually prove untenable.

Moreover, for the Iranians, the Iraqi elections in January have effectively delivered a Shi'a-dominated legislature. Even though the United States still controls the country through its massive embassy, economic influence and occupying forces, the

Iranian view is that the US will eventually be worn down and will be forced to withdraw most if not all of its forces.

Whether or not this is an accurate analysis is less important than that it provides a source of confidence to the Iranian political and theocratic leadership. There is little evidence that Iran is currently seeking much influence in Baghdad, but there is no doubt whatsoever that it has the ability to do so, should it so choose. Iranian intelligence operatives are embedded within Iraq, some of the Shi'a militias have close links with Iranian Revolutionary Guard units and, above all, much of the new Iraqi political leadership was in exile in Iran, not the United States, during the Saddam Hussein era.

The aura of confidence goes further, because the potential for what is effectively Shi'a rule in Iraq gives informal support across the wider Shi'a community in the region, not least in Bahrain and the oil-rich eastern regions of Saudi Arabia. Even in Lebanon, this week's huge demonstration in Beirut organised by Hezbollah is a salutary reminder that the Shi'a of Lebanon are that country's largest confessional group.

What is particularly striking, returning to Tehran after several years, is the transformation of the central residential districts, with many expensive new high-rise apartments, and of the growth of luxury residential areas close to the mountains to the north-east of the city. Part of the reason for this latter development is the heavy investment in land and property by rich Shi'a families from the western Gulf states, many of them using these rural properties to escape the summer heat of the Gulf. At an informal level this is a manifest example of the connectivity of Shi'a communities across the region, the irony being that this is a process given new heart thanks to Washington and its Iraq involvement.

Iranian Politics and the Economy

Iranian politics are particularly complex at present, with the political control by the theocrats not quite as clear-cut as is usually supposed. As a reformist, the outgoing President Khatami has clearly failed, and the Majlis is currently dominated by more conservative elements. The student revolts of recent years have been largely controlled, with leaders still in prison, and the overall human rights record has scarcely improved. At the same time, the economy is fairly buoyant. It may be highly inefficient and too closed to outside involvement, but the country is now self-sufficient in wheat production, petrol is well under a dollar a gallon, and Tehran's roads are beginning to approach the chaotic levels of Mexico City or Bangkok.

There is considerable corruption, extending to elements of the clergy, the revolutionary foundations still control significant parts of the economy, and there is no lack of poverty. At the same time, material life is improving to an extent sufficient to dampen outright opposition to the current theocratic rule. If anything, political apathy is more common than a vigorous civil society seeking political and social emancipation.

At the same time, one message is clear from a wide range of people holding diverse political views – if there was any kind of major attack from outside, whether from the United States, Israel or both, the effect would not be to threaten the current regime but to produce a degree of nationalist unity that would transcend the substantial political difference that exist within Iran.

The Nuclear Issue

Whether or not Iran does have such a programme, there is very widespread support within Iran for the civil nuclear-power plants such as the new reactor facility at Bushehr, and many Iranians also see nuclear weapons as essential to their security, deterring a United States administration that has declared Iran to be a part of the 'axis of evil' and in need of regime change.

Analysts in Washington argue that the Iranian civil nuclear-power programme *must* exist as a basis for weapons capabilities, given Iran's massive oil and gas reserves, but Iranians will point to their substantial investment in hydroelectric power, arguing that since Iran has its own uranium ore deposits, the civil programme is just part of a wider pattern of energy resource diversification.

Neither the Bush nor the Sharon administrations accept this argument, but it is highly unlikely that the Iranian government will back down on pursuing its nuclear power programme, and will be deeply reluctant to abandon its nuclear fuel cycle programme, even if it does provide Iran with technologies more relevant to a nuclear weapon capability.

Risk of War

In current circumstances the risk of a military attack on Iran, from Israel or the United States, looks all too plausible at some time in the next 18 months. This timescale relates to the fuelling of the Bushehr reactor – after that is complete, with the uranium fuel rods installed, any attack that includes the destruction of Bushehr could result in a Chernobyl-level disaster that could well affect Saudi Arabia and other western Gulf states as well as large parts of Iran.

As things stand, the Iranian government may go some of the way towards a long-term fuel cycle freeze, and may even accept higher levels of inspection, but it will not abandon its civil nuclear-power programme and will almost certainly continue to develop the technological abilities to produce nuclear weapons, even if it does not go the whole way. That is a situation unacceptable in Washington or Tel Aviv, yet it is becoming apparent, even in Washington, that an attack on Iranian nuclear facilities carries huge risks. Iran has a massive capacity to make things more difficult for the US military in Iraq, it could encourage Hezbollah against Israel, there could be a major oil price surge, and the current theocratic rulers could also confidently expect most Iranians to support their country strongly and, in doing so, help consolidate the power of the regime itself.

As a result, there are some small indications that neo-conservative elements in Washington are looking for other ways forward. Even the Committee on the Present Danger has recently put out a position paper that discusses the need for diplomatic pressure along with various forms of support for Iranian opposition groups.

Even so, what has to be remembered is the position of Israel, with all its support in Washington, set alongside the palpable self-confidence emanating from the current Iranian leadership. The ingredients for confrontation are most certainly there, and it is not at all clear that the Iranian leadership is prepared to make sufficient concessions to forestall that risk. Indeed, it simply does not see why it should.

Overall, it looks increasingly as though the recent Iraqi elections have given a real boost to Iran's perception of itself as a country with a major regional role. It is very far from what the Bush administration expected when it terminated the Saddam Hussein regime and it now looks as though that very action will, in a very unexpected way, make a confrontation with Iran more likely. At the very least, the Europeans are going to have to use a huge amount of diplomatic energy if they are to help avoid another very dangerous war in an already volatile region.

'IT'S OIL, STUPID' *24 March 2005*

This week's controversy over the attorney general's advice in the run-up to the Iraq war is just one further example of the persistent unease about the war and it aftermath. In the United States there have been concerted efforts to mark the second anniversary of the start of the war with suitable up-beat assessments, pointing to the recent elections and the decrease in insurgent activity, but even in the US, the controversy continues.

In part, this is due to the continuing casualties and the very high costs of the war. While there has been some decrease in the pitch of the insurgency, US forces still had 222 troops injured in the first three weeks of March, 82 of them seriously. The overall casualty figures – over 1,500 US troops killed, 11,500 injured and many thousands more evacuated to the US because of accidental injury, physical or mental illness – have resulted in a growing awareness, at the local level, of the costs of the war.

The Bush administration has been assiduous in downplaying the deaths and injuries, and the national media rarely pays much attention, a few papers such as the *Washington Post* being notable exceptions. At the same time, town and city newspapers right across the United States do cover the local stories of young men and women returning in coffins or, if surviving, having slowly to recover from serious injuries.

Even so, the overall argument is made that the war has brought democracy to Iraq, that Saddam Hussein was an increasing threat, and that the consequences of the war across the region are broadly positive. There are intense arguments from the other side. When he was a buffer against the Iranian revolutionaries, Saddam Hussein was very much the good guy. Back in 1988, with the Iran–Iraq war in virtual stalemate, his regime could rely on the US Navy taking on and destroying most of the key modern elements of the small Iranian Navy, just when he was conducting his most brutal *Anfal* campaigns against the Kurds.

As to the wider issues of democracy across the Middle East, again there is hollow laughter at the idea that such motivations are entirely innocent. Rumsfeld is currently deeply critical of Turkey, and reminded us this week that the war in Iraq would have been much easier for the United States if Turkey had allowed free military access, but that decision not to do so was taken by the elected Turkish parliament, not by an autocracy. Indeed there is a persistent suspicion that if a range of states across the Middle East really did embrace fully independent democratic processes, devoid of US pressure, then a repeated response of electorates would be demands for wholesale US withdrawal from the region and a cessation of support for Israel.

The Oil Factor

All of these aspects of the Iraq war may be relevant, but what is actually more striking about attitudes in the Gulf region itself is that there is a near-universal view among academics and policy analysts that the fundamental factor in all of the developments, far more important even then the US commitment to Israel, is oil.

When Clinton was campaigning for the White House, it is said that his team had constantly to be reminded that the election would be won or lost on arguments over the state of the economy. One way to do this was to have the slogan 'It's the economy, stupid', prominently displayed. Similarly, the further you get from the Washington and the closer to the Gulf states, the view hits you time and time again – 'It's oil, stupid'.

What is perhaps most curious is the way in which this contrasts so strongly with the views of many academics and others in the West, although it is an outlook that is slowly changing as the views of some analysts, such as Michael Klare, begin to be taken more seriously. One of the complications, and one of the issues that has made it more difficult to emphasise the oil factor, is that two different aspects have to be disentangled.

At the time of the war, one argument put forward by opponents of the war was that it was all about US oil companies taking over the Iraqi oilfields and reaping huge rewards in the process. In other words this was a matter of short-term gain or 'plunder', with the huge lobbying power of the transnational oil companies very much at the root of the rush to war. At a time of heightened tension over the presumed existence of those well-known weapons of mass destruction, this could easily be discounted as little more than conspiracy theory.

While such direct lobbying may have been largely irrelevant, the end result two years down the line is that the war has certainly been 'good' for the oil industry. Oil-related companies such as Halliburton have found Iraq immensely profitable, and the oil companies themselves are currently enjoying exceptional profitability.

At the same time, the oil companies' financial successes relate only indirectly to Iraq and follow a pattern well-known during the 1973–74 and 1989–90 oil price surges. In any period of suddenly rising oil prices, the big transnationals are adept at passing price increases to consumers with conspicuous rapidity. The practice is to transfer 'well-head' price increases to consumers within, at the most, a month of those increases taking effect. With the companies having perhaps a hundred days of supply at the old prices going through the complex system of tank farms, oil tankers plying the sea routes, refineries and final distribution, profit-taking becomes the order of the day.

The reality is that 'bull' markets are almost always good for resource industries, but this is not the key issue in the Gulf region. The real issue here is the long-term trend towards progressively greater reliance on Gulf oil. This is measured in terms of decades not months and is the core factor at the forefront of analysis and political viewpoints across the region.

On this analysis, the Gulf region has nearly two-thirds of all the world's known oil reserves, and more keeps getting found, in contrast to oilfields in the United States, the North Sea and elsewhere that are in decline. Moreover, Gulf oil is high quality, easy to extract and very cheap, much more so even than the much smaller reserves of the Caspian basin. In the short term, intense exploitation of reserves in Africa and Central America, coupled with drilling in Alaska, may ease US import demands, but the long-term trend is all in favour of the Gulf.

Furthermore, it is not just the United States that needs the oil – Europe, China, the East Asian tiger economies and increasingly India are huge oil importers and will require even greater resources from the Gulf region as that becomes *the* key oil-exporting region of the world. It is this kind of thinking that has prompted Iran's recent long-term deals with China and India, and also makes those countries, along with Japan, so deeply concerned over their increasing reliance on Gulf oil.

Based on this kind of assessment, the view across the region is that any talk of US commitment to democracy is peripheral and is only relevant if it ensures increasing US influence, backed by powerful military forces. In short, Washington is seen as engaged in a long-term process of indirect control of the region, that will, in the process, give it immense leverage over the world's oil resources in competition with China and India, an important and perhaps crucial part of ensuring the future of the New American Century.

Perhaps by the end of this decade the prevailing view among western analysts will be that the start of the second Iraq war in 2003 was essentially about oil. It may well even become the accepted view, forgetting that it was close to academic heresy at the time of the war. That time has not yet come, at least in the west, but it is thoroughly embedded in the Gulf region itself, with opinion formers in Iran and elsewhere long since recognising that this indeed is the 'great game' of the early twenty-first century.

9
Endless War

INTRODUCTION

During a five-month period from April to August 2005, opinion against the war in Iraq began to harden in the United States, the insurgency itself continued to develop, and a series of four coordinated bombing attacks on the London transport system demonstrated that radical groups loosely connected to the al-Qaida movement were still capable of major actions against western states. Not only did this appear to have no discernible effect on the policies of the Bush administration in the United States, but there were further indications of gathering tensions with Iran that could lead to a military confrontation.

The situation in Iraq was made particularly problematic as a result of two linked factors. One was that the insurgents were developing new tactics, not least the development of armour-piercing shaped-charge explosives that could destroy light armoured vehicles. They were also able to emplace very large explosive devices, despite the widespread US capabilities for observation and reconnaissance. The other was that the insurgents were becoming increasingly skilled at using the internet, videos and DVD to spread their own versions of events in Iraq to a receptive audience in many countries.

Perhaps most important was the growing possibility that the Iraq insurgency was developing a new attribute – as a combat training ground for paramilitaries that might, in later years, use their skills and experience in support of radical causes in the Middle East and beyond. In this respect, Iraq looked set to replace Afghanistan in this role, but to do so in the context of a largely urban guerrilla war that produced tactics and experience more closely allied to potential future conflicts than the more dispersed Afghan civil war of the 1990s.

In spite of all of these issues, though, there remained a belief in some key circles in Washington that Iran had to be targeted. In part this was because of a determination not to allow Tehran to develop nuclear weapons, but it was also in the face of increasing concern that an alliance between Iran and the majority Shi'a community in Iraq could lead to a reshaping of the political and security map of the Persian Gulf that would be highly undesirable for the United States.

A STATE OF INSECURITY *21 April 2005*

The desperate plight of Iraq is exemplified this week by a number of brutal incidents. The slaying of dozens of Shi'a civilian hostages by their Sunni insurgent captors in the town of Madaen, southeast of Baghdad, the killing of 20 Iraqi troops in the western town of Haditha and the latest attempt to assassinate interim prime minister Iyad Allawi – all represent a contrast to the impression of progress that Washington has been eager to portray. If these were isolated events they would be easier to dismiss, but it is more realistic to view them as part of a pattern of factors – seven in all – that show that the Iraqi insurgency is maintaining vigour while changing direction.

First, insurgents are mounting many attacks on Iraqi police and security forces, including numerous car bombs. Around 250 Iraqi security personnel were killed in March. On 19 April, four national guards were killed and 38 people injured in a car bomb in Baghdad, and five more people were killed in an attack in Khaldiya, west of Baghdad.

Second, US forces are concentrating on training and back-up for Iraqi forces, resulting in a decrease in US military patrols and therefore fewer targets for insurgents. In response, insurgents are mounting larger and more coordinated attacks on US bases. One assault on a US Marine base near the Syrian border involved 50–100 paramilitaries in a sophisticated multi-pronged operation utilising mortars, rocket-propelled grenades and three suicide-bombers (one of whom drove a fire-engine).

Third, the Americans are trying to build up a 142,000-strong Iraqi police force (far larger than the entire British police force for a population of around one-third of Britain's) by employing trainers from US companies – current contracts include $500 million to DynCorp, $200 million to SAIC, $200 million to US Investigation Services and $400 million to L-3 Communications Holdings (*Business Week*, 18 April 2005). The problem is that much of the training is in disarray: many local recruits see it as an opportunity to get a salary and have no intention of actually serving in the force. Matt Sherman, a US State Department official, says: 'It's safe to say there are tens of thousands on the payroll who aren't working.'

Fourth, the relatively low recent US death toll tends to overshadow the equally significant high level of combat injuries being suffered by US troops (the second week of April witnessed one of the highest totals since the war began in March 2003 – 224 people injured, 31 of them seriously). This reflects the fact that the sheer intensity and savagery of the conflict shows few signs of diminishing.

Steve Fainaru, a *Washington Post* reporter, describes an incident in Mosul where a US unit spotted insurgents transferring arms between vehicles. The sergeant in charge, Domingo Ruiz, ordered a soldier to respond:

> 'The sniper fired his powerful M-14 rifle and the man's head exploded, several American soldiers recalled. As he fell, more soldiers opened fire, killing at least one other insurgent. After the

> ambush, the Americans scooped up a piece of skull and took it back to their base as evidence of a successful mission.'
>
> The March 12 attack – swift and brutally violent – bore the hallmark of operations that have made Ruiz, 39 and a former Brooklyn gang member, renowned among U.S. troops in Mosul and, in many ways, a symbol of the optimism that has pervaded the military since Iraq's Jan. 30 elections. (*Washington Post*, 13 April 2005)

Such responses by US forces accompany a near-total failure to realise that large sectors of Iraq's population see them as an occupying power using violent methods against legitimate resisters, which have the effect of killing many innocent civilians; the bombing raid by strike aircraft near Haditha is only one example.

Fifth, the problems of reconstruction during an insurgency remain steep. Fallujah is a prominent example. The November 2004 assault on this 'city of mosques' damaged more than half of the city's 39,000 homes. Around 10,000 were destroyed or sufficiently damaged to render them unsafe to live in.

The great majority of the city's 250,000 residents had sought refuge outside the city before the assault began. Five months on, only 90,000 have returned: the majority of the city still has no electricity or piped water, there is 85 per cent unemployment and a moribund economy. Moreover, the city is ringed by four checkpoints controlling access, where returning residents have to queue for as much as four hours before observing a 7pm curfew if and when they are allowed through (*Washington Post*, 19 April 2005).

One Marine major comments: 'We have to be very careful how we repopulate the city. We paid too high a price to hand it back.' Once again, this seems entirely legitimate from an American perspective, but to many Iraqis it is a cogent reminder that the United States calls the shots.

Sixth, the issue of 'de-Ba'athification' – a purge of officials employed by the Saddam Hussein regime – is returning to shadow the work of the new Iraqi government dominated by Shi'a and Kurds. The US occupiers have sought to defuse the insurgency and increase efficiency by re-employing experienced Ba'athists, thus quietly reversing the immediate post-war policy of Paul Bremer's Coalition Provisional Authority. The incoming Iraqi leadership sees this shift as anathema, and are not persuaded by Donald Rumsfeld's efforts during his visit to Baghdad to prevent a new purge – even if this results in a boost to the insurgents.

Seventh, the determination of United States forces to stay in Iraq for years raises the question of whether Iraq will replace Afghanistan as a combat training-zone for paramilitaries from elsewhere in the Middle East.

The reliable Washington weekly *Defense News* (21 March 2005) notes that several of the young men detained after recent violent incidents in Saudi Arabia, Kuwait and Qatar had gained combat experience and training in Iraq. This trend is a reminder that the US invasion and occupation of Iraq, and the subsequent insurgency, involve long-term issues with strong regional ramifications. The question of the intensity and direction of the current Iraqi insurgency is small by comparison.

These seven elements of the Iraqi mosaic are enough to caution against the rhetorical optimism of the George W. Bush administration. Taken together, they suggest that we are still in the early years of a potentially decades-long conflict.

AN UNWINNABLE WAR *16 June 2005*

Donald Rumsfeld's remarks about the Iraq war on 14 June combined a widely reported admission that the security situation was no better than when the Saddam Hussein regime was terminated in April 2003 with a characteristic piece of convoluted logic: '...clearly it has been getting better as we've gone along', as 'a lot of bad things that could have happened have not happened'.

For a United States defense secretary even to acknowledge a military problem is unusual; the propaganda norm is to put a positive gloss on difficult situations. But more interesting still was Rumsfeld's comment that: '...this insurgency is going to be defeated not by the coalition – it's going to be defeated by the Iraqi security forces, and that is going to happen as the Iraq people begin to believe that they've got a future in that country'.

While many analysts would endorse the conclusion, the real point of Rumsfeld's comments is their marked contrast with his and his fellow Bush administration officials' repeated assertions over the past 27 months. Time and again they have proclaimed coalition successes over a retreating Iraqi insurgency: the killing of Uday and Qusay Hussein, the capture of Saddam Hussein himself, the major operation in Najaf, the destruction of rebel centres in Fallujah.

Now, Donald Rumsfeld himself – one of the war's leading architects – publicly accepts that the world's most powerful military force, deployed by a state that spends almost as much on the military as every other country in the world put together, cannot counter 20,000 or so determined insurgents backed by a minority of the population of Iraq.

It is an astonishing moment.

An Escalating Conflict

It also comes at a time when the tempo of the Iraq war is escalating in a way that is starting to have a sustained impact within the United States: on public and political opinion, on some senior military personnel, and – perhaps most importantly – on recruitment into the US Army and its reserve forces.

The wave of insurgent violence in Iraq, noted in recent articles in this series, has killed more than 900 people since the administration led by Ibrahim al-Jaafari was sworn in on 3 May. This week alone, 45 people died in two huge suicide bombings: on 14 June in Kirkuk, directed at civil servants queuing outside a government-owned bank, and on 15 June in an army canteen in Khalis, north of Baghdad, aimed at Iraqi soldiers.

The violence continues to exact its toll on the US military, even as it has increasingly switched from risky patrolling duties to training Iraqi security forces. In the first half of June, 41 US personnel were killed (more than in the whole of March); in the five-week period to 7 June, over 600 were wounded, more than half of them seriously.

The US military's training task is proving deeply problematic. There is, on paper, the appearance of progress. US military sources claim that 169,000 Iraqi police and security personnel have now been trained, with 107 Iraqi military and police special battalions now in operation. In practice, this is highly misleading, for only three of these battalions are assessed as being able to operate independently (*Washington Post*, 10 June 2005). Such details are part of a much wider realisation within the United States that the policy towards Iraq is deeply troubled, leading to a perceptible shift in public attitudes. Four indications of this shift are notable.

A New Pessimism

The first is public opinion. In a recent Gallup survey, nearly 60 per cent of respondents wanted a partial or complete withdrawal of US forces from Iraq, the highest figure since the war began. In a *Washington Post*–ABC News poll, the numbers believing that the Iraq war had not made the United States safer climbed above 50 per cent for the first time, and nearly 40 per cent thought that the situation was coming to resemble Vietnam (*Asia Times*, 15 June 2005).

The second is the changing mood in Washington. In the House of Representatives, which voted overwhelmingly for the war in 2003, a bipartisan group is drafting a resolution calling on the Bush administration to present an exit strategy. This follows a 32–9 vote by the House's international relations committee on a similar proposal (*Boston Globe*, 11 June 2005). The two-year term of members of the House, compared with six years in the Senate, make them frequently more responsive to changes in public feeling.

The third indication of Iraq's new impact is the doubt among senior US military officers in Iraq about the prospects for US strategy. In a sense this merely confirms Rumsfeld's emphasis on the need for a political settlement, but the officers go further in assessing the insurgency as deep-seated, resilient and adaptable. Its character is seen in the way that it can respond to major counter-insurgency actions by quickly relocating its efforts.

This aspect of the insurgency was already evident during the huge Fallujah operation in November. While it was under way, the insurgents transferred their attention to the larger city of Mosul and were able to occupy large sections of the city, forcing the US into an emergency transfer of troops to support the local Iraqi security forces. This, a common pattern throughout the insurgency, indicates the insurgents' remarkable ease of movement through many of Iraq's urban and rural districts.

A particularly telling recent comment came from Frederick P. Wellman, a US officer training Iraqi forces. In the words of a newspaper report:

> Lt. Col. Frederick P. Wellman, who works with the task force overseeing the training of Iraqi security forces, said the insurgency doesn't seem to be running out of new recruits, a dynamic fuelled by tribal members seeking revenge for relatives killed in fighting. 'We can't kill them all,' Wellman said. 'When I kill one I create three'. (*Knight Ridder Newspapers*, 12 June 2005)

The fourth example of worries on the American domestic front is the current state of US Army recruitment. In May, the army recruited 5,039 new soldiers – short of both the initial (8,050) and secondary (6,700) target. The reserve forces faced a similar shortfall – the Marine Corps reserve goal was missed by 12 per cent, the army reserve by 18 per cent, and the army National Guard enlistment was down by 29 per cent.

These difficulties arise despite the deployment of 1,000 more recruiters, a lavish TV advertising campaign, an increase in enlistment cash bonuses to $20,000, and a lowering of the educational requirements of new recruits (*Knight Ridder Newspapers*, 13 June 2005).

This is all a long way from the Pentagon's recent aim of increasing the army's strength by 30,000 to 510,000 while improving the educational standards of recruits to ensure that they can handle the increasingly automated battlefield and the demand for versatile forces available for rapid deployment.

A Cornered Policy

When Donald Rumsfeld became defense secretary in January 2001, he advanced the idea that the United States could achieve its strategic objectives with smaller but much more high-tech armed forces, using new generations of equipment and highly competent personnel to maintain 'full spectrum dominance' whenever and wherever required.

The war in Iraq has forced the US to modify this aim. The emphasis on huge technological superiority remains, but it is now matched by a need for much larger numbers of troops. Now, the sheer human costs of the war suggest that not even the amended policy is working.

If the United States' Iraq predicament gets much worse, it is conceivable that conscription will reappear on the military agenda. This is where Donald Rumsfeld and the Bush administration really are in a bind. With the mood in the US starting to swing away from the war, any talk of restoring the draft would be deeply unpopular. Perhaps this explains why Rumsfeld is now expressing the hope that political change in Iraq can end the insurgency. In plain logic: he has no other option.

TARGETING IRAN *7 July 2005*

The election of Mahmoud Ahmadinejad as president of Iran on 24 June is not an easy event for Washington to digest. The more convinced neo-conservatives find it especially difficult. The assumption on the American right has been that Iran is ripe for internally fomented regime change, with all that is required to bring people onto the streets being a perceived chance of success.

The United States can plausibly present Ahmadinejad as a hardline theocrat, and the Iran he leads as more dangerous than it would have been under the canny pragmatist he defeated, Hashemi Rafsanjani. The problem for the US right is that Ahmadinejad clearly has extensive popular support, and his sizeable victory cannot be explained away by any electoral irregularities.

Ahmadinejad has defended Iran's right to develop its civil nuclear-power programme, and in this too he is supported by much of the Iranian population. The reported resignation of Iran's nuclear negotiator, Hassan Rowhani, makes it more likely that talks with the 'EU3' (France, Germany and Britain) will not produce a solution acceptable to Washington.

In that case, any subsequent referral of the issue to the United Nations Security Council will face Chinese support for Iran, evidenced in the increasingly close economic links between the two countries. Moreover, Tony Blair's domestic political pressures would make it difficult for him to support another war. As a result, the United States would have to go it alone.

The US neo-conservatives would be unfazed: their clear-cut view (virtually synonymous with that of the Israelis) is that Iran cannot be allowed to develop a civil nuclear-power programme, let alone nuclear weapons; Tehran must be stopped, by military means if necessary.

America's Temptation

It is a difficult decision for the Bush administration, already mired in troubles in Iraq and Afghanistan, and facing the challenge of preparing American opinion for yet another conflict. But other factors work in its favour. The Iranian hostage crisis in 1980 is still etched into the American psyche; it would be easy enough to represent Iran as a potential nuclear threat and to condemn its support for terrorism; and there remains a deep well of support for Israel in the United States – reinforced by their shared views over Iran's military ambitions.

What all this means is that the risk of a US confrontation with Iran remains. It may even be time-limited by the need to act well before next year's mid-term elections to Congress and before the Bushehr nuclear power station begins to get its uranium fuel rods – with the consequent risk of a Chernobyl-type disaster from a subsequent bombing raid.

The US neo-cons still talk about the need for wholesale regime change in Iran, but they also recognise that military action to such an end would have to be substantial. It would involve attacks on the leadership, and the bombing of economic targets as well as destruction of a range of nuclear facilities, airfields, air defences, missile production plants and missiles already deployed. It would also even involve US troops on the ground, given the presumption that this time they really would be welcomed by cheering crowds in Tehran.

The political realities of Iraq make this prospect seem absurd, but it is worth noting that the more hawkish US commentators believe Iraq went wrong because the US military has been too constrained from using force against the insurgents. During the second Fallujah assault in November 2004, Mackubin

Thomas Owens of the Naval War College, wrote that the Fallujah tactics had to be applied to all major urban centres of insurgency if it was to be brought under control (*The Weekly Standard*, 6 December 2004).

Some on the American right certainly advocate regime change in Iran, but post-election realities in Iran and Bush's troubles in Washington make a narrower military option more likely: concerted attacks against Iranian nuclear facilities, missiles, air defences and airfields, together with any anti-ship missiles currently deployed close to the key oil shipment route through the Straits of Hormuz.

This might not lead to regime change but it would set back Iran's military developments by several years. At the same time, some kind of Iranian military response would be almost inevitable and this would enable the United States to escalate an air war against a much wider range of targets.

What has to be factored in is that the US Air Force and the US Navy are not experiencing the strains and tension that exist in the army and Marine Corps through the 'overstretch' caused by Iraq and Afghanistan. Substantial elements of the air force and also the navy's carrier-based air power are readily available for action against Iran. They do not currently have sufficient forces available in the region, but these could be deployed within perhaps six weeks of an attack being ordered.

Israel's Determination

All this means that US action against Iran is still possible, is made rather more likely by Ahmadinejad's election, and could come at any time in the next twelve months. More immediately, though, an attack by Israel is becoming relatively more likely. Ariel Sharon's government is simply not prepared to have Iran get anywhere near a nuclear-weapons capability, nor is it prepared to allow Iran to develop an integrated civil nuclear-power fuel cycle. It is also increasingly concerned over

Iran's recent developments in missile technology, especially the reported testing of a solid-fuel rocket motor for the Shahab-3 medium-range missile (*Asia Times*, 10 June 2005).

All of Iran's current medium-range missiles are essentially 1950s-vintage Scud derivatives with liquid fuel motors that are difficult to prepare and even more difficult to maintain in a condition to launch. Solid-fuel rockets are far more reliable, can be stored in remote places away from fuelling points and can be maintained at a high state of readiness. They are therefore difficult to find and destroy. In combination with any kind of nuclear-weapons programme, Iran could develop a deterrent capability that would make it very difficult for either the United States or Israel to interfere in its affairs.

The problem for Israel is that destroying Iran's nuclear and missile facilities is a much bigger military operation than the single air raid on Iraq's Osiraq nuclear research reactor back in June 1981. What would be involved now would be several days of raids against targets in many parts of the country. On the other hand, their military strategy could be more limited than anything the more powerful United States military might envisage yet still have a useful effect from Israel's perspective.

For a start, the Israelis would be far less concerned about the Straits of Hormuz, calculating that if Iran tried to close the straits in response to an Israeli attack, the United States would take vigorous counter-action against any threatening Iranian forces. Neither do the Israelis anticipate any kind of regime change in Iran in response to attacks from themselves or the Americans. They are far more realistic about internal Iranian politics and are aware that any military action would increase Iranian nationalist fervour, as well as support for the existing regime.

Israel has altogether more modest aims – the destruction of any facilities that could contribute to the development of nuclear weapons and the destruction of Iranian missiles and their production facilities. There is no expectation that any attacks would have long-term effects – all they would be seeking is a few years of delay, with the possibility of further attacks in the future. From their perspective, though, they might also have the added bonus of the Iranians retaliating against US facilities in the region, bringing the United States into a bigger conflict and at least ending up with substantial damage to the Iranian economy.

Until recently, the Israeli air force would have been hard pressed to even consider an attack on Iran, given that this would involve air strikes over a number of days at a range far greater than that of the Osiraq raid. What has changed is the systematic re-equipping of the Israeli air force with new longer-range US-built strike aircraft. One of these is the F-15I, a derivative of the American F-15E Strike Eagle. Israel has around 25 of these large and powerful planes that have a combat radius of 2,225 kilometres. Israel is also building up a fleet of over 100 of the smaller F-16I strike aircraft, a variant fitted with large conformal fuel tanks that give it a combat radius of 2,100 kilometres.

Most of the potential targets in Iran are within 1,500 kilometres of Israel and almost all are within 2,000 kilometres. Furthermore, Israel has a fleet of US C-130 Hercules transport aircraft modified for air-to-air refuelling and there are reports that it has been loaned some US KC-135 tanker aircraft. Israel also has a substantial number of redundant F-4 Phantom aircraft and some of these may have been modified to produce pilotless strike aircraft. All in all, Israel certainly has the capability for sustained air strikes against Iran, with the great majority of the equipment being of US origin. In any case, it would be impossible for Israel to attack Iran without US knowledge and approval, given that the United States has almost total control of the air space between Israel and Iran.

There are two further reasons why we should look to Israel rather than the United States. One is that any raid on Iran would be a massive and politically desirable diversion away from the internal upheavals being caused by the withdrawal from Gaza. The other is that a raid on Iran would almost certainly result in attacks by Hezbollah in southern Lebanon, giving the Israeli air force every excuse for a whole series of air raids against Hezbollah facilities, potentially setting it back years as a threat to Israel's northern territory.

What all this means is that it is dangerous to assume that the increasing problems being experienced by the United States in Afghanistan, and the much greater problems now evident in Iraq mean that Iran is no longer a potential focus for conflict. What may have changed is that the lead candidate for attacking Iran may well have shifted in the past three months from the United States to Israel, and it is just possible that Israeli military action could happen a lot quicker than most people expect.

THE LONDON BOMBS IN THE WIDER WAR

8 July 2005

The multiple bombings in London on 7 July were almost certainly perpetrated by a group allied to the al-Qaida movement. They were intended to kill and maim many people and to do so on the opening day of the G8 summit in Scotland for maximum international impact; in taking more than 50 lives and injuring 700 they have succeeded in this aim. The bombings came at a time when there were few if any indications of an attack – indeed the alert status in the United Kingdom had recently been downgraded from 'severe general' to 'substantial'.

They also came after a pause in such attacks outside of Iraq and Afghanistan. The most recent major incidents were in late 2004 – the attack on the Australian embassy in Jakarta in September (killing 11 people and injuring 161), followed by the bombing of the Taba Hilton in Sinai in October (killing 27 and injuring 122).

The London bombs were hugely destructive, and had many similarities to the larger Madrid attacks of March 2004. That carefully coordinated operation involved months of planning by people with access to finance, technical abilities and safe houses. The perpetrators planted ten bombs on four commuter trains, and set other bombs timed to kill people in the vicinity. 191 people died and 1,800 were injured in what became known as Spain's '11M'.

At the time, Spanish security and police forces were regarded as highly competent, and thought to have considerable knowledge of radical jihadist groups operating in the country; yet they were still unable to detect in advance the large contingent responsible for the Madrid attacks. British security organisations have been making similar intense efforts to uncover such networks, and the police have arrested dozens of suspects – very few of whom have come to trial. There has evidently been a failure to identify or track the group preparing the London explosions.

But this is less a reflection on the UK agencies than an indication of the viability, vigour and persistence of the range of groups linked under the 'al-Qaida' banner. Since 9/11, such affiliates have conducted far more actions than in a similar period beforehand. They have ranged across the world: Islamabad, Casablanca, Mombasa, Djerba, Karachi (twice), Istanbul (twice), Bali, Riyadh, Yemen, Tashkent, Madrid and now London, as well as failed attempts in Paris, Rome and Singapore.

The War of Perception

All these actions have taken place despite George W. Bush's equally wide-ranging 'war on terror'. United States-led forces have terminated regimes in Afghanistan and Iraq, and over 200,000 foreign troops are now deployed there fighting the insurgencies that have since developed. At least 40,000 people have been killed in the two countries, most of them civilians, up to 20,000 people are in detention without trial, and rigorous new anti-terror laws have been brought in by many countries.

The 'war on terror' has not curbed al-Qaida and its associated groups. Instead, they have received an influx of new recruits. There has also been a marked rise in anti-Americanism, especially in the Middle East, much of it focused on the impact of coalition actions in Iraq. In the wake of the London bombings, western political leaders instantly denied that the attacks could have anything to do with their actions in Iraq; in reality, the conduct of this 'war on terror' is proving deeply counterproductive. The London atrocity, following Madrid, is the latest example of this in Europe.

From a United States perspective, the different military actions in Iraq and Afghanistan are essential parts of a vigorous military campaign to defeat extremists. But many sectors of society across the Middle East perceive the US (in coalition with Britain and a few other states) as an occupying power that uses massive force to maintain control.

In Fallujah in November 2004, a sustained assault employed extraordinary firepower to leave a city the size of England's Hull, France's Lille, Italy's Imola or Poland's Wroclaw with a good deal more than 1,000 people killed or injured, half the dwellings wrecked, almost every school, mosque or public building destroyed or damaged, and most of the population fleeing the city as refugees.

The images of Fallujah, and of other degraded towns and cities in Iraq – from Baghdad to Najaf, from Baquba to Ramadi – are as familiar in the Middle East as are those of the London bombings in the British press today. A real tragedy of the London bombings, to put alongside all the raw human losses and wounds, is that very few people in Britain will make the connection between the two realities; yet, as with Madrid, the war on terror has come to those of us living in Europe.

Retrospect and Prospect

After the Madrid bombing, an earlier article in this series commented:

> Madrid forms part of a much greater pattern of human loss. On 11 September 2001, 3,000 people died in New York and Washington. Within four months, about 3,000 civilians had died in Afghanistan in the first phase of George W. Bush's war on terror. Until last week, another 400 people had died in further paramilitary attacks across the world, and more than 8,000 civilians had died in the initial three-week phase of the Iraq war in March–April 2003.
>
> Almost all of the loss of life after 9/11 was outside the countries of the Atlantic community. That is now no longer the case.

In the past 16 months, many more thousands of people have died in Iraq and Afghanistan. Now, London has become a target. For now, everyone mourns the loss of life and expresses sympathy with the injured and bereaved, but the greater tragedy would be to avoid starting the serious and difficult process of rethinking the conduct of this 'war on terror'.

If we do not, the prospect is of a potentially endless war, involving thousands more deaths and tens of thousands maimed, in a bitter cycle of violence. Breaking that vicious cycle will be immensely difficult but it has to be done. If we don't succeed, then the suffering in London will be just one more part of a widening human disaster.

A JEWEL FOR AL-QAIDA'S CROWN *11 August 2005*

Once again there have been suggestions from Washington that it might prove possible to cut back on US troop deployments in Iraq, perhaps by 20,000 troops early next year. Yet again, though, the timing of these statements has been singularly unfortunate, with the first ten days of August being one of the worst periods for American troops since the war began. In these few days alone, 44 have been killed and, in the two weeks to 9 August over 200 were injured, two-thirds of them sustaining serious injuries.

Moreover, the attacks on US convoys have become particularly damaging as the insurgents further develop their abilities. Earlier this week (10 August), four US soldiers were killed and six injured when a patrol was attacked in the northern town of Beiji, but this was not a roadside bomb but a careful attack by a substantial number of insurgents using rocket-propelled grenades on troops in two armoured Humvees and an armoured Bradley Fighting Vehicle.

At the same time, when improvised explosive devices (IEDs – roadside bombs) are used, their manner of deployment is getting far more dangerous. Three weeks ago, a massive IED was laid under a road south-west of Baghdad Airport and was detonated under another Humvee. The IED was constructed from a 250 kg bomb normally carried by aircraft and produced a crater 6 feet deep and nearly 17 feet wide. The Humvee was completely destroyed and the four US soldiers in it were killed instantly. More recently, an attack on a large 25-ton Marine Corps amphibious assault vehicle on 3 August near Haditha used an IED that was so powerful that the entire vehicle was blown into the air, killing 14 Marines and an interpreter travelling with them (David S. Cloud 'Insurgents Using Bigger, More Lethal Bombs, US Officers Say', *New York Times*, 4 August).

When these major attacks affect US forces they are covered by the domestic media and this is adding to the changing mood in the United States, but far more Iraqis are being killed every day, with little or no coverage outside the region, apart from a few specialist websites such as Iraq Body Count and Professor Juan Cole's Informed Comment (<www.iraqbodycount.net/> and <www.juancole.com/>).

As the insurgency continues to develop, it is becoming apparent that Iraq is developing into a training ground for paramilitaries that will have a significance far beyond Iraq and could be measured in decades. In relation to such a role, two issues are immediately apparent – the evolving structure of the insurgency and the persistence with which events in Iraq are being used for much wider propaganda purposes by the loose group of networks that we still label 'al-Qaida'.

A Different Insurgency

As to the insurgency, a remarkable account of its current development, by far the most detailed assessment to appear in the open defence literature, was published last week in the Washington-based *Defense News* (Greg Grant, 'Inside Iraqi Insurgent Cells', 1 August 2005). Currently, an average of 40 IEDs are deployed each day in Iraq and there is a steady improvement in capabilities. According to the Head of the US Army's IED Defeat Task Force, Brigadier General Joseph Votel, 'The enemy is evolving and constantly innovating. If there were any thoughts that this is a rudimentary and unsophisticated enemy, those thoughts have been replaced.'

Most insurgencies have a highly structured organisation with key leaders coordinating attacks and communicating down a chain of command. According to *Defense News*, though, in Iraq there are large numbers of small free-standing insurgent cells that operate with only the loosest of coordination. Those cells that are engaged in bombing activities may individually number only a handful of people, and each is likely to concentrate on a particular area, keeping a close watch on US patrols and even using hoax IEDs to see how the US troops react.

While US military convoys may be attacked, insurgent cells also like to target convoys of civilian SUVs as these often carry US personnel and intelligence officials. Tankers are also favourite targets because of the spectacular effects of burning fuel. These attacks provide strong TV coverage for the satellite channels but insurgents video the great majority of attacks in order to study the effectiveness of their own tactics, to train new recruits and to provide raw footage for propaganda purposes.

Some insurgent cells operate on what amounts to a freelance basis, developing particular skills and then hiring themselves out to al-Qaida associates such as Al Zarqawi or the Sunni Ansaar al Sunna. Video footage of attacks can then be used to demonstrate their capabilities. The *Defense News* analysis also confirms other reports that the insurgents are continually developing their capabilities, sometimes with very straightforward tactics, and at other times with high levels of sophistication. Placing a roadside bomb can be a dangerous activity, particularly given the levels of observation that US forces can achieve with their long-range observation capabilities. One method used by insurgents is to have bombs placed in cars that have large holes cut in the floor. A car can then be driven along a road and the bomb dropped into place without the car even stopping.

At the other end of the scale, much larger bombs are now being used, as well as modified explosives designed to penetrate armoured vehicles. The device that destroyed the Marine Corps assault vehicle near Haditha is reported to have used three landmines exploding simultaneously. For armour-piercing, one form of shaped charge consists of a concave-shaped ingot of a metal such as copper placed on an explosive charge so that when the latter is detonated, much of the energy is absorbed by the copper, turning it into a high-velocity 'slug' of molten metal that goes right through the armour plating of a vehicle travelling above it. Shaped-charged explosives are widely used in modern munitions deployed by a number of regular armies, but these are being built and deployed by insurgents using hidden workshops and relatively unsophisticated equipment.

The great majority of the insurgents carrying out bombing attacks are Iraqis, many of them drawn from the previous armed forces, especially some of the elite troops such as the Special Republican Guard. Suicide bomb cells are organised in a broadly similar way, but most of the suicide or martyr bombers are from outside the country, especially from Saudi Arabia.

Unlike the bomb-making cells, the actual bombers receive little training, and then only in target acquisition and how to detonate the device. According to *Defense News*, the actual suicide missions are carefully planned and executed. According to information gained from a captured suicide bomber:

> Two vehicles are commonly used. The first transports the bomber to the location of the prepositioned car bomb and then follows behind to guide the bomber along the route and videotape the attack. The captured car bomber said it would be easy to drive around Baghdad and pick out up to 20 soft targets.

An Information War

When the frequency of attacks is put together with this kind of information about the organisation of just one part of the insurgency, we begin to get some idea of the problems facing the US and Iraqi security forces. Furthermore, given the current intensity of the insurgency, there must be substantial community support for these attacks across large areas of central Iraq.

An added factor is the way in which the publicising of insurgent activities is now a highly developed international activity, especially by groups allied to Zarqawi (Susan B. Glasser and Steve Coll, 'The Web as Weapon', *Washington Post*, 9 August 2005). The production of videos by insurgent groups is nothing new – there were examples from Chechnya in the 1990s, but the Zarqawi group has taken it to new levels since its initial recording of the beheading of hostages a year or more ago. One of its first major video productions was an hour-long film distributed last year that started with the US bombing raids on Baghdad at the outbreak of the war, and went on to show graphic footage of civilian victims. Because of its length, it was distributed via the net in a series of parts or chapters, but more recent productions have taken on much more efficient distribution techniques.

According to the *Washington Post*, the latest release is the 46-minute 'All Religion Will be for Allah', a video that attains almost professional qualities of production. Released just over a month ago the organisers distributed it worldwide with

> a specially designed Web page with dozens of links to the video, so users could choose which version to download. There were large-scale file editions that consumed 150 megabytes for viewers with high-speed Internet and a scaled-down four-megabyte version for those with limited dial-up access. Viewers could choose Windows Media or RealPlayer. They could even download 'All Religions Will Be for Allah' to play on a cell phone.

A School for Insurgency

The combination of an increasingly effective insurgency with the use of innovative worldwide information distribution has to be seen in the context of the tough measures and heavy firepower that the US forces believe is necessary as they try to control the insurgency. These, too, are being heavily publicised, so that all of these issues – US actions and insurgent 'successes' – are circulating widely in sympathetic communities across the world, adding to support for the insurgency and the wider activities of al-Qaida affiliates.

It is at this level that we have the real significance of what is happening in Iraq. As mentioned in earlier articles in this series, Saudi security agencies are already concerned that young Saudi radicals are travelling to Iraq and getting combat experience before returning home, and there is even evidence that tactics being learned in Iraq are being applied in Afghanistan, a hugely ironic development as this was the previous combat training zone for al-Qaida supporters.

What we are now just beginning to see is the appearance of paramilitary recruits from countries outside the immediate region, including Western Europe and Australia (*ITN News*, 10 August). This is almost certainly only in its early stages, but we should also expect it to grow, given the resonance that the Iraq insurgency is having with disaffected young people beyond as well as within the Middle East.

The aims of al-Qaida and its affiliates – including the expulsion of 'crusaders and Zionists' from the Islamic world, destruction of corrupt and elitist regimes and the re-establishment of an Islamic Caliphate – are all measured in decades, not years. To achieve these goals, tens of thousands of paramilitaries will be required, and although Afghanistan remains unstable, it is not the combat training ground it might once have been.

Instead we have Iraq – an absolute 'gift' to bin Laden, Zarqawi and others. Not only are there well over 150,000 'crusader' troops occupying the historic home of the Abbasid Caliphate, the insurgency is primarily one of urban conflict, providing a training environment very much more relevant to future 'anti-elite' actions than the largely rural civil war in Afghanistan a decade ago. Moreover, the oil motive is one of the core driving forces of Washington's policy towards the Middle East and there is therefore a determination by the United States to remain in control of Iraq and the wider Gulf region for many years to come. From the perspective of bin Laden and the wider al-Qaida movement, it could scarcely be better.

IRAN: CONSEQUENCES OF A WAR *18 August 2005*

George Bush's comments at the weekend on a military confrontation with Iran have raised fears that the United States might still be prepared to attack Iran's nuclear facilities, despite the risks and likely consequences. Bush was interviewed by Israel's state-owned Channel 1 TV and, speaking from his ranch in Crawford, Texas, commented 'As I say, all options are on the table. The use of force is the last option for any president and, you know, we've used force in the recent past to secure our country.'

His comments may have been directed primarily at Israeli public opinion, perhaps to discourage the more hawkish elements there that want Israel to go it alone, but there was an immediate response from German Chancellor Gerhard Schroeder: '...let's take the military option off the table. We've seen it doesn't work.' Perhaps more significant has been the comment from an official at the British Foreign Office: 'Our position is clear and has been made very, very clear by the foreign secretary... We do not think there are any circumstances where military action would be justified against Iran. It does not form part of British foreign policy.'

While President Bush may have had an Israeli audience in mind, his comments stem from a deep-seated view within the administration that Iran is the major threat in the region and that it simply cannot be allowed even the basic means to produce nuclear weapons, whether or not it intends to do so. This means that Iran must not develop the nuclear fuel cycle, including uranium enrichment, which is integral to a civil nuclear-power programme but involves technologies that could be diverted into a nuclear weapon programme.

The Fuel of Enmity

With its origins in the traumatic events of 1979/80 – the fall of the Shah, the Khomeini revolution and especially the hostage crisis – Iran has long been seen as the real threat to US and Israeli interests in the Middle East. For many on the neo-conservative wing in Washington, terminating the Saddam Hussein regime in Iraq may have had its own intrinsic merits, but was also designed to send a strong message to Iran that the United States was the dominant power in the region, and that Tehran simply had to live with that. Regime termination in Tehran might be the ultimate aim, but, in the interim, US military dominance in Iraq would also serve to keep the Iranians in their place.

The bottom line for Washington, though, was that even an isolated and circumscribed Iran could not be allowed to develop nuclear weapons, and that issue remains, even if it has now been supplemented by a real concern that Iran is also highly capable of interfering in Iraq. There was particular concern in Washington at the way the Prime Minister, Ibrahim al-Jaafari was able to take a powerful group of ministers to Tehran last month and do a series of deals that served to cement a new Iraqi–Iranian relationship, not least in terms of the joint development of some of Iraq's oil resources.

The dilemma for Washington is that the Shi'a majority in Iraq wants those links, in spite of a history of Iraqi–Iranian antagonism stemming from the bitter 1980–88 war, not least because a close relationship with Iran gives greater security for Iraqi Shi'as in a wider region that is largely Sunni. It may well be the case that the Iranians have been careful not to interfere too much in the Iraqi insurgency, but extensive links have been made with many Shi'a political and paramilitary organisations in Iraq, and there is no doubt that the Iranians could cause major problems for US forces if they chose to do so.

Indeed there is recent evidence that there has been a substantial increase in Iranian involvement in the Iraqi insurgency (Michael Ware, 'Inside Iran's Secret War for Iraq', *Time Magazine*, 15 August), including aid with the design of new weapons. The new shaped-charge explosives that are capable of penetrating US armoured vehicles are reported to be based on a design developed by Hezbollah paramilitaries for use against Israeli forces in southern Lebanon, and to have been introduced into Iraq by a group linked to the Iranian Revolutionary Guard Corps.

For the Bush administration, therefore, the outlook is bleak, with Iran holding some of the key cards in the political evolution now going on in Iraq, possibly involved more directly in the insurgency and seemingly determined to face down the EU3 (Germany, France and the UK) over their attempts to negotiate an end to Iranian plans for uranium enrichment.

A Triple Dilemma

Furthermore, there are three other factors that are causing problems for Washington when it tries to make a case against Iran. For some years, now, the US has claimed that Iran has been developing a clandestine nuclear weapons programme, keeping it hidden from the International Atomic Energy inspectors. One of the major charges is that one particular IAEA inspection found traces of highly enriched uranium in an experimental centrifuge complex, with this cited by the US as proof of a nuclear weapon programme. Unfortunately for Washington, it now appears that the IAEA has technical evidence that this was actually due to contamination which was already present in the centrifuges when they were obtained from Pakistani sources (*Independent on Sunday*, 14 August).

The second factor is that if Iran has been decidedly tardy in its openness with the IAEA in recent years that is also a criticism that can be laid at the door of the Egyptians and the South Koreans. Both countries have had to admit recently to activities that, if not actually proscribed under the terms of the Non-Proliferation Treaty, were certainly at the margins of legality.

Finally, the prospect of referring Iran to the UN Security Council has its own problems. Many members of the IAEA Governing Board are deeply reluctant to support such a move and, even if it went ahead, China would be almost certain to veto any resolution antagonistic to Iran, not least because of the very close economic links that the Iranian government has recently forged with Beijing.

The Tehran Lens

Within Iran itself, there is widespread public support for a civil nuclear-power programme, not least because it is seen as conferring advanced industrial status on the country. Support for a nuclear weapons programme is less evident, but there is a deep-seated suspicion of the United States, especially as it is now so prominent in the region. The US military has close to 200,000 personnel more or less surrounding the country, in Iraq, Afghanistan, western Gulf states such as Kuwait and Qatar, and on the ships of the Fifth Fleet in the Persian Gulf and the Arabian Sea. The Bush administration has labelled Iran as part of the 'axis of evil' and has made it clear that regime change is the firm policy.

Iranians also point to US infringements of Iranian air space by reconnaissance drones and to the clear commitment that the Bush administration has to modernising its own nuclear arsenals including the probable development of small earth-penetrating warheads that could be used for fighting 'small nuclear wars in far-off places' such as Iran.

Perhaps most pertinent of all is the Iranian view of the non-proliferation regime – namely that the Non-Proliferation Treaty involves a tacit bargain between the nuclear weapons states and those without. This bargain involves the latter forgoing the nuclear weapons option in return for being helped to develop civil nuclear power. Most countries in the NPT accept this bargain, but the United States no longer does. Iran simply will not accept that Washington has the right to exclude it from this bargain, and the leadership knows full well that any major confrontation with the United States would bring the great majority of the Iranian people fully behind it.

What Kind of War?

If the United States is determined to force Iran to give up its nuclear ambitions, and if diplomatic and economic pressure fails to have any effect, what kind of military confrontation might ensue and what might be the consequences? This is a scenario that is uncomfortable to consider, but could well become reality, either involving Israel or the United States.

If Israel decided to take action, then this could come at any time, not least as a possible diversion from its difficult domestic environment as the Sharon government presses ahead with the Gaza withdrawal. Israel is particularly concerned about Iran's newer medium-range missiles such as the Shahab-3, as well as the longer-term prospect of a nuclear-armed Iran. It has the capability to attack a wide range of Iranian nuclear industry targets over a number of days, using its newer F-15I and F-16I extended range strike aircraft, quite possibly aided by the Israeli presence in the Kurdish region of north-east Iraq.

If Israel did attack Iran's nuclear facilities it would be using American equipment and would have to do it with the tacit support of US forces in Iraq, Kuwait and the Persian Gulf. Any such operation would clearly be seen by Tehran as essentially a joint US–Israeli operation. Indeed, the possible Iranian responses would probably be similar to those it would make to a direct US attack.

Although the United States is thoroughly mired in the Iraq insurgency, that is being fought very largely by the US Marine Corps and the Army. There are very substantial air and naval forces available both in the Gulf and in the wider region that would be able to mount a sustained attack on Iran's putative nuclear facilities. Although a range of air force and navy strike aircraft might be used, the US Air Force would want to make full use of the B-2 'stealth' bomber. This particular plane would be central to any air attacks on Iraq but its radar-avoidance capabilities depend on it being housed in expensive climate-controlled hangars.

Until recently, the B-2 was restricted to being deployed from its home base at Whiteman Air Force Base in the United States and Diego Garcia in the Indian Ocean, where portable hangars had been erected. At the end of last year, though, two new permanent hangars were opened at RAF Fairford in Gloucestershire in a $19 million programme completed seven months ahead of schedule (details from <www.globalsecurity.

org>). This means that any US attack on Iran would almost certainly involve planes flying from the UK.

The main aim of US military action would be to set back Iran's nuclear and missile development programmes by several years and to serve notice on the regime that any further developments would not be tolerated. If there was any kind of immediate Iranian action against US forces, further raids might well target elements of the leadership and the economy in the hope of destabilising the regime.

Even to write about such actions when the United States has such major problems in Iraq and Afghanistan seems pointless, but it has to be remembered that many analysts were saying that a war with Iraq was highly unlikely, even three months before it started. Furthermore, there really is deep unease within the Bush administration that it is beginning to lose its grip on the region, especially as Iranian influence in Iraq is clearly increasing. In these circumstances, a real shock to Iran is readily seen in some circles in Washington as a means of re-establishing dominance. It therefore makes sense to consider just how the Iranians might respond, and whether the consequences would compare with the unforeseen aftermath of the termination of the Saddam Hussein regime in Iraq.

Iranian Responses

The first point to emphasise once again is that any attack would serve a powerful unifying function in Iran, bringing together most shades of opinion in support for the civil, religious and military leadership in the face of an evident external threat. Contrary to much opinion in Washington, it is highly unlikely that the Tehran regime would become unstable. Therefore, and in such circumstances, it would have a wide range of political and military options to exercise in response to a US attack.

It would face a US air assault that would be directed not only at the Iranian nuclear facilities but also medium-range missile batteries, airfields and command and control systems, so that Iranian responses would factor in the likelihood that all these systems would be damaged if not destroyed in a matter of days. Even so, there are several immediate Iranian responses available, three of which could have substantial impacts.

Firstly, Iran could encourage Hezbollah units in southern Lebanon to engage in attacks on northern Israel, using the huge numbers of unguided short-range missiles that have been accumulated there. Israel would be almost certain to respond with overwhelming force, causing outrage across the region, not least among the majority Shi'a communities in Iraq.

Iraq itself could be the second centre of operations, with numerous Revolutionary Guard units filtering into the country to join up with Shi'a militias in opposing the US occupation. This would be a massive additional problem for the already overstretched American forces, and the US would be likely to retaliate with multiple air strikes against Iranian military targets and transport and communications systems, further escalating the war, yet almost certainly uniting the Iranian population even more firmly behind the leadership.

Finally, Iran has multiple means to disrupt Persian Gulf oil exports. These include the capacity to close the Straits of Hormuz using anti-ship missile batteries acquired in recent years from China. They also have up to 2,000 naval mines, including some very modern types (Michael J. Maazarr, 'Strike Out', *The New Republic*, 6 August 2005). Furthermore, irregular units could infiltrate into western Gulf states including Kuwait, Saudi Arabia and Abu Dhabi, intent on sabotaging oil facilities down the Gulf coast. With oil prices already at a singularly high level, any such disruption would have worldwide economic effects.

Iran also has potential influence in Afghanistan, where it could complicate matters for the United States, although its potential for action in Iraq is much more potent and immediate. Given the very difficult circumstances that the US faces in Iraq, that is the real context in which Iranian action could be so effective.

Against each prognosis, it might be argued that the Iranian leadership would be reluctant to engage in a major war with the United States, but there is a counter-argument that is much more persuasive. A common view in Tehran is that since the United States simply will not let the Iranians develop a nuclear industry, an attack is more or less inevitable. If Iran does not respond forcefully to such an attack, the presumption is that it will encourage the United States to act repeatedly and with impunity against any future Iranian attempt to reconstitute a badly damaged nuclear and missile infrastructure. In this line of thinking, there is no option but to respond with maximum impact, especially when US ground forces are so overstretched.

The Risk

Much of this analysis may seem excessive and even scare mongering. It is surely difficult to contemplate even the Bush administration getting embroiled in a new conflict, or even enabling the Israelis to do so. Against that, though, two issues remain.

One is the 'bottom line' of the Bush administration that Iran cannot be allowed to develop nuclear weapons. The other, which is rapidly growing in importance, is the increasing influence of Iran in Iraq. That trend is becoming more evident week by week, and may eventually be the 'tipping point' that leads Washington into the highly dangerous route of military action against Iran.

10
Afterword – A War Too Far?

In reviewing the first two and a half years of the Iraq War, three groups of issues are apparent – trends, events and determining factors. Taken together, they suggest that Iraq has not yet proved to be 'a war too far' and that it would be wrong to assume that the neo-conservative vision of a New American Century is being lost in the evolving American predicament in Iraq and Afghanistan.

TRENDS

Of the many trends that have become evident, several have a long-term significance. The first is casualties – both civilian and military. Before the start of the war, there were predictions from several analysts and policy groups that there would be a high incidence of Iraqi civilian and military casualties and that the United States might itself suffer considerable losses. In the first flush of optimism following the destruction of the Saddam Hussein regime, these were discounted, and it is clear from the weekly analyses reprinted here that it only became apparent over many months that the Iraqi civilian casualties were considerable. Moreover, with the coalition refusing steadfastly to provide figures, it was left to voluntary non-government groups such as Iraq Body Count to attempt to assemble the necessary data.

The impact of US military casualties was also slow to develop, partly because of the anxiety of the Bush administration to downplay their significance and partly because it took many months for the high level of serious injuries to be appreciated. Only after well over 1,000 US troops had been killed and many thousands seriously injured did the impact start to emerge, and then frequently through the accumulating impact of stories in numerous local media outlets rather than in the network media.

A second trend that was slow to have an impact outside of the region was the combination of sustained lawlessness in many of the major cities, especially Baghdad, and the persistent problems of reconstruction, made so much worse by an insecure environment. The early looting in the weeks immediately after the war was widely reported, but its transformation into systematic lawlessness was not so easily recognised. It remains an issue of very little concern in the United States.

As the insurgency evolved, a further factor that attracted increasing attention in the Middle East but was largely ignored outside of the specialist defence press in western countries, was the close links developing between the US military and their Israeli counterparts. By the end of the second year of the war, frequent exchanges of ideas on training and doctrine were evident, as was the US employment of Israeli military equipment in Iraq. Most of this had been developed in connection with Israel's control of Palestinian populations in the occupied territories, and was being used by the US forces as their own methods and equipment frequently proved inadequate for the urban guerrilla campaign they were facing in Iraq.

To the US forces these were reasonable developments that might serve to decrease the many risks to their own troops, but across the region this served to confirm the widely held view that the occupation of Iraq was, to some extent, a US/Israeli operation, especially when reports emerged of the presence of Israeli forces training Kurdish militia in north-east Iraq. What is pertinent is that the adverse impact of such a relationship across the region was either not recognised in Washington or was thought to be a price worth paying.

The fourth trend has been the relatively recent development of substantial opposition to the war within the United States itself. This became more sustained and deep-seated during the course of 2005, not least as the casualties increased, and became focused on the campaign by Cindy Sheehan, the mother of a young soldier killed in Iraq, to bring home the issues to President Bush while he was on vacation at his ranch in Crawford, Texas.

The administration also came under unexpected pressure through early failures to respond to the emergencies caused by Hurricane Katrina in New Orleans and along the Gulf Coast at the end of August, and by substantial increases in fuel prices across the country. While it is too early to say whether the developing anti-war movement could ever match the campaign against the Vietnam war in the late 1960s, there are indications that it could have a cumulative impact for the current administration and its successor.

The final trend that is worth noting here is that early predictions of the systematic involvement of US contractors in lucrative reconstruction contracts and the deep involvement of the United States in the political evolution of Iraq have proved all too accurate. This is particularly noticeable in terms of the penetration of US influence into all the major instruments of government, to the extent that Iraq can most certainly be considered to be a client state of Washington.

EVENTS

Of the events of the past two and a half years, five stand out as having a particular resonance. The first is the early guerrilla-like responses to the coalition's invasion of Iraq, especially the manner in which some of the very earliest troops' movements met unexpected resistance. This was largely discounted in the wake of the collapse of the regime, but can be seen as being far more significant than was recognised at the time.

The second is President Bush's 'mission accomplished' address on the aircraft carrier USS *Abraham Lincoln* on 1 May 2003, even if his speech was not quite as self-congratulatory as the banner displayed so prominently behind him. Even so, there really was a belief in administration circles in Washington that Iraq was a largely completed mission; it took many more months for the full gravity of the situation to be recognised.

The third event was not recognised as being particularly significant at the time, but has certainly proved to be so. This was the refusal of India, in mid-2003, to commit a full division of troops to a peace-enforcing role in Iraq. As India was one of the few countries with the spare capacity in its armed forces to make such a commitment, once it had been decided not to do so, there was little likelihood of any other country providing large-scale support. From then on, the United States was largely on its own, with a dwindling band of military support that has substantially ebbed away since.

Fourthly, President Bush's re-election in November 2004 may have come at a time of considerable military difficulties in Iraq, but it was immediately seen as a vindication of the Iraq policy in particular and the conduct of the global war on terror in general. Given the trend of domestic opposition outlined above, this event may have an effect that is relatively short-lived.

Immediately after the election came the assault on Fallujah, an event of enduring relevance and one born out of a determination to erase what was seen as the most important single focus of the whole insurgency. Although the city was severely damaged, over a thousand people killed and over 200,000 forced to leave the city as refugees, the impact on the overall insurgency proved minimal, with outbreaks of considerable violence in Mosul and elsewhere developing even before the Fallujah assault was completed.

Moreover, since then images of the destruction in Fallujah, the 'city of mosques' have had a substantial resonance across the Islamic world, adding to anti-American sentiments. Furthermore, even the dedicated efforts to maintain control over the city after its occupation by US and Iraqi forces proved exceedingly difficult, with insurgents re-establishing substantial activity within months of the assault.

DETERMINING FACTORS

Although opposition to the occupation of Iraq has become progressively more marked in the United States as the war moves towards its third year, there are five factors that are likely to ensure that the war will be protracted. One is that the insurgency retains considerable support amongst many Sunni communities and is evolving rapidly in terms of techniques, tactics and munitions. The Pentagon is planning to maintain large numbers of troops in Iraq until 2009 so military planners do not expect an early end to the conflict, whatever some politicians may wish.

Secondly, while opposition to the war is growing in the United States, the neo-conservative influence in the administration remains strong, and much of its outlook is shared by the large Christian Zionist lobby that is highly supportive of the State of Israel. This lobby is almost certainly more significant for Zionism than the traditional Jewish lobby which is now divided over its support for the hard-line Sharon government. In combination with neo-conservatism, the defence lobby and the many commercial interests that are benefiting from the global war on terror, it constitutes a force with substantial continuing power in determining US security policy.

The third factor is the role of oil, not in terms of short-term profitability for transnational oil companies but in relation to the longer-term role of the Persian Gulf as easily the most important location of oil reserves worldwide. With close to 70 per cent of the world's oil reserves located in the region, and with China joining Japan, the United States and Western Europe as dominant oil importers, the significance of Gulf oil is already substantial and will increase greatly over the next two decades.

For this reason alone, a full US withdrawal from Iraq is so unlikely that, if it were to happen, it would be the biggest foreign policy disaster for the United States in 60 years. It also remains a core reason for the US antipathy to Iran. Although western analysts frequently ignore the oil factor, it is widely recognised across the region, where the US military occupation in Iraq is thought to have little or nothing to do with the promotion of democracy and much more a matter of an American/Zionist plot to control the oil. That is a perception that is not easily dispelled.

Fourthly, there are clear indications of a potential crisis in relations between Iran and the United States that could involve a military attack on Iranian nuclear facilities, either by the United States or by Israel. The motivation for such an attack has so far come from a fundamental belief, especially in neo-conservative circles that Iran, as a 'rogue state', cannot be allowed to acquire weapons of mass destruction. In addition, the growing links between Tehran and the Shi'a majority in Iraq is raising concerns that the US may experience increasing difficulties in trying to maintain Iraq as a client regime.

Finally, there is the role of al-Qaida, as outlined in the previous chapter. For the al-Qaida movement, Iraq is probably the greatest single gift that it could imagine receiving. Al-Qaida associates can all too easily claim that the US presence in Iraq is a neo-Christian crusade, aided by Zionists, to take control of a country that was, for nearly 500 years, the seat of the Abbasid Caliphate. Whatever the historical realities of the relative powerlessness of that Caliphate for much of its existence, the near-mythical aim of the al-Qaida movement to create a Caliphate embodying an Islamist polity means that Iraq can serve as a beacon for paramilitaries to aid the cause. Furthermore, Iraq can now be treated as a combat training zone for paramilitaries from across the region, gaining skills and experience in asymmetric warfare that can be applied elsewhere.

PROSPECTS

The al-Qaida aim of establishing a Caliphate is one that is measured in decades rather than years, and it is in the interests of the movement for the United States to stay in Iraq for as long as possible. Even if an early withdrawal would be seen as a valuable sign of weakness to the movement, the role of US forces in Iraq as providers of long-term combat training is even more useful. On the US side, the importance of the region's oil is such that withdrawal simply cannot be considered. Without the oil factor, it would be quite realistic to argue that a withdrawal of US forces from Iraq would be feasible, given the manifold problems facing the US military as the insurgency evolves. This, though, is missing the point. The United States is locked into Iraq for the foreseeable future primarily because of the oil factor, and the al-Qaida movement, with its many associates, is similarly engaged for the long term. As a result of the confluence of these two conflicting aims – the US need to control the Gulf and the militant response to this policy – it is wise to expect the Iraq War to form one major part of a wider regional conflict that might soon come to include Iran and may well last for many more years or, more likely, decades.

Index